SNAFU

THE DEFINITIVE GUIDE TO
HISTORY'S GREATEST SCREWUPS

ED HELMS

GRAND CENTRAL PUBLISHING

New York Boston

Cover and interior illustrations by Mark Harris. Cover and interior design by Headcase Design. Cover images by Getty Images, Shutterstock, and Adobe Stock. Cover copyright © 2025 by Hachette Book Group, Inc.

Grand Central Publishing
Hachette Book Group
1290 Avenue of the Americas, New York, NY 10104
grandcentralpublishing.com
@grandcentralpub

First Edition: April 2025

Grand Central Publishing is a division of Hachette Book Group, Inc. The Grand Central Publishing name and logo is a registered trademark of Hachette Book Group, Inc.

The publisher is not responsible for websites (or their content) that are not owned by the publisher.

The Hachette Speakers Bureau provides a wide range of authors for speaking events. To find out more, go to hachettespeakersbureau.com or email HachetteSpeakers@hbgusa.com.

Grand Central Publishing books may be purchased in bulk for business, educational, or promotional use. For information, please contact your local bookseller or the Hachette Book Group Special Markets Department at special.markets@hbgusa.com.

Library of Congress Cataloging-in-Publication Data
Names: Helms, Ed, author.
Title: Snafu : history's greatest screwups / Ed Helms.
Description: First edition. | New York : Grand Central Publishing, 2025. |
   Includes bibliographical references.
Identifiers: LCCN 2024051875 | ISBN 9781538769478 | ISBN 9781538769485
   (ebook)
Subjects: LCSH: United States--History--Errors, inventions, etc. | Common
   fallacies--United States.
Classification: LCC E179 .H475 2025 | DDC 973--dc23/eng/20241106
LC record available at https://lccn.loc.gov/2024051875

ISBNs: 9781538769478 (hardcover), 9781538769485 (ebook), 9781538775806 (B&N signed edition), 9781538775615 (regular signed edition)

Printed in the United States of America

LSC-C

Printing 1, 2025

IMAGE PERMISSIONS

CONTENTS

INTRODUCTION

SNAFU is an acronym that stands for "Situation Normal: All Fucked Up." It was military slang during World War II, and the soldiers who coined it were essentially saying, "Yeah, everything's a disaster—but hey, isn't it always?" Over time, the term traveled beyond the battlefield and made its way into our everyday language. Today, according to Oxford Dictionaries, SNAFU means "a confused or chaotic state; a mess." A definition that, frankly, could apply to everything from assembling IKEA furniture to your last family vacation.

But the SNAFUs in this book are not your run-of-the-mill slip-ups, like accidentally using ranch dressing as coffee creamer (in my defense, it was in a very tiny, fancy-looking carafe). No, these are the big mamas—the epic blunders that unravel like slow-motion train wrecks, except it's like ten different trains derailing in every direction, with clueless officials insisting, "Everything's fine!" while entire towns get leveled in the chaos. And these disasters aren't confined to one poor soul making a bad decision—they're massive, institution-shaking calamities that drag entire governments, corporations, and far too many innocent bystanders along for the ride. And yet, like rubberneckers at a car crash, we just have to watch. There's something weirdly irresistible—almost primal—about witnessing a colossal screwup.

That's why I started the *SNAFU* podcast a few years ago (available wherever you get your podcasts—five-star reviews welcome!). But I was quickly awed by just how many catastrophic screwups litter our past. The deeper I dug, the more I realized that humanity's hall-of-fame-worthy blunders needed more than just a podcast; they needed pages—glorious, printed pages—to fully capture the breathtaking scale of our collective idiocy. And thus was born the book you now hold in your hands (or see on your screen or hear on your Air-Pods—hi there!).The stories in this book crisscross America and span every decade since World War II, revealing a rich tapestry of human folly that, frankly, makes me feel a lot better about many of my own life choices.

Now, you've probably heard the old saying that tragedy plus time equals comedy. Mark Twain supposedly said that (or was it Carol Burnett? Either way, I'm stealing it). And that's certainly true, but I would argue this book is about much more than retroactive comedy—it's also about reassurance. Because if history teaches us anything, it's that we've been royally screwing things up for centuries, and yet, somehow, we're still here. In other words, no matter how disastrous things have gotten, whether it's world wars, financial collapses, or the time someone decided to put pineapple on pizza, humanity has demonstrated an uncanny ability to bounce back.

And that actually feels like a pretty useful lesson right now. We are living in a time of nonstop anxiety, where every news update feels like we're inching closer to oblivion. Climate change, global conflicts, social upheaval—sometimes it feels like the whole planet is just one bad decision away from getting snuffed out like a birthday candle in a tornado. But guess what? That feeling isn't new. People in the 1950s were terrified of nuclear annihilation. The 1970s brought an energy crisis and disco. The 1980s had acid-washed jeans and actual acid rain. And somehow, despite all of it, life moved forward. Humanity stumbled, adapted, and—against all odds—kept going.

That's the strangely uplifting message buried in all these SNAFUs. No matter how idiotic, shortsighted, heartbreaking, or downright absurd our mistakes have been, they haven't taken us out yet. And it turns out studying them can be a weirdly optimistic exercise. Sure, it's easy to despair when the world feels like it's unraveling, but looking back at our collective blunders serves as a powerful reminder: We've been here before, and we'll get through this, too.

So, consider me—Ed Helms—your unofficial history teacher. Grab a number two pencil, dust off that three-ring binder, and pull up an unreasonably tiny school desk. I'll be at the front of the class lecturing with gusto and just a hint of coffee breath. Together, we'll explore the wonderfully insane world of SNAFUs, and who knows? You might just learn something.

Let's dive in, shall we?

PART ONE

THE
FIFTIES

NUTS OVER NUKES

Welcome to the Nifty Fifties! A conservative era and a golden age of growth, science and technology, and...some other, less pleasant things. More on that soon.

As the country bounced back economically after the *biggest* and *deadliest* war in history, we also saw a population explosion (gotta love those Boomers!). New technology was on the brink of blowing up, too. Radios were moved to the back of the living room, as boxy black-and-white television sets made their way into American homes. Households could now gather around the television to see the *ideal* nuclear family à la *The Adventures of Ozzie and Harriet, Leave It to Beaver, The Donna Reed Show,* and *Father Knows Best.*

World War II had ended five years prior to the fifties, and the Cold War clash between the Soviets and Americans was just getting started. In reality, the decade wasn't *all* an American Dream full of shiny automobiles and Elvis Presley. The McCarthy hearings led to Hollywood blacklists; even icons like Orson Welles and Charlie Chaplin were accused of being communists. Not to mention there was a growing sense of nuclear dread casting a dark chill over American life.

Ah, yes. The economy, population, and tech weren't all that was exploding...nukes were perhaps the most major (and most radioactive) threat uniting 1950s America. Investment in the development of military-grade weapons was finally paying off post–Manhattan Project. From uranium in baby toys to accidental detonations, it was a decade we look back on fondly—if that fondness means bold-faced fear of nuclear annihilation. Grab that TV dinner and settle in on that Scandinavian sofa—it's time to go nuts for nukes in our first decade full of SNAFUs.

ATOMIC ENERGY LAB:

AN ENRICHING RADIO*ACTIVITY* FOR THE OPPENHEIMERS OF TOMORROW

In 1951, an iconic toy-maker
decided kids could have a little
radium, as a treat.

It's Christmas Day 1951. Bing Crosby's voice blares from the radio, and little Johnny's lungs are full of secondhand smoke from Dad's first cigarette of the morning. His eyes drift to that fat package under the tree. What could it be?

He tears through the paper to reveal a bright red box made to look like a briefcase. Splashed across the top in bold yellow letters are the words GILBERT U-238 ATOMIC ENERGY LAB, with some illustrated atoms to complete the effect. He opens it, revealing an honest-to-God miniature lab, complete with test tubes, a spherical glass cloud chamber, and instruments with intriguing and mysterious names like "deionizer" and "spinthariscope." There's even a short comic titled "Learn How Dagwood Splits the Atom!," the title page of which features a grateful Blondie kissing the titular hero on the cheek as he stares into the middle distance, lost in contemplation of the unspeakable powers he has unleashed.

Promotional materials boast of "awe-inspiring sights!" and the ability to "actually SEE the paths of electrons and alpha particles traveling at speeds of more than 10,000 miles per SECOND!" On the box, beneath an image of a rosy-cheeked lad gazing in wonder at a working version of the set, are the words "Exciting! Safe!" But only one of those is accurate...because those four little jars next to the base of the cloud chamber are full of freaking *uranium*.

SCIENCE IS COOL, KIDS!

Let's begin by reminding ourselves that it was a different time. Advances in chemistry and nuclear physics were front-page news, just like advances in AI and deep-fake technology are today. In 1898, Marie and Pierre Curie discovered radium. In 1913, Niels Bohr introduced the world to quantum mechanics. Budding young chemists wondered if they could be the next Albert Einstein or Alfred Nobel. By the turn of the twentieth century, companies were marketing chemistry sets for teenagers, typically portable copies of the tools used by actual chemists, and they became popular toys.

Enter *another* Alfred: Alfred Carlton Gilbert. A man of many talents, Gilbert was an accomplished athlete who once held the world record for most consecutive chin-ups *and* won a gold medal in the pole vault at the 1908 Olympics. He studied medicine at Yale but decided to forsake that career path for a more noble calling: magician.

Gilbert paid his way through college by performing magic tricks. After school, he began producing magic kits stuffed with trick coins and playing cards, founding the magnificently named Mysto Manufacturing. Gilbert crossed over into the chemistry set game as early as 1917.

THE ERECTOR WHO SAVED CHRISTMAS

According to toymaker lore, Gilbert's greatest idea came to him during a train ride in 1911. Electricity was all the rage back then, and the tracks between New York and New Haven were being electrified. As Gilbert wondered at the high-voltage power line towers rising beside the tracks, he became enamored with the complicated network of girders and scaffolding that made their construction possible. He immediately set to work on what may very well have been a bolt of genius: a miniaturized but extremely lifelike toy version of the engineering marvel he'd witnessed. The Erector Set was born.

In 1913, he debuted a wooden case containing a set of small steel beams, gears, pulleys, and everything the user needed to build a wide variety of miniature mechanical wonders. Gilbert's sets included a tiny motor, allowing kids to create small working cranes and other devices that functioned just like their grown-up counterparts. The Gilbert Erector Set was an immediate hit.

During World War I, Gilbert earned the enviable moniker "The Man Who Saved Christmas" after he appeared before the US Council of National Defense to argue that toy factories should be allowed to continue production during wartime. "America is the home of toys that educate as well as amuse," Gilbert said at the time, "that visualize to the boy his future occupations, that start him on the road to construction and not destruction." This noble sentiment— and, possibly, the fact that Gilbert's toy factories were *also* churning out machine-gun parts, gas masks, and Colt .45s throughout the war—swayed the council. Christmas 1918 was saved.

Boys (and, surely, girls, too, even though there was *zero* mention of girls among decades' worth of Erector advertising materials) loved the hands-on and true-to-life construction experience, while parents appreciated the educational value of Gilbert's invention. A generation of anxious parents must have breathed sighs of relief as they watched their sons eschew a career in magic for something more practical. (Though Steve Martin still did pretty well for himself.) But that solace wouldn't last long.

POWER IN THE PALM OF YOUR HAND

On July 16, 1945, in a remote desert basin in New Mexico, a select few witnessed the awesome power of atomic energy for the first time in human history as the United States tested its first-ever nuclear weapon.

Famously, the sight caused Dr. J. Robert Oppenheimer to reflect upon lines from the Bhagavad Gita: "Now I am become Death, Destroyer of Worlds." There's no record of Oppenheimer or anyone else thinking anything along the lines of "Wow, if only I could expose my son to a small amount of that!" But they weren't thinking like A. C. Gilbert.

Thus, in 1950, Gilbert unveiled the U-238 Atomic Lab, the most sophisticated chemistry set ever to hit the market, and almost certainly the most ill-advised. By assembling the cloud chamber and activating the deionizer, kids could watch the "delicate, intricate paths of electrical condensation" formed by the decay of the samples of radioactive material.

Yes, *radioactive material*. The kit contained four jars of *radioactive uranium-containing minerals*: autunite, torbernite, uraninite, and some carnotite, just for good measure. "There was nothing phony about our Atomic Energy laboratory," Gilbert would later boast.

But maybe there *should* have been? I mean, there's a reason the Easy-Bake Oven is just a warm light bulb.

To be fair, the isotopes included in the set were less dangerous than those used in the Manhattan Project—what higher standard could you ask for in a children's toy?—but they could still cause long-term organ damage if ingested. To Gilbert's credit, the manual did caution users not to break or unseal the jars containing the samples. "You would run the risk of having radioactive ore spread out in your laboratory," it warned.

It also glossed over the fact that said "laboratory" was almost certainly either a child's bedroom, or maybe a family's kitchen table. Also, giving kids a bottle with *special stuff inside* and telling them *not* to open it seems like an exact recipe for the aforementioned tots getting hammers to crack into those little glowing tubes.

Gilbert insisted that none of the radioactive materials used in the set "might conceivably prove dangerous," a patently false claim that stands as a testament to the unwisdom of allowing magicians to market radioactive toys to children. God only knows what might have happened if the Atomic Lab kit had proven as successful as the Erector Set. Thankfully for the lungs and kidneys of America's youth, the set was only available for about two years before Gilbert shut production down.

"Wait a minute," you might say, "did it really take Gilbert an entire year to decide that Baby's First Nuclear Device was a bad idea for a toy?"

No! It's actually worse than that. Safety concerns were *not* the reason that Gilbert ceased production. Instead, it was a matter of dollars and cents: The kit was extremely expensive to produce. Even at $50 a pop—well over $500 in 2025 money—Gilbert was selling the kits at a loss. The high price prevented the Atomic Lab from selling well—no wonder, given that any family living within a few hours' drive of a nuclear plant could expose themselves to radiation for a *fraction* of that price.

Shockingly, there are no recorded instances of radiation poisoning stemming from the kit. And, while the threat of radiation escaping was very real, the estimated radiation exposure from playing with the kit amounted to roughly the same amount one receives from spending a sunny day outdoors without protection. Given that a recent study found that as many as *half* of children's toys contain harmful chemicals, the U-238 Atomic Lab is somehow *not* the most dangerous plaything ever conceived.

If we had learned our lesson from Gilbert, maybe toxic playsets would have gone the way of the lawn dart. But the powers-that-be never do seem to learn. Take for example the Hassenfeld Brothers' (later, Hasbro) actual attempt to make Flubber for children in 1962, a product tie-in for Disney's first-ever sequel to *The Absent-Minded Professor*—yes, *that* Flubber, from the 1997 Robin Williams flick—which left so many kids with bubbling rashes that the manufacturers buried their entire stock under the parking lot. Or take the CSI Fingerprint Analysis Kit, which was available until 2009. The front of the box shouts that little Johnny can "lift prints just like a real CSI." What it doesn't tell you is that the fingerprint powder is 7 percent tremolite, an extremely toxic form of asbestos, which causes lung cancer.

"Toy has never seemed to me to be the right word to apply to such things," Gilbert later wrote of kits like the Atomic Lab. He wanted it to be a serious educational tool for young neutron enjoyers, not something frivolous five-year-olds would dump into the pile of action figures under their bed.

By the time he retired in 1954, Gilbert had accumulated no fewer than 152 patents, the most famous of which was undoubtedly the Erector Set. Ever the innovator, he also set an example for other businessmen by providing a company lawyer for his employees free of charge, paying some of their medical expenses, and embracing the then-radical concept of maternity leave.

Ironically, the failure of the Atomic Lab did wonders for Gilbert's legacy: Today, he's remembered for saving Christmas and inventing the wildly popular Erector Set, and not as the infamous defendant in the hypothetical class-action juvenile radiation poisoning lawsuit that would have arisen if his radioactive toy had caught on.

THE CHOSIN FEW:

MORE THAN THEY COULD CHEW

That time during the Korean War when
American troops got bad orders...
but at least they got some candy?

It was November 28, 1950. And high atop the icy mountains of North Korea, the US First Marine Division found themselves in what can only be described as a really bad situation. Trapped in the unforgiving terrain around the Chosin Reservoir, near the village of Hagaru-ri, they were joined by a small detachment of British commandos and a handful of South Korean police—about 30,000 troops in total. Not exactly a small gathering. Unfortunately, they were about to get ambushed by 120,000 soldiers of the Chinese Communist Army. That's a 4 to 1 ratio, which in military terms translates roughly to: "we're screwed."

The marines fought valiantly, holding their position for almost two weeks. Munitions dwindled, and temperatures dropped far below freezing, frostbite setting into extremities and exposed skin.

The marines needed a miracle, but all they could do was call for more airdrops. And what kind of reinforcement did they receive? Enough firepower to blow the enemy back into the hills? Nope. A hundred thousand more men? No, sir. Captain America, perhaps? Sorry, not even his plucky sidekick, Bucky.

No, the thing that saved these marines on the edge of disaster?

The penny candy classic: the Tootsie Roll.

THE CHOSIN PATH

You might be wondering how the US 1st Marine Division ended up in the frozen mountains of North Korea in the first place. The simplest answer: to fight America's endless war on communism. On June 25, 1950, North Korean forces, backed by the Soviet Union, crossed the Korean Peninsula's thirty-eighth parallel, an ideological dividing line that separates the communist North from the democratic South.

Naturally, Western powers started freaking out. It took President Truman all of two days to pledge US warships and planes to South Korea. But finding men to go and fight across the Pacific Ocean was another story. In the five years following the end of World War II, the Marine Corps had shrunk by more than 50 percent. Perhaps American men simply had other interests, like polishing their Oldsmobiles or picking up ladies at sock hops.

This made Chicago native George McMaster a bit of an anomaly. George was so eager to be a member of the esteemed Marine Corps that he enlisted when he was just seventeen years old. In fact, because he was still a minor in 1948, young George actually tricked his mother into signing the enlistment paperwork.

"World War II was over and we had no one else to fight," George recalled in an interview with the Korean War Educator Foundation. You can probably imagine George's shock—and his poor mother's concern—when two years later, he was deployed to fight overseas. He was assigned as squad leader of the Third Rifle Platoon, Dog Company. Cute name, huh? Unfortunately, the road ahead for Dog Company would be far less simple than a game of fetch.

George and the rest of his dogs boarded a ship bound for Korea on September 21. By September 27, they had North Korean troops fleeing north from Seoul, the South Korean capital. Initially, General Douglas MacArthur, who led the attack, reckoned that the war would end there. But he just had one more *teeny-tiny little* task for the marines: Get back on ships, sail all the way around the tip of the Korean Peninsula into enemy territory, and then chase the North Koreans all the way to the Chinese border.

Sure, no problem, General! It'll be like taking a Tootsie Roll from a baby, right? Well...maybe if that baby were an infant Clark Kent with the grip of a rusty steel vise.

The first hiccup came right off the bat. MacArthur's men were delayed for twelve whole days while minesweepers cleaned the water around their landing zone. George and his pals were left at sea, just waiting. I like to think of them playing pinochle while they cracked jokes about "His Royal Highness Douglas MacArthur and his lapdog staff."

One of those lapdogs was General Edward Almond. If MacArthur was Michael Scott, regional manager, then Almond was Dwight Schrute, assistant *to* the regional manager. He was MacArthur's chief of staff, or as George liked to say, his "chief ass-kisser." While MacArthur commanded the whole operation in Korea, Almond commanded the whole ragtag corps on its way inland to enemy territory. Beneath him was a practical and modest general named O. P. Smith who commanded the marines' 1st Division. Despite literally being in command of George's Dog Company, among many others, General Smith was by all accounts *not* a lapdog. In fact, he'd been butting heads with Almond since day one.

Smith's skepticism of the American tactics would only intensify in the weeks ahead. And it was all justified. Months earlier, President Truman had asked General MacArthur the likelihood of the Chinese entering the war. MacArthur knew that the Chinese had up to 125,000 troops stationed just over the border between China and North Korea, but he insisted that they weren't much of a threat.

So Truman gave MacArthur the order to give Almond the order to give Smith the order to march the marines inland toward the border, around the Chosin Reservoir, and deep into the mountains of North Korea. That order gave no indication that more than 20,000 men would face a fight unlike any they'd ever seen before.

A FROZEN BATTLE

George and the rest of his company stepped ashore in North Korea on October 26. While hiking north, they spotted a handful of South Korean soldiers, as George said, "running hell-bent" in the other direction, abandoning their position and their weapons. The South Koreans tried to warn them: The Chinese were advancing.

But the marines had to obey their command: Keep moving. So they took the abandoned weapons for themselves and assembled atop a nearby hill. Then, out of nowhere, enemy bullets started flying. The marines spent the rest of the day defending themselves from the hills. By George's account, his company lost two men in the surprise attack, but they had the area secured by nightfall.

This unnerving new development didn't seem to upset MacArthur and his intelligence staff. His earlier assumptions had been proven wrong, but he still thought that China's "peasant army" didn't pose a significant threat.

Almond ordered Smith to get his men up the road to the Chosin Reservoir as fast as possible. After doing so, Smith set up his headquarters in a town called Hagaru-ri, complete with a medical clearing center and—the keystone of Smith's whole operation—an airstrip. Until the airstrip was complete, planes couldn't land to deliver supplies to the troops, but they air-dropped plenty of C rations, ammo, and medical equipment. In those rations? You guessed it: some delicious Tootsie Rolls. But we'll get to that.

Almond ordered Smith to send George's regiment up through the mountains northwest of the Chosin Reservoir. They departed on Thanksgiving Day and stopped in the evening for a modest feast, airdropped from the sky. George said it felt strange to have real food after eating out of C-ration cans for so long. The only problem was that this was *solid food* in every sense: The weather was so cold that their turkey and potatoes were chunks of ice by the time they dug in.

The cold intensified in the days ahead. George heard someone mention that it was thirty-five degrees below zero. He and his section were assigned a patrol in the nearby hills. As they approached a small village, a few Chinese soldiers emerged with their hands raised in surrender. But George's squad smelled a rat and approached the soldiers with caution—and with reinforcements.

Their instincts were spot-on. Out of nowhere, Chinese troops in the hills above started firing down at them from all directions.

That elevation gave the enemy a slight edge, but the marines had more advanced weapons, and soon they had backup. They called for air support, and American planes roared in—dropping napalm on Chinese soldiers taking cover in the upper hills. By dusk the fighting settled down, but the carnage was far from over.

At around eleven P.M., George's squad faced the first of several waves of Chinese soldiers. He said their method of attack was simple: "Mass a large number of men, get as close to us as possible without being detected, and charge, hoping that we would run out of ammunition, our weapons would jam, or we would run out of men defending our positions."

Throughout the night, ammunition did indeed begin to run out. George was hit in the pinky. Luckily, it was so cold that his blood just froze to his glove instead of leaving his body in large quantities. I guess that's good? Then he got hit below the armpit. He felt the flow of blood and held his arm up to the night sky to see if it was still there. Thankfully, it was. George remained on the ground, unable to move. As the light broke on the morning of November 28, he finally stood on his feet and walked around the battlefield. There were bodies everywhere.

Back at headquarters, Generals Almond and MacArthur were reeling from their missteps. So General Smith took matters into his own hands. A classic case of managing up. He ordered the marines in the north to halt their attacks and fight their way back south down the reservoir to headquarters at Hagaru-ri. But they would need reinforcements for the fourteen-mile journey.

Airdrops had been the marines' saving grace since the beginning of their mission in the Chosin Reservoir, and they'd need a lot more to make it out of the mountains alive. Planes scattered the hills with re-ups of medical supplies, ammunition, C-rations, and more. And here's where the Tootsie Rolls save the day. A big stock of the tubular taffy candy arrived at the Post Exchange at Hagaru-ri, and in a moment of desperation, General Smith rationed them among troops. In George's memory, the candy was available by the truckload. Other accounts have lieutenants fighting over their allotted candy stashes.

So why on Earth were our marines gorging on empty calories during the Korean War? Well, the US military actually started feeding Tootsie Rolls to the troops during World War II, when the candy's property of unmeltability proved advantageous in the sweltering heat. In North Korea, George and his fellow soldiers discovered that Tootsie Rolls were just about the only food that would *warm up* easily despite the freezing temperatures. Frozen meat and potatoes? Not so useful. But a blast of sugar did the trick. They'd use their body heat to soften the candy, and the sugar gave them the energy they needed to survive.

In fact, there were *so many* Tootsies rolling around between the men, and so *few* bullets, that the complete catastrophe of the situation birthed a legend. As the story goes, a supply drop that was supposed to contain ammunition was filled with candy instead, because they were using the code name "TOOTSIE ROLLS" for mortar rounds. Someone in the telephone chain between the surrounded marines and the supply depot had a brain fart. Whether the legend is true or not, one thing's certain—the First Marine Division ended up with a mountain of Tootsie Rolls. And in the brutal cold of the Chosin Reservoir, calories were as crucial as ammunition. It's safe to say that without the sweet, chewy sustenance of those little chocolatey lifesavers, the marines might not have made it out of the mountains alive.

After a three-day hike, George and his company arrived at Hagaru-ri. Bullets flew from the hills as they approached headquarters. George stumbled

into a makeshift hospital tent. There, he was told he would likely be flown out
to safety and receive further medical treatment. But at that moment, he had
other, more pressing priorities. He went straight to the cook shack, thrilled to
eat a meal that didn't come in a wrapper.

THE CHOSIN FEW

On December 5, George boarded a plane with other wounded and frostbitten
soldiers and evacuated Hagaru-ri. He was among the last of those to be flown
out, eventually arriving at a hospital in Japan for proper treatment. Ten thousand still remained at basecamp.

By now, it was evident that MacArthur's grand fantasy of taking the Chosin
Reservoir and advancing on to the border of China was a no-go. With his and
Almond's egos badly bruised, it was up to General Smith to get the rest of the
men to safety. Over at the command center, reporters asked Smith his next
move. His answer went down in marine history: "When you're surrounded, it
is impossible to retreat. We're simply attacking in a different direction."

And so the marines prepared to backtrack—a backtrack attack, you might
say—along the icy, narrow road that brought them to the Chosin Reservoir,
down the mountains, and to the coast, where they could evacuate from enemy
territory. The frigid temperatures persisted, and walking was the only way
they could keep warm.

You can bet your bottom dollar that the marines relied on Tootsie Rolls
for this trek, too. In fact, candy was just about the only thing left to chew on.
Then, on December 10, 1950, they finally cleared the last treacherous mountain pass and boarded flat train cars that took them to the coastline. There,
ships awaited them with showers, hot food, medical relief, and rest.

The whole ordeal at the Chosin Reservoir lasted just thirteen days. Thousands of men were killed, wounded, or missing in action. But the legacy of the
marines who fought there endures far longer than a Tootsie Roll's shelf life.
Survivors of the battle are called the "Chosin Few," and they're honored today
with a monument at Dallas–Fort Worth National Cemetery.

George McMaster received a respectable bundle of awards, including
the Purple Heart, Navy–Marine Corps Combat Action Ribbon, and two Navy
Presidential Unit Citations. He also brought the bullet he took at Chosin
back home inside him. When he talked about the experience, he said he could

still feel it in his chest sometimes. Understandably, General Smith became a highly decorated war hero, receiving a lengthy list of awards and medals that would take up half the page.

General Almond didn't face much backlash for his tactical mistakes. After all, he was just a dog in MacArthur's lap. As for MacArthur, the Korean War badly tarnished his otherwise stellar legacy. He was relieved from command by President Truman.

Decades later, the marines gave one more award to an individual who was not at the Chosin Reservoir—Ellen Gordon, chairman and CEO of Tootsie Roll Industries. And if you assume that the Chosin Few couldn't bear to chew up another Tootsie Roll after their return from Korea, you'd be wrong! Tootsie Roll Industries continued to supply 1st Marine Division members with gift boxes of the candy long after the war. Fortunately, this time around, they weren't frozen.

JIMMY CARTER'S NUCLEAR NUTS

What happened when the 39th president was twenty-eight years old? He was sent into the heart of a nuclear reactor's meltdown.

At 3:07 P.M. on Friday, December 12, 1952, a cold wind blew over the ice-flecked shores of the Ottawa River. Squat brick buildings lined the riverbank as snow fell gently on the hillside. It was like an illustration from a little old Canadian grandma's Christmas cookie tin. If Grandma's cookie tin was decorated with festive illustrations of...a nuclear research facility. Weird choice for a cookie tin, Grandma.

But inside this facility, Chalk River Laboratories in Deep River, Ontario, Canada, the scene was anything but calm and bright. Well, maybe a little bright. Red lights were flashing in the facility's control room because their fancy new nuclear reactor, NRX, was seconds away from melting down.

At the time, NRX was the most powerful research reactor in the world. And in those early days of the nuclear power boom, it was an atomic scientist's dream—an enormous cylindrical beast straight out of a 1950s drive-in sci-fi flick. It stood in the center of a light-filled redbrick building, the reactor vessel housed in concrete. It was ten feet tall and twenty-six feet wide and could conjure up to thirty megawatts of nuclear power—enough to light up three US cities for a year—with supremely radioactive uranium fuel rods at its core.

So when the Chalk River plant supervisor—decked out in thick Buddy Holly glasses and a plastic pocket protector, no doubt—saw those red lights go on, he started shaking in his plant-issued underwear. Those lights meant that the boron carbide safety rods inside the reactor core, the ones that kept NRX from overheating and unleashing a tidal wave of radiation across the picturesque cookie-tin shores of the Ottawa River, were dangling *out* of the reactor.

Ol' Buddy freaked out and ran downstairs to stop the operator in the basement from giving everyone in the plant a nasty case of radiation sickness right before the holidays.

He arrived just in time to stop the basement operator in his tracks. But they weren't out of the woods yet. Buddy still needed his assistant upstairs to push a specific combination of buttons to reset the reactor and fix the basement operator's mistake. He grabbed the phone and spewed out the button combo to his assistant, but in a turn of events straight out of an *I Love Lucy* episode, just moments after issuing the order, Buddy realized that he'd asked the assistant to push the *wrong* buttons! He screamed through the phone for the assistant to stop, but alas, the assistant needed *both* hands free to push the buttons, and he had already put the phone down. He was now out of earshot.

Buddy screamed into the void. The reactor was toast. Hydrogen gas explosions hurled NRX's gasholder dome four feet into the air—accounts differ, but some say it quite literally hit the roof—releasing radiation into the atmosphere and flooding the basement with about a million gallons of radioactive water. As this mess unfurled, there were some 1,800 workers going about their business on-site.

A radioactive lagoon had formed in the basement at Chalk River Labs, and the damaged NRX was a ticking time bomb that had to be disassembled, fast. On their shortlist of worries: The radioactive water could start leaking into the Ottawa River, the uranium hydride on the melted fuel rods could oxidize and start a fire, or the hydrogen that escaped during the explosion could mingle with the irradiated water and burn in the air, starting a raging bonfire that'd put a level ten pyro to shame. I repeat: The literal AIR around them could have caught on fire. Plus, the radiation levels around the damaged reactor were *extremely high*, so they couldn't just send in someone like our civilian friend Buddy the Plant Supervisor to repair it.

It was a mess. And on top of that, it was a *secret* mess sparked by mechanical issues and operating errors. This was the first nuclear core meltdown to *ever* happen, and at that time there were only a few people in the whole world with the necessary skills, security clearance, and a *"Sir, I'm willing to get radiation poisoning to serve my country, yes sir!"* type attitude, someone willing to go into the belly of the damaged reactor and fix it. In short: Chalk River needed help. So when a top secret, state-of-the-art nuclear reactor is in need of disassemblin', who's the Canadian government gonna call?

They punched their fingers into their rotary phones and dialed up Captain Hyman Rickover, the man in charge of the top secret US atomic submarine program. Rickover's men knew their way around a nuclear reactor. And since this was the first nuclear mess of its kind, it seemed like...an opportunity. A shining chance to give his men real-life experience with nuclear cleanup. *Gee, thanks, Captain Rickover.* So he bellowed down to his star subordinate, a young, up-and-coming lieutenant, to task him with leading this idiotically dangerous cleanup job.

And who was that naval officer? It was none other than twenty-eight-year-old Jimmy Carter.

JIMMY TO THE RESCUE

Around the time that the NRX was melting into a puddle of radioactive goo over in Canada, Jimmy Carter was posted just across the border in Schenectady, New York, as the senior officer of the USS *Seawolf*, one of the first US atomic submarines. He'd been getting up to all kinds of eggheaded nuclear hijinks, teaching his men about everything from math and physics to reactor technology. Then he heard Captain Rickover's bellowing call.

Suddenly, Carter and his team of twenty-four atomically inclined navy men found themselves whisked away from Schenectady and plopped on a train, watching the snow-dusted Canadian forest roll by out the window. Sounds kind of romantic...if they weren't on their way to disarm the melting heart of a super-radioactive nuclear device. They weren't allowed to tell their wives, or any other family members, where they were going. As Carter's biographer Jonathan Alter put it, "Carter had essentially been drafted into battle."

Once Jimbo and his team rolled up to Chalk River, they were greeted by more than 800 staff and 170 Canadian military personnel. It was like a small city of people bustling around in hazmat suits with mops and buckets. They briefed Jimmy and his team on the stupidly dangerous mission they were about to undertake: The reactor core was deep underground and, as Carter writes in his autobiography *A Full Life*, "surrounded by intense radioactivity...each of us would absorb the maximum permissible dose with just ninety seconds of exposure."

Just *ninety seconds.* In 1952, the maximum amount of radiation the government deemed acceptable for its officers to endure each year was *1,000*

RADIATION

times higher than it is today. And the "protective clothing"? Basically a bee-keeper outfit with a gas mask. So Jimmy devised a plan to make this dangerous job *slightly* less terrifying—essentially, a nuclear relay race with deadly consequences for dropping the baton. He divided his men up into teams of three. Each team's mission was to go into the reactor and disarm it quickly and efficiently, in ninety-second increments, hurriedly unscrewing one nut and bolt at a time.

They practiced their nuclear relay race on an exact replica of the damaged reactor that the personnel at Chalk River had built on a nearby tennis court in the days right after the NRX meltdown, time being of the essence, and a safe, non-irradiated place to practice being crucial to their success. So the faux reactor was ready and waiting for Jimmy and his crew when they arrived on-site.

The teams of three practiced jumping into their heavy white suits and masks, then running like madmen into the faux reactor to replace the relevant parts of the machine. As Jimmy recounted in *A Full Life*, "We tried again and again until we were as proficient as possible."

Only then did they descend into the true belly of the beast.

For the radioactive relay, the team relied on primitive CTV: Big, bulky TV cameras were set up underground inside the reactor. Jimmy and his men watched carefully as each team ran into the reactor, unscrewed the proper nuts and bolts, and tore right back out. Then, outside on the tennis court, the men made those exact same repairs to the faux reactor, bolt by bolt—monkey see, monkey do.

Jimmy's relay team was the last group to go down. He wrote in his 1975 autobiography *Why Not the Best?*, "We descended into the reactor and worked frantically for our allotted time." Well, all that tennis court practice paid off—Jimmy and his partners finished disassembling the reactor in one minute and twenty-nine seconds, with one extra second of exposure to spare.

Finally, NRX was neutralized.

Jimmy and his team breathed a sigh of relief through their gas masks, patted one another on the back, and hopped on the train back to Schenectady. But even though their mission was a success...Jimmy and his team still weren't free from NRX.

NO MORE NEUTRONS

In the 1950s, very little was understood about the aftereffects of radiation. The fallout from Hiroshima and Nagasaki was still being studied. So, for several months after their nuclear relay, Carter and his team were required to submit urine and fecal samples to the government, which were monitored for radioactivity. In fact, doctors told Carter that after being exposed to this much radiation he probably wouldn't be able to have any more children.

All in all, Carter's pee was radioactive for a full six months! But despite his glowing urine, "there were no apparent aftereffects from the exposure—just a lot of doubtful jokes among ourselves about death versus sterility." (And, in spite of the navy doctor's predictions concerning Jimmy's future fertility, he still had four healthy kids.)

In 1953, after the death of his father, Carter was honorably discharged from the navy, and he headed back to Plains, Georgia, to take over the family peanut business. Despite his distance from the budding nuclear power boom, his experience at Chalk River remained fresh in his mind—he'd return to that experience, speaking and writing about it, over and over throughout his lifetime. On the campaign trail, in his presidential autobiographies...maybe even

in a pair of Levi's on the front porch of the Georgia governor's mansion, spinning his yarn about the Chalk River fiasco to Gregg Allman—of the Allman Brothers, of course—over a bottle of J & B Scotch.

In a 2008 interview with the *Ottawa Citizen* aptly titled, "When Jimmy Carter Faced Radioactivity Head-on," Carter's close friend and personal biographer Peter Bourne said that prior to the incident with NRX, Carter approached nuclear power in a "very scientific and dispassionate way." But after descending into a melting nuclear reactor, his outlook changed. He saw and felt firsthand nuclear power's ability to destroy, as he fumbled with NRX's radioactive nuts and bolts in a flimsy hazmat suit.

Bourne said he believes the *emotional* fallout of the experience influenced Carter's thinking during his time as president. As Bourne recounted in the 2008 *Ottawa Citizen* interview, "not just in terms of having his finger on the nuclear button, but in his decision not to pursue...the neutron bomb as a weapon."

Carter said it best in his inaugural address:

We pledge perseverance and wisdom in our efforts to limit the world's armaments...and we will move this year a step toward the ultimate goal—the elimination of all nuclear weapons from this Earth. We urge all other people to join us, for success can mean life instead of death.

To this day, neither the United States nor any other nation has deployed a neutron weapon. So maybe ol' Jimmy peed neon for months, and heck, he even made it to the ripe old age of 100 (RIP, Jimmy), but this is the rare case in which sending a future US president into the heart of danger also changed the course of history...for the better.

MKULTRA:

ONE MAN'S MISSION TO TRIP AMERICA'S BALLS OFF FOR FREEDOM

In the 1950s, a CIA scientist secretly bought the entire world's supply of LSD, embarking on a horrific attempt to discover the secrets to mind control.

On a summer's night in 1955, federal drug enforcement agent George White sat on a custom porta-john, poured himself a drink from a pitcher full of premixed, pre-chilled martinis, and watched a CIA-funded sex worker secretly slip one of her clients a dose of LSD. From libations, to fornication, to pillow talk, White gawked at their every move from behind a two-way mirror, listening to every sound via microphones tucked into electrical outlets. He downed his martinis, scrawled observations on a notepad, and occasionally unzipped to make use of his toilet-turned-office-chair, so he wouldn't have to miss a second of the action.

This was a dishonest day's work in what White dubbed "Operation Midnight Climax": a government-funded peep show that itself was part of a CIA "research" program code-named MKUltra, which ran 149 projects across universities, hospitals, and prisons, to develop methods of mind control on civilians, patients, and the incarcerated. Originally an attempt to beat the Soviets in a contest of brain warfare, MKUltra grew into an abusive, unaccountable research program that covertly drugged thousands of Americans for twenty years and expanded the CIA's arsenal of unethical interrogation practices.

And if you want to (ahem) *wrap your brain* around how and why a program funded to prevent Americans from being mind-controlled would pay for the installation of a portable toilet behind a false wall in a San Francisco apartment, then you need to understand the man who approved that purchase order: a CIA chemist named Sidney Gottlieb.

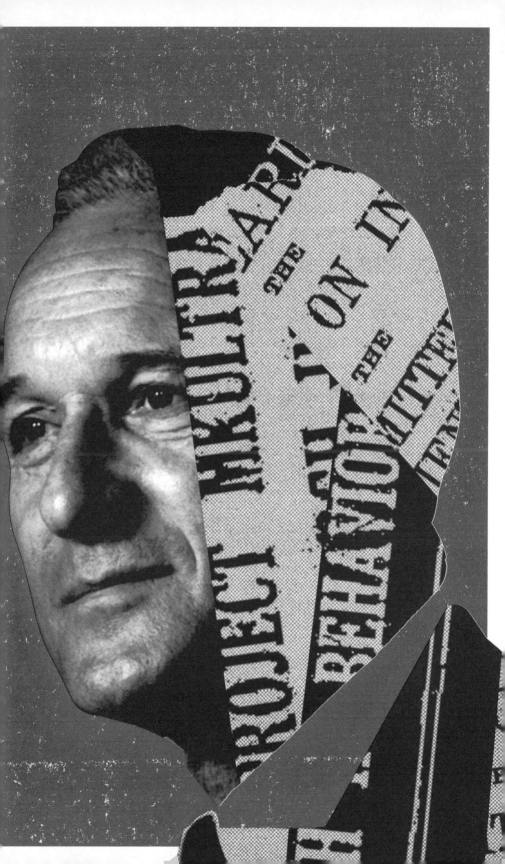

JUST THE (EVERY)MAN WE'RE LOOKING FOR

Gottlieb was the son of Hungarian Jewish immigrants and grew up in New York City. Born with a clubfoot and battling a stutter through childhood, he struggled with bullies as a child. But he excelled at academics and grew into a brilliant scholar. He earned a PhD in biochemistry from Caltech, then settled down with his wife and two daughters and went to work for the US Department of Agriculture to research...soil. Typical "hero's journey" stuff.

Now, you may be asking, "Ed! Why would a soil-sniffing family man with no history of violence become a shadowy scientist for the CIA?"

Well, that's exactly the point of this particular SNAFU: Gottlieb was, by all accounts, a gentle researcher who loved folk dancing, meditation, family, and goat's milk. He felt terrible when his physical disabilities stopped him from fighting in the Second World War. And when the CIA came calling, he was more than ready to answer, like so many patriots at the dawn of McCarthyism.

By the time Gottlieb joined the CIA's Technical Services Staff in 1951, the US government had already recruited former Nazi and Japanese imperial scientists to continue human experiments they had begun for the Axis Powers during World War II. And if testing interrogation methods on concentration camp prisoners could become a résumé builder for the sake of fighting the USSR, then the call of patriotism would be more than enough for Gottlieb to embark on a career that was literally toxic.

In 1953, Gottlieb's boss and benefactor, CIA Director Allen Dulles, delivered a speech to an audience of Princeton alums, painting a picture of imminent "brain warfare" to be waged on the free world by China and the Soviet Union. He cited interviews with American POWs who had been treated harshly by their North Korean captors, and a missionary who was interrogated for seventy-five days by Chinese Communists.

Dulles was alarmed that these prisoners had made anti-American statements or betrayed fellow Americans by giving false testimony. Detailing the extensive torture that caused these prisoners to break down and confess to things they hadn't done, he warned that America's enemies were on track to scale their mastery of mental conditioning through chemical agents, threatening to brainwash the world with "lie serum." To Dulles, it was time that we got serious about catching up with them in the war to control the human mind.

That's how—in an America where authority figures spread fears of "brain warfare," then responded to their own fearmongering by committing secret brain warfare on their own countrymen—Sidney Gottlieb was given a blank check to do anything, to anyone, without their knowledge or consent, as long as it was in the name of outracing the Communists to produce effective techniques for mind control.

ONE BUILT A CUCKOO'S NEST

Even before MKUltra was in full force, Gottlieb had already drugged and killed people in the name of freedom. Just a couple of years before Dulles declared brain war, Gottlieb had flown to Japan with a CIA team to drug and question four Japanese nationals who had been suspected of spying for the USSR. During this interrogation, the four suspects confessed, after which Gottlieb's team shot them and dumped their corpses into the Tokyo Bay.

I know, I know. You're reading this book in the twenty-first century, so you're probably already assuming that the CIA does some incredibly shady stuff in the name of national security.

Well, that classic CIA playbook took a psychedelic turn when Gottlieb spent 240,000 American taxpayer dollars (around $2.8 million when adjusted for inflation) to buy the entire world's supply of LSD—then used his power at the CIA to set up experiment after experiment at various universities, hospitals, and prisons.

You may have heard that Ken Kesey (author of *One Flew Over the Cuckoo's Nest*) volunteered for CIA experiments at the VA hospital near Stanford University. Not only did this actually happen, but Kesey was paid $75 each time he got high on LSD. Then he got a job as a night attendant on the psychiatric ward so he could steal stashes of the drug and throw psychedelic parties with his buddies. These experiences would become the inspiration for his first novel.

That's right, folks. The CIA gave the world *One Flew Over the Cuckoo's Nest*! But hold your breath, because this is about to get extremely upsetting...

Gottlieb's LSD experiments were often performed on people who were supposedly being cared for or rehabilitated by the government. At the National Institute of Mental Health's Addiction Research Center in Lexington, Kentucky, a doctor put seven substance-addicted Black patients into isolation quarters and dosed them with LSD, without their knowledge, for seventy-seven days. At Ionia State Hospital in Michigan, patients who had been declared criminally insane were secretly given LSD and interrogated. And at the Atlanta Federal Penitentiary, mafia soldier James "Whitey" Bulger was injected with LSD almost every week for fifteen months. He thought he was helping doctors find a cure for schizophrenia, and his reward was a lifetime of violent visions and haunting nightmares.

Then there was the heinous series of "experiments" at the Allan Memorial Institute in Montreal, where Dr. Ewen Cameron used MKUltra money to "treat" patients with electroshocks, forced paralysis, and more than 150 hours of forced listening to hypnotic recordings of his own voice—intended to "depattern" (basically, destroy) their minds.

These experiments were conducted with no more than the vague notion that if one was to reprogram a human brain, then one must surely wipe it clean first. And Dr. Cameron was so trusted as an authority figure that he was even allowed to put a pregnant nurse named Esther Schrier into a series of drug-induced comas.

Schrier, who had struggled with anxiety and postpartum depression after the sudden death of her first child, admitted herself to Cameron's care for treatment. She had hoped to become a more capable parent to the child she was carrying. But one month later, she couldn't speak or get up from bed on her own. Seven months later, at the end of her third trimester, Schrier had forgotten even the basics of caring for a newborn.

Gottlieb systematically evaded accountability for these unspeakable horrors. Most of the people who actually ran these experiments had no idea they were being used by the CIA for the purposes of weaponizing LSD. The puppet strings that Gottlieb used to weave MKUltra into these institutions were often made of research grants, and Gottlieb funded subprojects through shells and fronts, making every effort to keep his identity and true purposes secret.

And so, hidden behind layer after layer of CIA subterfuge, Gottlieb created the Greatest Generation's own twisted version of "fuck around and find out"—which brings me back to Operation Midnight Climax, the MKUltra subproject where federal agent George White spied on government-funded sex workers from a secret porta-potty in a San Francisco apartment.

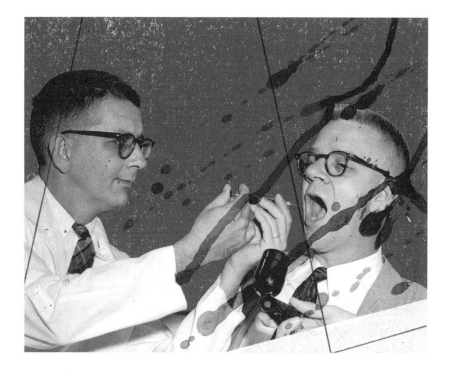

CURIOUS GEORGE

White, unlike Gottlieb, wasn't a hippie-adjacent scientist. He was a burly pug of a man, with a barrel chest and a balding forehead that could take down all ten pins at the end of a bowling lane, no problem. When hunting down an enemy spy in India for the US military, he fought and killed the guy with his bare hands and reportedly kept a photograph of the corpse pinned to a wall in his office. As a drug enforcement agent, he once put a silencer on his pistol so he could carve his initials into the ceiling of a hotel room with bullets. And White was so committed to busting illicit drug dealers that he infiltrated the Chinese American Hip Sing Association for two years to build a case against the group's drug-trafficking leaders.

White also had a substance use problem. When others would drink a glass of gin, he'd drink a bottle, and he would take the very drugs that he seized during busts. He had no scruples and every willingness to break rules behind closed doors. And in 1953, he and Gottlieb set up an apartment in the West Village in New York City, where White would dose unwitting guests with LSD to determine if an acid trip had loosened their lips.

Two years later, when the Bureau of Narcotics transferred White to San Francisco, Gottlieb paid him to set up new "safe houses" there and continue moonlighting for the CIA. White began paying local sex workers kickbacks to bring clients from nearby saloons to his Telegraph Hill apartment, which overlooked the San Francisco Bay.

White decorated the walls of the apartment with boudoir paintings of French cancan dancers, filled its cabinets with sex toys, and watched every scene from behind his two-way mirror. There, deep into the night, he would sit on his portable toilet, take sips of premixed martinis, record post-coital chitchat, and take "research" notes about the behavior of complete strangers whom he had never met, never followed up on, and never engaged for any kind of serious clinical work.

This is how Gottlieb and his associates fought the big brain war that CIA director Dulles had launched. Operation Midnight Climax delivered zero insights of scientific value, unless you're under the impression that ten years of studying kinky, drug-enhanced sex were necessary to prove that some men like to talk after they've had an orgasm.

FROM GOTTLIEB TO GUANTANAMO

On the other hand, what Operation Midnight Climax did *well*—and this is what stories about MKUltra sometimes leave out—was to field-test the CIA's growing arsenal of chemical weapons. White and his team didn't limit their drug experiments to the bedroom; they routinely drugged unsuspecting victims in San Francisco bars with substances that had just been cooked up by the CIA for testing—including sarin, amphetamines, barbiturates, and mustard gas. White's right-hand man, Ike Feldman, once claimed in an interview that he and White tested the prototype for pepper spray.

Remember how Sidney Gottlieb got his start in the CIA as an interrogator, drugging and killing suspected spies overseas? Well, as MKUltra's network of spooks, scientists, and narcs illegally tested drugs on untold numbers of people on American soil, Gottlieb also traveled to clandestine detention centers in Europe and East Asia so he could torture the CIA's prisoners abroad.

Journalists and legislators would eventually discover that MKUltra was just one of six relevant programs run by the CIA—with cooperation from the army and the navy—to grow the CIA's capability to question, coerce, and violate the humanity of anyone it considered to be an enemy of the state. When the program was uncovered by a much more reasonable CIA agent in 1963, the CIA began shrinking its budget. They shuttered Operation Midnight Climax in 1966, and they attempted to destroy all records that the program had ever existed in 1973. In 1976, President Gerald Ford signed an executive order banning executive agencies from experimenting on human beings without consent and established oversight by review boards.

But the CIA's worldwide network of interrogation and torture is alive and well. And if you consider how the CIA and the US military have abused their still-active network of detention centers to detain and torture "enemy combatants"...then the echoes of MKUltra feel less like a mind-bending acid trip and more like a sobering wake-up call.

Remember those American POWs that Allen Dulles had claimed were "brainwashed" by Communists? It just so happens that between 2002 and 2005, US military trainers at Guantanamo Bay taught an interrogation class full of "coercive methods for eliciting individual compliance." They had copied these methods verbatim from a 1957 air force study of "brainwashing." And *that* study had ripped off its own menu of prescribed torture techniques from interviews with...those very same American POWs after they had returned home from the Korean War.

As of the publication of this book, the detention center at Guantanamo Bay has been operating for twenty-three years—though I'm pretty sure they're not dosing people with LSD.

THE HARSH TRUTH

So did anyone in this story learn *anything*? Maybe a teeny-tiny lesson about the dangers of hiding evil behind the veil of patriotism?

Well, in 1977, two decades after the peak of Operation Midnight Climax, Gottlieb testified to the Senate under immunity from prosecution that "I considered all this work...to be extremely unpleasant, extremely difficult, extremely sensitive, but above all, to be extremely urgent and important." In their closed-door session, where he refused to claim any crime against humanity, he said, "Harsh as it may seem in retrospect, it was felt that in an issue where national survival might be concerned, such a procedure and such a risk was a reasonable one to take."

George White, on the other hand, wrote a letter full of more...robust reflections to Gottlieb, as he was dying from cirrhosis. In it, he found the courage to look back on his misdeeds and admit: "I was a very minor missionary, actually a heretic, but I toiled wholeheartedly in the vineyards because it was fun, fun, fun. Where else could a red-blooded American boy lie, kill and cheat, steal, deceive, rape, and pillage with the sanction and blessing of the All-Highest? Pretty Good Stuff, Brudder!"

I can see you face-palming over there, but at least one of these guys was honest. Grotesque, but honest.

Gottlieb eventually realized that LSD wasn't a magic potion for controlling people's minds, but during his career, he crafted a number of good old-fashioned poisons to be used in CIA operations—including attempts to assassinate Chinese prime minister Zhou Enlai, Congolese prime minister Patrice Lumumba, and Cuban revolutionary Fidel Castro.

In 1975, when Gottlieb was called out of retirement to testify about MKUltra, he seemed to be seeking penance by helping treat leprosy in India. He began a late-life career as a speech-language pathologist, and in his final years (while making every legal effort to delay going on trial for drugging people) he worked in a hospice, caring for people who were on their deathbeds.

Pretty much everyone who's written about the life and times of Sidney Gottlieb is mystified by the glaring contradictions that defined his life. But even if Gottlieb went to his grave trying to balance his own moral scale, I think there are some unambiguous truths that we can learn from the man who's been called "the CIA's Gentle-Hearted Torturer."

Even the best of us can commit unspeakable acts of evil. The road to hell is paved with unchallenged intentions. And the ends rarely, if ever, justify a non-consensual, drug-fueled sex show. If we can all agree on that much, then maybe there's still hope for our big American brains to survive the twenty-first century.

MARS BLUFF BOMB

When the US military accidentally
dropped a bomb on the small town of
Mars Bluff, South Carolina.

Nine-year-old Ella David Hudson was playing house in her cousin's yard when she heard the whistle. It sounded like something out of *Looney Tunes*— bending in pitch and getting louder, fast. Ella had just enough time to think to herself, "Is that a jet flying low over us?" before...*PWWUCCCHHHHHHH!*

The world around her exploded. Dirt, buzzing electrical wires, and smoke hung thick in the air. Ella ran as fast as she could. Blood gushed from a gash in her forehead. Her ears rang from the blast, and she could barely hear the muffled sound of screams.

When Ella finally stopped running, she found her cousins standing in the garden, on the edge of a crater fifty feet wide and thirty-five feet deep.

Meanwhile, 15,000 feet above them, US Air Force Captain Bruce Kulka was hanging above an open trapdoor, staring down at the plume rising toward him...and probably thinking something along the lines of "Oh *%$!"

SAFETY FIRST

The plan on the morning of March 11, 1958, was never to drop a bomb on Mars Bluff, South Carolina. In fact, when Bruce Kulka boarded the B-47E bomber that day, he and his three crewmates were planning on flying to England.

They were part of Operation Snow Flurry—what was meant to be a simulated combat mission. Four planes intended to ferry four nuclear bombs across the Atlantic from Hunter Air Force Base in Georgia to Bruntingthorpe. Before they landed in England, each crew would simulate a bomb drop. Emphasis on *simulate*! Instead of dropping an actual, thirty-kiloton explosive on an unsuspecting British town (which would be frowned upon), the crew would hit a button at exactly the right moment, transmitting an electronic signal to a computer on the ground, which would calculate their accuracy.

You might be wondering, why bother carrying an actual nuclear weapon on a training mission? Well, Cold War–era wisdom dictated that you could never be sure when a fake war might suddenly be interrupted by a real one. Thus, the US Air Force liked to keep their aircraft armed and at the ready.

With that in mind, at eight A.M. on March 11, a two-man crew loaded the 7,600-pound bomb into Bruce Kulka's B-47E. The bomb, which was ten feet, eight inches long with a belly sixty-one inches around, hung snugly from a pneumatically powered catch in the back of the plane. For most of the flight, it would also be held securely in place by a steel locking pin, which when inserted made it impossible for the bomb to be released from the catch.

But as the crew loaded the bomb, they found a small problem with the aforementioned locking pin. For some odd reason, it wouldn't engage. Per air force safety regulations, the locking pin had to be removed for both takeoff and landing. Yes, you read that correctly: The *safety regulation* called for unlocking a bomb. This was because the B-47 was *heavy*—so heavy that it couldn't land safely with a full tank of fuel. Most of the time, this wasn't a problem; a B-47 crew could simply fly around until they'd burned off enough fuel weight to land without crashing. But in case of an emergency landing, they needed a way to jettison a bunch of weight, and fast.

Unlike other aircraft, the B-47 wasn't built to dump its fuel tanks during flight, so the engineers looked around for another easy solution. And the 7,600-pound explosive hanging out in the bomb bay seemed like a good one. In case of emergency on takeoff or landing, all the crew had to do was hit the pneumatic trigger in the cockpit, and the bomb would tumble out of the bomb bay door, freeing up enough weight for the heavy plane to land safely. On training flights, the plutonium and uranium core of the bomb was either stored separately within the plane or not carried on board at all. So, either way, while the ditched bomb would explode upon impact, at least it wouldn't be a nuclear explosion.

But don't worry, folks, this was just a worst-case scenario. For almost all of the flight, the locking pin would be engaged, and the bomb definitely, surely, don't be silly, wouldn't go anywhere. Safety first!

On the morning of the eleventh, the loading crew wasn't too worried when they couldn't get the locking pin to engage right away. They called in a supervisor, who helped them hoist the bomb into a sling, taking its weight

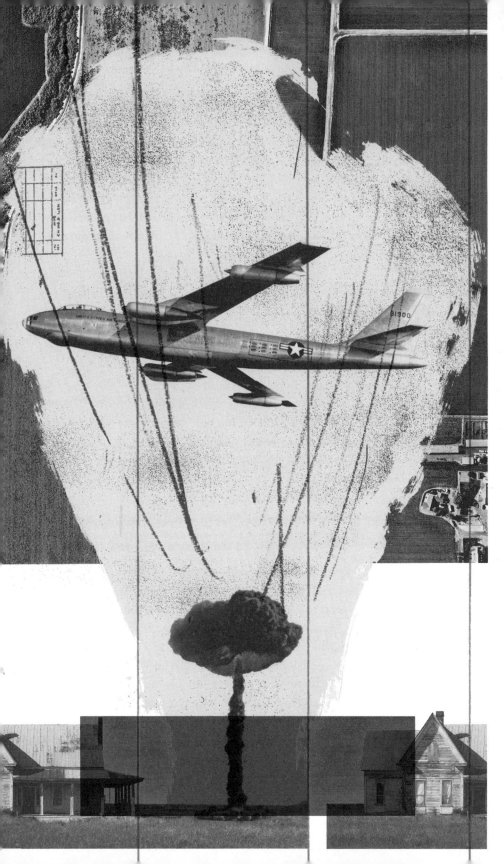

off the pneumatic catch. Then, they were able to jiggle and hammer the pin into place. Satisfied, they put the weight of the bomb back on the shackle, and moved on with the rest of their preflight checks. The team would be awarded points if they finished up by ten-thirty A.M. as part of a recently implemented performance review system. Down the line, those points could be traded in for a promotion. So, feeling highly motivated to wrap things up, the loading crew didn't bother double-checking the locking pin with the full weight of the bomb in place.

EMERGENCY RELEASE

Four hours later, at 3:51 P.M., the B-47 was preparing for takeoff. The copilot pulled a lever in the cockpit to disengage the locking pin.

Within a few minutes, the plane had reached an altitude of 5,000 feet. The copilot reached for the lever again, to re-insert the pin. But, just like it had been that morning, Chekhov's locking pin was stuck in its disengaged position. The bomb was hanging loose on its shackle.

Twenty-nine-year-old Bruce Kulka was the bombardier and navigator on the flight. His job was to help identify the bombing targets on the mission and to operate the equipment when they simulated the drops. Not in his job description? Crawling back into the depressurized bomb bay with an oxygen mask to search for the pin and insert it by hand. But a man's gotta do what a man's gotta do.

Bruce wasn't wearing a parachute when he shimmied through the narrow opening to the bomb bay. He'd never inserted a locking pin before, so he didn't know where to look for one. With the threat of the loose bomb quite literally hanging over him, Bruce spent about twelve minutes searching around the bomb's release mechanism before deciding the pin was probably above the bomb, attached to the shackle. He wasn't wrong. But, inconveniently, this was the only part of the bay Bruce couldn't see. The bomb was hanging in the way.

So he perched his weight just forward of the bomb's smooth, curved nose. He reached up toward the ceiling and felt a solid metal handhold. He began to pull himself up, to see over the top of the bomb.

But, suddenly, there was no bomb. Because the lever Bruce had chosen to pull was the emergency release mechanism. In a flash so quick it was hard to comprehend, the dark green mass of metal dropped. As he fell with it, he felt it land for just the briefest of moments on the closed bomb bay door. And then, in the span of a millisecond, Bruce reached out for something, anything, to hold on to, because the bomb was crashing through the trapdoors, hurtling toward Mars Bluff, South Carolina, 15,000 feet below.

FREE SWIMMING POOL

Ella David Hudson's family drove her to the hospital in a car doing eighty miles per hour on country roads. When they reached the emergency room, the wound on her head required thirty-one stitches and an overnight stay. Everybody else was okay for the most part—one of her cousins was treated for a cut behind her ear, and another for back and side pain. Doctors scanned all of them with Geiger counters. The air force knew the bomb hadn't been loaded with the plutonium and uranium core, but, you know...best to check, just in case.

When Ella's cousins, the Gregg family, returned home, they found their house knocked off its foundation, and the garage and tool shed flattened. Their Chevrolet sedan was totaled. The pine trees surrounding their property had been blasted to smithereens, and most of the family's fourteen free-range chickens had apparently been vaporized by the blast.

"It's incredible, if you think about it, that nobody got killed," Walter Gregg told a reporter from the *Sun News* years after the accident. And it's true that things could have ended far worse. When the bomb collided with the Gregg family's garden, the earth was soft and soggy from weeks of rain. So upon impact it sank into the ground, and when the TNT nestled in its core detonated, the surrounding dirt cushioned the blow.

At first, Walter Gregg appeared to have had a pretty good attitude about the whole situation. He'd served as a paratrooper during World War II, so maybe he was predisposed to give the air force the benefit of the doubt? In a quote that was reprinted over and over again, he said, "I always wanted a swimming pool, and now I've got the hole for one at no cost."

But when the air force official who was dispatched to evaluate the family's property claims denied them a housing allowance (they were staying with a friend, so he argued they didn't need to be reimbursed), Gregg's feelings started to sour. When the air force generously provided the family with a rental car for one week (plenty of time for Gregg to secure the insurance money to buy a new one, they thought!), he was unimpressed. And when the air force ultimately offered the family only $44,000 ($474,109.17 today) in restitution for the destruction of their home and most of their belongings, Gregg had had enough. He called a lawyer.

After years of back-and-forth, the family settled for about $10,000 more than they were originally offered. "The way it's written up, it sounds like a lot of money," Gregg told a local paper in 1961, "but it doesn't go far when you are trying to replace almost everything you've got."

The Gregg family never moved back to the house the air force accidentally destroyed. They never filled in the crater in their front yard. Every year, it becomes a little more overgrown, a little harder to spot. But it's still there.

SOUL-SEARCHING IN THE SKY

After accidentally dropping an (unloaded) atomic bomb on Mars Bluff and the Gregg family, Bruce Kulka scrambled back into the cockpit of the B-47. The crew radioed an airport six miles west of Mars Bluff to report a lost "device."

It may or may not surprise you to learn that this was not the first "whoopsie" involving a nuclear weapon on American soil. According to a Department of Defense report, the United States was involved in at least thirty-two such accidents between 1950 and 1980. Just a month before the Mars Bluff incident, *another* B-47 based out of Hunter Air Force Base had dropped an unloaded atomic bomb after it collided with another aircraft. But that time, the drop occurred over the Atlantic Ocean, so it didn't make the news.

The Mars Bluff bombing, however, put an unwanted spotlight on the air force's activities. In London, perhaps sensing a dodged bullet (or, more accurately, a dodged MK-6), members of the British Parliament demanded that American bombers stop carrying nuclear weapons over their territory. Which...fair. Not that we listened. Meanwhile, in Moscow, the Soviets pointed out that if the bomb *had* been loaded with a nuclear weapon when it dropped over South Carolina, it likely would have started World War III. The United States could have retaliated before realizing the bomb came from one of their own planes. Whoops.

So, under some pressure, the mishap in Mars Bluff motivated the US Air Force to do a little soul-searching. First, they re-engineered their nuclear weapon triggers so they'd be set off by an electrical impulse instead of concussion. If—or when—an unintended explosive fell from the sky again, it wouldn't explode upon impact.

Within days of the accident, the air force also issued a new regulation concerning locking pins. Moving forward, the locking pin was to remain inserted in the nuclear bomb shackle for the duration of the flight, including during takeoff and landing.

Better safe than sorry.

A119:

SHOOT THE MOON—LITERALLY!

That time when the United States
tried to detonate a nuke on the moon.

THE SPACE RACE

In our history, there have been some pretty strange scientific experiments, but few projects were stranger than the one given to Dr. Leonard Reiffel of the Armour Research Foundation. Dr. Reiffel was one of the nation's foremost nuclear physicists. He was tasked with an odd job: Study the effects of a nuclear explosion on the moon.

But why would *anyone* want to nuke the moon? The short answer: The United States was peeved that the Soviets had beat them to space, and they wanted the world to see a permanent reminder of US superpower technology.

See, when the Soviet Union's satellite, Sputnik, was launched on the back of a ballistic missile on October 4, 1957, it scared the *crap* out of Americans. I mean, by that point China had fallen to communism, and the Soviet Union had detonated a nuke in Kazakhstan in 1949. We were already doing civil defense drills and ducking under desks in case the communists pressed the proverbial button. Now there was a silver Soviet bubble beeping along in freaking ORBIT AROUND THE EARTH. It was a couple of atmospheric layers better than anything the United States had managed so far.

It was time to respond the American way: Blow some shit up.

So even though the moon ain't really made of Swiss cheese, Dr. Reiffel needed to find out how to make it look that way.

The institute set to work right away on the super-duper secret project called A119. What better way to show those commies who's the space boss than blowing a chunk out of the moon? Oh, yeah. Maybe put a man *on* the moon—but that wouldn't happen until the late sixties.

One veteran reporter even received a tip from a "senior intelligence official" that the Soviets were *also* planning to nuke the moon with a hydrogen bomb. The Soviets had been the first to put a satellite in space. No way was the United States going to be second in blowing up part of the moon...

The race was on!

ONE STEP BACK FOR MANKIND

Dr. Reiffel's first order of business was to understand the environmental impact of detonating a nuke on the moon. He worried the cosmic firework might end in a cataclysmic facepalm. His second task was determining the bomb's visibility from Earth, especially from Eurasia. After all, what's the point of an interstellar explosion if your adversary can't see it?

Dr. Reiffel quickly realized he needed more brainpower and brought on board Gerard Kuiper, a planetary physics whiz, along with a promising University of Chicago grad student named Carl Sagan. That's right! The same Carl Sagan who pretty much made astronomy cool. The same guy who would later co-found the Planetary Society and put messages onto the *Voyager* probe. And of course, he was the author and host of the Emmy-winning show *Cosmos* and the 1985 best-selling novel *Contact*. Yeah. *That* Sagan! In the seventies and eighties, if science had been a chart-topping, hit-producing band, Sagan would have been the front man.

But in the late fifties, Sagan was just getting started. Reiffel handed him his mission: Calculate if and how this lunatic, err...*lunar* explosion could be seen from Earth.

Between 1958 and 1959, Kuiper and Sagan churned out several detailed monthly status reports. And their findings? Let's say they were *not* what the air force wanted to hear.

While technically feasible, the risks were astronomical. Miss the moon, and the bomb could return to Earth in true Wile E. Coyote fashion—but with much more catastrophic consequences.

The team also worried that even hitting the target could have some negative consequences, to put it politely. While defacing the moon with an ugly crater worse than a New Jersey pothole concerned the scientists, project sponsors were less concerned.

Reiffel and the team reported that even if they detonated a warhead on the moon, the Soviets *wouldn't* see a massive pyrotechnic mushroom cloud screaming "Who's your daddy now?"

Nope. Even if they hit their target *just* right, they'd get nothing more than a big, disappointing dust cloud. Poof! So anticlimactic. And let's not forget the potential for radioactive contamination, ruining future moon missions before they even started. Oh, and the cost? Astronomical.

The public outcry? Guaranteed.

Tail between their legs, the air force neatly filed away the reports in confidential folders. Embarrassment avoided.

Life went on.

And that was that. Well, until the late 1990s. That's when it came out that Sagan had mentioned the project on an application for a prestigious fellowship back in 1959. Oops! Hey, even geniuses like Sagan can slip up. At least he got the fellowship, and went on to do work at the University of California, Harvard, the Smithsonian Astrophysical Observatory, *and* Cornell.

However, the information didn't make it to the general public until Keay Davidson, a biographer, stumbled upon the details while working on Sagan's biography in 1999. When the book hit the shelves, the moondust hit the fan. Especially since Davidson pretty much accused Sagan of "willfully and illegally" disclosing details surrounding a top secret project.

It's safe to say that those who wanted the project to remain secret weren't doing a joyous version of the moonwalk.

ON SECOND THOUGHT, LET'S NOT BLOW IT UP!

Of course, there was no *official* statement from the United States regarding A119.

Finally, Reiffel stepped forward to address the situation, confirming that he had been Sagan's boss, and that, yes, the project existed, but had long been scrapped. He stated that he was unaware that Sagan had provided the information on his application and had not granted him permission.

So just how much did Sagan reveal on the application? That's as mysterious as the moon itself. And it wasn't like anyone could ask Sagan about it, either. He died from cancer in 1996.

Looking back, I guess the plan backfired like a piece of the *moon* hitting the air force's eye. Not the *amore* they expected. But hey, no nuke, no foul, right? So the moondust settled once more.

Fortunately, Project A119 never moved beyond the theoretical stage. Whew! Even the Soviets determined that it wasn't the brightest idea. In 1963 and 1967, both sides agreed to sign treaties preventing future attempts to bomb the moon. Think of it as a pact of, "This was the dumbest idea ever. Let's not even contemplate it again."

Even George Bailey was speaking metaphorically about lassoing the moon and yanking it from the sky. I'm certain a radioactive moon is not what Creedence Clearwater Revival had in mind with "Bad Moon Rising," either.

Thankfully, the moon remained unscathed. In 1969, when Neil Armstrong set foot on the lunar surface, the only glow was from the sun, not anything radioactive. Instead of a crater, the United States left only footprints and the American flag—a testament to our human achievement instead of our destructive tendencies.

Years later, *Voyager 1* and *Voyager 2* would send back photos of Earth. Sagan infamously referred to the planet as a pale blue dot in the universe. And the moon? Well, it's the only one Earth has. Carl Sagan once wrote that Earth was home—to everyone we've ever known, every religion, every family, and every couple in love. And, we'd like to point out, Earth has just *one* beautiful moon.

So, remember this bizarre chapter of history the next time you gaze up at the moon. It's a reminder of the lengths to which nations will go to prove their prowess, even if it means contemplating something as astrologically ludicrous as nuking the moon.

Perhaps the best scientific decisions are the ones where cooler heads say, "You know...Let's *not* blow it up."

PART TWO

THE SIXTIES

THE COLD WAR'S BIG CHILL

Entering the Cultural Decade—groovy! Though the 1960s were synonymous with hippies and the peace movement, political turmoil at home and abroad solidified a shift: Gone were the days of the Golden Age fifties as counterculture took over. By the early sixties, Beatlemania crossed the Atlantic as mop-tops, black suits, and Liverpudlian accents invaded the *Ed Sullivan Show*. JFK took office on a platform to eliminate injustice, while Cold War tensions with the Soviet Union continued to escalate. By 1962, the "thirteen days the Earth stood still" during the Cuban Missile Crisis shook the country with the prospect of nuclear war. And when 1964 brought the torpedoing of US Navy boats in the Gulf of Tonkin, soon American forces were headed to Vietnam—a bitter proxy war between the United States and the Soviets.

But as the world grew more tumultuous, friction also helped solidify the decade as one of counterculture and rebellion, of feminism, environmentalism, anti-Vietnam activism, and civil rights protests. As young men all over the nation were drafted into the army and shipped off to South Vietnam, discontent grew at home—not only over the war, but over civil rights. Malcolm X and Martin Luther King Jr. were both killed. Together with the assassinations of JFK and RFK, the sixties would become synonymous with these four major tragic moments.

Despite it all, the United States was getting more innovative (or shall we say...desperate?) with ways to defeat the Soviets. Spying cats, explosive seashells, and nuclear ice sheets: America tried it all, and no idea was too *far out* to survive the Cold War's Big Chill.

PROJECT ICEWORM:

EVEN WITHOUT ICEMAN MISSILES, WE'RE IN THE DANGER ZONE

That time the US government developed a secret—and highly unwelcome—nuclear missile launch site under Greenland's ice sheet.

As eighteen-year-old Boy Scout Kent Goering traveled across the ice fields of Greenland in October 1960, surely he must have thought, "We're not in Kansas anymore." He had left behind his small town of Neodesha, Kansas, for a sweet internship. He and fellow eighteen-year-old Boy Scout Søren Gregersen from Denmark would spend 270 days in Camp Century, a futuristic US Army underground research station, which was touted in the press as "the City under the Ice."

Known for ice, snow, glaciers, and generally avoiding the color green, Greenland would not appear to be the first place one would want to summer. Yet in 1959, the US Army Corps of Engineers, along with a sled dog named Mukluk serving as base mascot, packed their bags and did exactly that. They took advantage of a location with minimal summer thaw, but *with* the luxuries of warm summer temperatures (below freezing each day!) and never-ending sunlight due to the high latitude. The engineers hauled out equipment over several days, dug into the ice, and placed prefabricated buildings into trenches, which were then covered by snow. Twenty-five feet beneath the ice, more than a hundred people worked to maintain base operations. After traveling 150 miles from Thule Air Force Base on Greenland's western coast, Kent and Søren arrived to join them. Søren's main draw? He would be able to study a nuclear reactor. Yes, in the middle of Greenland, the Americans dragged a nuclear reactor to power their base.

The two boys threw on their Boy Scout uniforms and faced the first of their trying tasks: photo ops. While they proudly wore the title of "junior scientific aide," their main purpose was to be a propaganda outlet for Camp Century. Sure, they would shadow scientists conducting experiments and see an operational nuclear reactor up close, but they also wrote articles for their respective nation's publications, talking about the wonders and hardships of their temporary home.

Kent's and Søren's tasks ranged from organizing the camp's library to monitoring the ice tunnels. As Kent wrote in *Boys' Life* magazine, "We helped survey the width and depth of the trenches. These measurements keep us informed on the rate at which the snow walls, floors, and roofs are closing in." Little did the two boys know that they were unwitting props in a cover story for a plan much more explosive than measuring some Arctic ice.

And Kent's words were a harbinger for issues to come. By 1966, Camp Century would be completely shut down. Because not only were the tunnels unstable, but they also hid a dark secret: the radioactive waste of the Cold War's nuclear standoff.

GREENBACKS FOR GREENLAND

But, hey, a discerning person might say, "Isn't Greenland part of Denmark? Why would the United States be able to build a base there in the first place?" Yes, great question, Discerning Person. Indeed, when the US Army Corps of Engineers began construction, Greenland was a country of Denmark, fully under Danish control. So why did the Danish government allow a US Army camp replete with a nuclear reactor less than nine hundred miles from Santa's workshop?

During World War II, Denmark was occupied by Nazis. Unable to protect Greenland due to the occupation in the homeland, the Danish ambassador to the United States asked the Americans to protect it until the war was over. So the US of A answered the call and our boys came marching in. The US military built several bases there, including Thule Air Force Base. After the war, the United States proposed to Denmark that it would be ever so kind as to purchase Greenland from them. To which Denmark essentially said, "Thanks, but no thanks. We're good keeping our land."

Well, the United States decided to wait Denmark out, holding its breath until Denmark gave some ground by settling for the 1951 Defense Agreement.

The agreement allowed the United States to stay...if it behaved. Is it just me, or did Denmark talk to the United States like it was a stray cat constantly carrying in dead rats? Anyway...

Greenland was in what we might call a *strategically optimal* position as the Cold War commenced. It allowed the United States to monitor the USSR and defend against any movement in the Arctic Ocean. And as with any good defensive position, it could also serve as an offensive position. Yeah, that's right, the United States wanted to do something a little spicy with Thule Air Force Base: install nuclear missiles.

The Danes, seeing the nuclear arsenal being dragged up onto the porch, said, "Hell no. You can't bring that crap in here."

Across the Arctic Sea from Greenland, the Soviets weren't any happier with the nuke installation plan. The Soviet premier sent a message to Danish prime minister Hans Christian Hansen: "The destructive power of modern weapons is such that for a country with a territory such [as the] Danish, the granting of bases to a foreign state would be tantamount to suicide in case atomic war breaks out." And to the USSR, if an opponent died via "suicide," it was usually assisted by a swift bullet from the KGB.

Hansen made it clear to the USSR that the Americans had a right to be in Greenland, but that nuclear weapons were not going to be tolerated on its soil.

Behind closed doors, the United States asked Denmark, "So, do you want to know if I bring nuclear weapons to Greenland?" And Hansen let the United States know—on the down-low—that it would *not* investigate if nuclear weapons showed up.

So officially, there were to be no nuclear weapons inside the main house of Denmark, but as far as the porch of Greenland was concerned, the prime minister decided to turn a blind eye.

CAMP CENTURY GETS COLD

By 1959, the plan for Camp Century was underway. The United States asked Denmark for permission to build the site, which would include a nuclear reactor to power the base. Of course, they didn't ask until well after the base's construction started. At that point, Denmark could only ask to please minimize the waste pushed out by the nuclear reactor. Good Danish Boy Scout Søren wrote that the Danish government told Americans they had to send all solid nuclear waste back to the United States for disposal. And the United States said, "Sure, no problem!" They agreed to take home all their cool, glowing souvenirs.

But the Danes made one concession that they would *definitely* come to regret. See, the solid waste wasn't the only *extremely dangerous* product of the reactor. It was also dishing "up to 50 millicuries of liquid waste out into the ice per year." For this, the United States asked for a little exception. Couldn't we just...flush that into a hole somewhere? Hansen's government was like, *Sure, why not?*

So a sewage hole was also set up to capture all the liquid runoff, but a couple of things didn't go quite to plan. First, it was much closer to camp than originally intended. Second, it had horrible ventilation. Both of which meant that the personnel at the base lived trapped beneath the ice, smelling the reactor's radioactive piss for a good portion of their time there.

That might have been bad enough, but after the construction wrapped up, the camp changed hands. Away went the Army Corps of Engineers. In came the reactor technicians, scientists, and soldiers. The only one who stayed behind was Mukluk, the mascot sled dog whose notes on the record have been described as "terse and to the point, but without significant improvement in human/canine translation, completely incomprehensible." I kid!

Oh, and there were the two Boy Scouts, assigned to run around and measure the trenches. Danish Boy Scout Søren said that he worked in the mess tunnel, where his job was to hammer marker pegs at different heights along the wall. Over time, as they moved, they showed the dire state of the base. Walls moving. *Floors* moving. Oh, and the ice cap overhead? Yeah, moving—straight down. It was crushing the base underneath. On top of all that, Søren also hung some good old-fashioned plumb lines so a soldier could read measurements every week of just how far down the ceiling had come. He put it succinctly, with the Danish penchant for understatement: "It's becoming a problem, that mess tunnel."

That pesky old mess tunnel.

Other base workers were there to see how the camp would hold up beneath the ice, to monitor a nuclear reactor, and to conduct scientific experiments.

One scientific study seemed, on the surface, to be for the good of the planet. Scientists at Camp Century headed a research project to drill ice cores down to the bottom of the ice sheet. By drilling into the ice, scientists could determine the temperature at different points in time and corresponding CO_2 levels. Essentially, they could study humanity's effect on climate change.

This scientific exploration was not just for the benefit of humanity. The same US Army folks who were allowing sewage and nuclear waste to disperse into the ice didn't suddenly become environmentalists. What they really wanted to know was how the Arctic landscape would change so that they could leverage that info in any future confrontation with the USSR. By studying the ice melt, they could possibly predict the lay of the land—and where "land" would melt away to create waterways. If they knew where ice would melt, they would know where they could maneuver submarines, and would thus have the advantage against the Soviets in Arctic confrontations. To sum it up, the study wasn't being used to save the Earth—it was being used to gain a military advantage against the enemy.

What Denmark didn't know until much later was that the United States wanted a whole lot *more* than just a nuclear reactor in Camp Century. You remember that agreement about how the United States wasn't supposed to bring nukes into Danish territory? Yeah, the US negotiators did that with fingers crossed behind their backs. In fact, the whole base—with its Boy Scout propagandists leading the way—had been one big smoke screen to hide the real goal.

The truth was: They wanted a whole *arsenal* of nuclear missiles underneath the entirety of Greenland. And they already had Hansen's secret promise to look the other way.

ICEMAN MISSILES INCOMING

In particular, the Americans who wanted to start planting missiles in the Greenland trenches were the good old boys of the US Army. You see, they wanted to establish their own nuclear missile program within the military. The navy had Polaris. The air force had Minuteman. But the army? Nothing. It wasn't fair. If their sibling forces got to have them, why couldn't they? *Come onnnnnn. They get all the cool toys.*

So the army put together a little scheme they called "Project Iceworm," a defense system based in, you guessed it, Greenland. Specifically, it was located—wait, I bet you can guess it again!—directly in Camp Century.

To *improve* on the air force's Minuteman missile program, Project Iceworm would have the advantage of needing shorter-range missiles, capable of striking the USSR without being based on American land. Most important, the missiles would be called Iceman missiles, which means that they could have plastered Val Kilmer's face all over them several decades later. Missed opportunity.

As for the missile bases: The Defense Department proposed an underground railway system that would carry 600 nuclear missiles beneath the entire ice sheet of Greenland. These missiles would be constantly moving between silos so that the Soviets would not be able to pin them down. So one of the *real* missions of Camp Century was to see what it would take to build a whole stinking railroad under the ice.

Which brings us back to our intrepid Boy Scouts. Thanks to Kent Goering and Søren Gregersen dutifully running from trench to trench with their tape measures, hammering little pegs into walls, the army knew *just* how bad things were getting by 1963. It was, in short, a sort of reverse ice pop. Instead of the kids squeezing the ice, it was going to be the ice squeezing the kids.

Take one crazy example: Day by day, the ice tunnels of the base were getting narrower—as all the heat and steam from human cooking and human breath was freezing into the walls. If the base was going to stay operational, the tunnels would have to be dug out again, or they would get too narrow to pass through.

Like the moving walls, the icy railroad used to get around the base was also slip-sliding hither and yon. Not great for keeping things lined up, like, you know, train tracks.

And then there was the fact that the roof over the base was sagging to a dangerous degree. In 1962, the army reworked the roofs of four different tunnels, recutting them and adding big metal arches to hold them up. But it was a huge amount of work, and let me tell you, we're not talking about a four-tunnel base. There was a *lot* more work needed if the army was going to keep the doors open. Every day they didn't do their ice-ceiling reno, the ceilings threatened to make the final descent: straight down onto the people below.

Now, I don't know about you, but being trapped under a metric base-flattener (official measurement) of solid ice has never been a dream of mine. And it turns out, it was never a dream of the US Army, either. Then there was the particular point above the nuclear reactor: The engineers determined that it was in danger of a sudden and catastrophic collapse.

Once the word went up the chain of command that things were getting dangerously *squeezy*, they gave the order: Shut it down.

It was the beginning of the end. At the same time, the reactor's fuel rods were practically spent. The choice to replace them and redig the base was

completely untenable. So in 1964, the reactor was broken down and shipped off to Idaho, another desolate place to hang out for the rest of its nuclear lifetime.

Also, the United States definitely *did* know that Denmark would not be happy with a bunch of missiles on their soil, if the word ever got out.

Indeed, when Denmark found out that the army had planned to put missiles into their godforsaken reverse ice pop, they were not happy. In 1995, as a result of news stories about cancer-stricken workers near Thule Air Force Base, the Danes decided to look into the possibility of American nuclear missiles being held there. The report revealed the hall pass signed by long-deceased Hansen. The United States, sure enough, admitted to having had nukes at Thule Air Force Base. Another report revealed the even bigger truth: The United States had also plotted to establish its own nuclear arsenal in Greenland via Project Iceworm.

Luckily, it never came to be. Camp Century closed up shop and let the ice take over.

CLIMATE CATASTROPHE

But that doesn't leave the good old US of A completely off the hook. Remember the "liquid runoff" from the nuclear reactor? Yeah, we can't forget about that.

It will take at least a hundred years (so Camp Century can live up to its name), but with global warming on the rise, eventually the ice will melt over Camp Century and all the waste left behind by the engineers will run off—out of the sewage hole and into some great places like, oh, you know, the water supply of the entire Greenlandic population.

And who is that? Well, Greenland's population today is *still* mostly Indigenous Inuit people, despite still being under the umbrella of Danish rule. When the Danes made Greenland an official country in 1953, it demanded that the Greenlandic population become Danish. Greenlanders were expected to attend Danish schools, live by Danish cultural norms, and speak the Danish language.

Greenland finally established itself as an autonomous territory in 2009, but its colonial past is difficult to ignore. And with Camp Century, we get a little frozen yogurt swirl of *two* colonial powers who have essentially done what they always do: violated the natural resources of an Indigenous population and then ignored the consequences. Par for the course in world history.

One vocal opponent was Vittus Qujaukitsoq, a tae kwon do champion, gem collector, and—oh, right, the important part—the former foreign affairs minister of Greenland. Coming from a family of Indigenous hunters in Qaanaaq, Greenland, near Thule Air Force Base, he was understandably pissed when he found out about the pollutants left behind by Camp Century. In 2016, during his tenure as foreign affairs minister, he wrote,

> *In reality, there are only very few places in the world where the rights of indigenous peoples, including their right to self-determination, are fully respected. This is most evident when governments and large, private corporations in other countries far from Denmark freely and without permission take land and natural resources from indigenous peoples.*

Qujaukitsoq made it his mission to bring some justice to Greenland, pointing out that even though there was radioactive waste at Camp Century, there were things left behind by the Americans that were even *more* dangerous. He was right. Oil and polychlorinated biphenyls (PCBs) make up 200 metric tons of chemical waste left behind by the US Army. PCBs are incredibly damaging to the environment, being highly carcinogenic. The physical

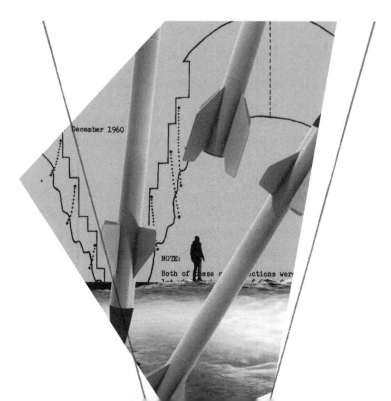

waste, including those railway lines and prefabricated buildings that were left behind to rot, comes to about 9,200 metric tons. There's also the 6.3 million gallons of literal raw sewage.

Like any good martial artist, Qujaukitsoq didn't run away from a fight. He demanded that Denmark do something and then insisted that their response was not enough. In his view, they were sticking Greenland with the cleanup job and hadn't done enough to get the Americans to pay for it. He even lodged a complaint against Denmark with the United Nations. He also stepped down from his role as foreign minister to challenge his own party leader, Greenland premier Kim Kielsen. His relentless dogging of the issue forced Denmark to act; they agreed to pursue financial reparations from the United States on Greenland's behalf. They haven't really *pressed* the issue since then, but in the meantime, the United States signed an agreement with Greenland to help pay for the cleanup.

While Denmark insists that the United States should foot the bill, there will be very little movement until the ice starts to melt. For now the physical waste is around 118 feet deep, while the liquid waste is around 213 feet deep. To access either would require a drilling operation. And I don't know about you, but I've never met someone who wanted to drill through one hundred feet to scrape up some frozen dooky. The likeliest future is that no cleanup gets done until global warming does the hard part. Looks like we'll need some Boy Scouts to head back out on the ice sheet with tape measures. Let us know when it's time to start the cleanup, guys! You're doing great out there.

And sure, climate change *was* studied at Camp Century. Those ice cores that were drilled ended up being key elements in studying climate change for the greater good. Scientists were able to measure isotopes of oxygen and CO_2 levels, showing exactly how human interaction had changed the temperature in the environment.

Yet the camp will most likely be remembered as a place where massive harm was done to the environment in the name of possibly stockpiling Earth-ending weaponry.

ACOUSTIC KITTY:

CAN YOU HEAR MEOW?

The redacted life of the CIA's cyborg cat.

Sometime in the early 1960s, the CIA's gadgets and gizmos team wanted to develop a new kind of spying device: implantable microphones. Over the years, they'd found success shrinking and disguising microphones and transmitters in all kinds of ways, but they always seemed to run into trouble with interference: The microphones picked up *everything* audible. That made it difficult to isolate conversations or specific details—the kinds of things that spying is all about. What they needed was something that could function like a human ear, tune in to distinct noises, and filter out the rest. After years of research and development, they selected an agent to undergo a historic surgical procedure to implant a microphone and transmitter. According to one account, the agent they chose was an adult female with long gray-and-white hair.

She was also a cat.

DUELING PERSPECTIVES

We owe the majority of our nameless heroine's legacy to two characters: Victor Marchetti and Robert Wallace. Both worked directly for the CIA and on Project Acoustic Kitty—yes, that's the actual name of the project.

Bespectacled with thick frames and tousled curls, Marchetti joined in 1955 and steadily climbed the ranks and security clearance levels, eventually working as a special assistant to the executive director, and as the executive assistant to the deputy director. I don't know the difference between those last two, but the point is, he was an important guy who had a good look behind the curtain. Which matters, because he would eventually resign in 1969, grow a truly epic set of lush sideburns, and become an outspoken critic of the agency—but we'll get to that later.

Then there's Robert Wallace. While most of his pictures are post-retirement, they feature icy blue eyes and the smallest tweak of a know-ing smile. He joined the CIA in 1971 and was appointed deputy director of the Office of Technical Service in 1995 before being promoted to office director in 1998. He was heavily awarded for his service, earning multiple medals and recognition from the inspector general, and retired in 2003. He spends his days now giving talks about spies and espionage on a cruise ship circuit.

While these two agree on the broad strokes of what Operation Acous-tic Kitty entailed, they directly *contradict* each other on several key points, including the fate of our feline agent.

So we're going to tell you her story, but we're also going to tell you the story behind her story: the catty dispute between the only two people to go on record with her tale.

WHY A CAT?

One thing Marchetti and Wallace do agree on: There was a cat. Now, while Marchetti wasn't *directly* involved in Operation Acoustic Kitty, I like to imag-ine how he got the inside scoop. I picture him sidling up to the watercooler while the brainiacs from the research team noodled on what kind of animal would best suit stealth surveillance.

"A rat?" says Brainiac 1, leaning to fill his paper cup.

"No way! *Way* too small. The thing would be dragging a mic half its size around, and the battery pack alone would be too big to implant! Besides, peo-ple run from rats," replies Brainiac 2, grimacing at the thought. "They are everywhere, though. You may be on to something there."

"A pigeon, then."

"Eh, too compact. They'd have to wear it as a backpack or something. It'd be too obvious. What we need is an animal with a proper ear canal, something that can channel noise toward the mic."

"What, like a cat?" scoffs Brainiac 1, lifting his cup for a sip and pausing when he sees the glint in his coworker's eye. "Seriously? A *cat?!*"

I like to imagine Marchetti doing a spit take here, just for fun.

But these hypothetical brainiacs were onto something. Like humans and other mammals, cats have a cochlea, the part of the ear we're interested in for secret spy sound. Thanks to thousands of years of evolution, felines have excellent directional hearing. The triangular curved shape of their ear funnels noise directly into the ear canal, a perfect location for a tiny microphone. They're also known to be particularly adept at silently skulking about.

Another evolutionary factor that proved helpful is that every cat has plenty of loose skin built in. Have you ever watched a well-fed, older cat saunter, hypnotized by the majesty of their swaying belly pouch? Just me? Well, cats have two main loose-skin locations: the aforementioned pouch—which exists to protect their organs from disemboweling kicks—and the scruff of the neck at the base of their skull, which exists so their mothers can carry them while they're still kittens and too small and new to move on their own. Remember these pouches. They'll come into play later.

Beyond the anatomical advantages, back in the 1960s—decades before the cat rescue hobbyists of Instagram popularized the trap-neuter-return method of population control—feral cats were *everywhere* you could find people, trash, and rodents. If you were a foreign agent having a clandestine meeting on a park bench or in a seedy alleyway, you probably wouldn't think twice if you saw a cat hunched next to a trash bin or under a nearby tree. That's what the CIA was counting on.

If Operation Acoustic Kitty was a success, the United States could deploy a team of cyborg kitties to listen in on conversations anywhere in the world and no one would ever be the wiser. All they needed to do was figure out how to A) wire a cat and B) get a cat to listen. Super-simple stuff.

MORE THAN ONE WAY TO WIRE A CAT

When the CIA's research and development team got down to work, they faced a few hurdles. They would need to design a microphone, transmitter, and power source that could withstand the warmth and dampness of the implant site. They also needed to make sure that the device wouldn't be perceivable or annoying to Acoustic Kitty when it was on the move. Once they were satisfied with their designs, it was time to wire the cat.

Here's where the tussle between Marchetti and Wallace came into play.

On November 22, 1983—twenty years *after* Operation Acoustic Kitty— Victor Marchetti sat down for an interview with John Ranelagh, author of

The Agency: The Rise and Decline of the CIA. And he laid out in detail every-thing he knew about the project. Contrary to Wallace's account, Marchetti told Ranelagh that the cat was a tom, and along the way to launching the first mission, he underwent multiple procedures:

> *They slit the cat open, put batteries in him, wired him up. The tail was used as an antenna. They made a monstrosity. They tested him and tested him. They found he would walk off the job when he got hungry, so they put another wire in to override that.*

So that's the Marchetti version. Short and, if we're being honest, a little tough to read. It's not like our kitty pal was willingly going through a *Rocky* montage or something.

When Wallace put his own account of events into print in 2008, he added some details Marchetti left out. He said the researchers worked with an audio equipment contractor to produce a three-quarter-inch transmitter that would be implanted in the cat's scruff (remember that neck pouch from earlier?). The microphone was nestled in the ear and a thin wire antenna connected to the transmitter was braided into the cat's fur. The transmitter was powered by the smallest batteries available, which limited how long the device could transmit. His account makes no mention of the cat's tail acting as an antenna (which would be an impressive surgical feat considering the intricate musculature), nor does he mention any subsequent wiring to over-ride the cat's hunger.

As Wallace tells it, after an hour-long operation with no complications other than some onlooker queasiness, the anesthetized cat was put into a recovery area for observation. There must have been at least a few people in that room who were bracing for failure. Imagine that vet, wiping their brow after successfully implanting a listening device in a cat, wondering if this bizarre surgery was all for nothing. Or the brainiacs from earlier, chewing at their cuticles over the feasibility of their pitch. After all, how could it possibly work? How could the transmitter and power supply withstand all that gushy internal cat stuff? The device would almost certainly short out before it could relay anything of use back to the listening agents.

And yet, to everyone's immense surprise, the implanted microphone and transmitter worked. Agent Acoustic Kitty was live and generating a viable audio signal. Now all they needed to do was see if the cat remembered its training.

A declassified 1968 document titled "Behavioral Program" outlines some of the methods used by the CIA to train animals. Safe to assume it applies to our own feline agent. The program sought to direct animals to specific points and back using audio cues. The animals started their training in a pen and then moved into more complex environments once a foundation of behavior was established. It's not clear if this was a description of the methods used in Acoustic Kitty's regimen, but one way or another...it didn't take.

According to Wallace, when it came time to send the cat into the wild, its movements "proved so inconsistent that the operational utility became questionable." Or, in other words, "Acoustic Kitty had a mind of its own."

That's right, through an expansive process of trial and error, the CIA learned just how hard it is...to herd cats.

ROADKILL OR RETIREMENT?

Here we come to one of the most critical deviations between Marchetti's and Wallace's Acoustic Kitty accounts: What happened to the cat?

Victor Marchetti presents a colorful if devastating conclusion to Acoustic Kitty's first field test. According to him, Acoustic Kitty's handlers took it to a nearby park and directed it to approach and listen to two men on a nearby bench. Deposited out of the van and paws on the ground, Acoustic Kitty had graduated from the sterile confines of the training program. The cat saw its target and remembered its training. It defied its nature and ignored the birds. Acoustic Kitty sauntered forth and...was promptly struck by a passing taxi. "There they were," says Victor Marchetti, "sitting in the van with all those dials, and the cat was dead!"

This tragic version of Acoustic Kitty's fate went undisputed for more than twenty years. In 2008, with the publication of *Spycraft: The Secret History of the CIA's Spytechs from Communism to Al-Qaeda*, Robert Wallace offers a less salacious conclusion: Trying to direct a cat in a foreign environment was simply deemed impractical and the project was closed, sans dramatic demise.

The only declassified government evidence of the project comes in a heavily redacted document from 1967: "Views on Trained Cats [redacted] for [redacted] Use." The document concludes that while successfully training a cat was clearly a "remarkable scientific achievement," the amount of money and training required was simply not practical.

After fourteen years of service, Victor Marchetti left the agency disillusioned with both the agency's policies and operations and the US government at large. In 1975, when he published *The CIA and the Cult of Intelligence*, he came out guns blazing. While he admitted that gathering intelligence was necessary—even if it involved eavesdropping spy cats—he took issue with the CIA being used as an "operational arm, a secret instrument of the presidency and a handful of powerful men, wholly independent of public accountability, whose chief purpose is interference in the domestic affairs of other nations (and perhaps our own)."

Robert Wallace, on the other hand, retired from the CIA in 2003 after thirty-one years of service. During those years, he was awarded recognition from the CIA's inspector general, the Intelligence Medal of Merit, the Distinguished Career Intelligence Medal, and two Clandestine Service Donovan Awards. In other words, he was definitely an Agency Man. So you have to wonder: Was his cleaner account of Acoustic Kitty an attempt to tie up a loose ball of yarn left out in public by Marchetti?

While we may never know whose account is closer to the truth, the fact that Acoustic Kitty existed at all is stranger than fiction. With the Cold War looming and well over a decade before the founding of PETA, there were virtually no ethical checks and balances to deter the researchers at the CIA from pursuing this ludicrous endeavor. They were so eager to determine if it could be done that no one bothered to question if it *should* be. But in a time of heightened political tension and no public scrutiny, the concept of a bugged cat who could gather intel without arousing suspicion was too tempting to pass up.

Whoever the Acoustic Kitty was, it endured some uncomfortable handling in becoming the CIA's first cyborg spy. You never want to be the first trial in a *trial-and-error* process. It took the US government's best and brightest at the Central *Intelligence* Agency approximately five years and several million dollars to determine that turning cats into bionic spies just didn't have legs.

OPERATION POPEYE:

MAKE MUD, NOT WAR

Why the United States launched a top secret
military effort ... to make it rain.

By 1967, the Vietnam War had reached new levels of disapproval with the American public, causing the US government to grow desperate for solutions. The war had gone on for a decade, and there were almost 20,000 Americans dead and nearly 60,000 South Vietnamese killed in action with another 21,000 North Vietnamese dead. The following year, 1968, would be the bloodiest on record for the US forces. Though they were outgunned by American artillery, the Vietnamese were on their home turf defending their independence, and they weren't going to give up without a serious fight. It didn't help that the United States had underestimated the amount of foreign support North Vietnam would receive from communist allies China and the Soviet Union— support to the tune of $2 billion just between 1965 and 1968.

The Vietnam War, perhaps more than any other American conflict, is synonymous with protests. It was also the first truly televised war, bringing the terror and carnage of combat to American living rooms. Americans were *afraid*. And so was the US government.

Losing on both fronts, against the North Vietnamese and with the American public, a group of "high-level experts" was convened in Washington to brainstorm creative solutions to end the war ASAP.

Now, I wasn't at this meeting, but I imagine their conversation went something like:

> **Expert 1:** Gentlemen, we have to end this war. At home, they're raiding the draft boards...Out here the troops are getting soaked to their skivvies six months of the year thanks to the monsoons. Plus, there's the dying. Morale overall...it's low.

Expert 2: Could we try...bomb...more?

Expert 1: We've tried "bomb more" a lot of times already. It hasn't worked yet...but I'm not against it.

Expert 2: Mass poisoning could be fun!

Expert 1: We're on that, too. We've been using Agent Orange to absolutely ruin the entire landscape. But we're doing it so much it's even poisoning our own guys!

Expert 3 gazes meaningfully into his water glass.

Expert 2: You've been awfully quiet over there. Got any bright ideas?

Expert 3 slowly looks up.

Expert 3: What if we made...bigger monsoons?

Experts look around the room in silent wonder.

And thus, Operation Popeye was born.

MAKE IT RAIN

Imagine for a moment you're outside and it's hot, like ninety degrees Fahrenheit hot. On top of that it's raining. It's been raining for months and will continue to rain for the foreseeable future. The humidity is inescapable. Your skin looks like you've been in the bath too long. (Maybe you're reading this in Florida, and you don't have to imagine, but go with me here.) That is what it's like during monsoon season in Vietnam. From May to October, as much as eleven inches of rain per month falls on Ho Chi Minh City. Now imagine trying to travel and fight an enemy in those conditions. It was, no doubt, punishing.

The jungles of Vietnam were also thick and difficult to navigate. The North Vietnamese had an intricate understanding of how to use the jungles to their advantage, creating tunnel systems, building booby traps, and hiding in the jungle cover. Their fighting techniques were unlike anything US troops had faced before. Fighting in those jungles was terrifying—and not just because, you know, war is terrifying. It was difficult to even find the

North Vietnamese (unless they had already found you), let alone beat them on their home turf.

The United States tried many tactics to tame the jungles—bombing them, cutting them down, and dousing them in herbicides like Agent Orange, which went on to have devastating, long-lasting health effects for both Vietnamese civilians and US servicemen. It will surprise no one that bombing the jungles and drenching them in toxic chemicals did not make them any easier to fight in.

As challenging as monsoon season was for the Americans, it was an even greater challenge for the North Vietnamese. Each year, the rains flooded the Ho Chi Minh Trail, which was the primary route the North Vietnamese used to transport troops, weapons, and other supplies. So, the ever-enterprising US military decided to weaponize the weather.

Operation Popeye was top secret and thus a lot of the backstory about its inception is either lost to time or sitting in a classified folder in some damp, dark closet in the basement of a government building. What we do know is that Operation Popeye was willed into existence in 1966 under President Lyndon B. Johnson. And the idea itself sounds as if it's pulled from a sci-fi novel: Manipulate the clouds, causing them to release more rain.

This is fantasy, right? Au contraire, mon frère. This is reality. It's called *cloud seeding,* and this wasn't the first time anyone had ever done it.

HOW TO SEED A CLOUD

Back in November 1943, a scientist named Dr. Vincent J. Schaefer became the first person (that we know of) to successfully seed a cloud. He did this by hiring a pilot to fly him through a storm cloud where he then released three pounds of dry ice. Lo and behold, it started snowing. When Dr. Schaefer died, the *New York Times* wrote in his obituary, "He was hailed as the first person to actually do something about the weather and not just talk about it."

I hope you guys are ready to take a trip down science lane, because that's where we're going next. If you're like me, you may be trying to remember what the heck a cloud even is. Well, thankfully, my ninth-grade earth science teacher, Mrs. Miller, taught me very memorably that a cloud is basically a bunch of water droplets or ice crystals that form around dust or salt particles floating in the air as they are cooled by the atmosphere. *Cloud seeding* is just flying a plane into a cloud and introducing tiny ice nuclei so that more ice crystals can form.

Most of the time, this is achieved with a compound called silver iodide. To be clear, cloud seeding can only happen when there's existing weather to amplify.

The US military had first toyed with weather manipulation in South Vietnam in 1963, three years before Operation Popeye. The Central Intelligence Agency seeded clouds in an attempt to break up a protest led by Buddhist monks after observers had noticed that the monks stayed in position through tear gas but for some reason disbanded when it rained. It's unclear how successful the CIA's efforts were at that time, but it's safe to say that dipping a toe into the pond of meteorological warfare left it top of mind for the US military.

In October 1966, the military began conducting cloud seeding tests over a strip of the Lao Panhandle. Their report on the effort, which also acted as a recommendation to expand the project under Popeye, states that they did so as a "non-publicized effort"—meaning, they did not tell the Lao authorities what they were up to. The report went on to boast that, in one instance of their testing, "the rainfall continued as the cloud moved eastward across the Vietnam border and inundated a US Special Forces camp with nine inches of rain in four hours." Personally, I wouldn't brag to the president that I drenched his army while simultaneously trying to get him to sign off on my new project. But maybe that's just me.

However, as one government official later noted, there was no possible way to predict the results of a cloud seeding operation. Measuring a science experiment of this grandeur would require years of research and mundane measurements. Seeing as the military is not funded to embrace the scientific method, you can guess that they didn't implement any sort of system. Perhaps they should have looped in someone else who was funded to give a damn about the long-term effects of tinkering with weather.

Not everyone within the Johnson administration was in agreement about Operation Popeye. A group of State Department officials and attorneys—let's call them *Blutos*—were quick to point out that weaponizing the weather was an alarming precedent for the United States to set. And they pointed to the same report that was used to justify the project, which also expressed possible changes to climate and landforms, or injury to civilians. Simply put, they said, changing the weather could kill innocent people. The effects of tinkering with the rain were understudied (or not really studied at all). For all they knew, their efforts could go around causing severe flooding and landslides, or even damaging crops that feed entire villages. A legal adviser was tasked with putting together a comprehensive study on the impacts of the operation to determine all of its possible legal implications—a study that would unfortunately not be ready until the project was well underway.

The other issue raised by the Blutos was the absolute secrecy surrounding the project. The authors of the original proposal had suggested that when the government was accused of playing fast and loose with the weather, they should just...admit it! Their idea was that the best way to deal with criticism would be to point out that destroying the roads between North and South Vietnam was actually less violent than a bombing campaign or a massive ground invasion. In a twist of uncanny foreshadowing, though, the authors of the original proposal *also* noted that "this line would not satisfy critics...and it is possible that the issue could be brought before the UN." Like, *Hey, here's how we suggest bullshitting this thing. Nobody's really gonna buy it, but it's the best we got!*

Did any of the significant hesitations from within the Johnson administration put the brakes on Operation Popeye? Dear reader, would we be here if they had? Proponents of Popeye claimed that earlier testing was "too successful." They also went on to say that costs would be so low, they were baaaaasically insignificant. Who could say no to that?

Certainly not Lyndon B. Johnson, who gave the project his sign-off, thus approving the first large-scale effort to use weather as a weapon. The plan was to extend the monsoon season in Vietnam by thirty to forty-five days, thus disrupting the ability of North Vietnamese soldiers to travel with muddy roads, landslides, and flooding. The air force would begin seeding the clouds over crucial regions of Vietnam, and if all went as planned, they would make it rain (or at least, make it rain *more* than it was already going to).

Soon, Operation Popeye even had a catchy slogan: Make Mud, Not War. But to be clear, they were still making war, sooo...yeah.

Over the next five years, from 1967 to 1972, both the US Air Force and the US Navy would participate in 2,600 cloud seeding runs. Brian Heckman, an air force pilot who belonged to the Fourth Weather Reconnaissance Squadron, was given limited information about what he'd be doing in the war. He was very surprised, upon being briefed, to discover that his mission was to make it rain. On the podcast *99 Percent Invisible,* he said, "We just went around looking for clouds to seed." And once they found them, they'd ignite silver or lead iodide flares and hope that it would begin raining.

And remember how in the proposal the cost was so low as to be "insignificant"? Well, steel yourself for some napkin math. All in all, the project cost about $3.6 million a year—yeah, flying planes ain't cheap. And before

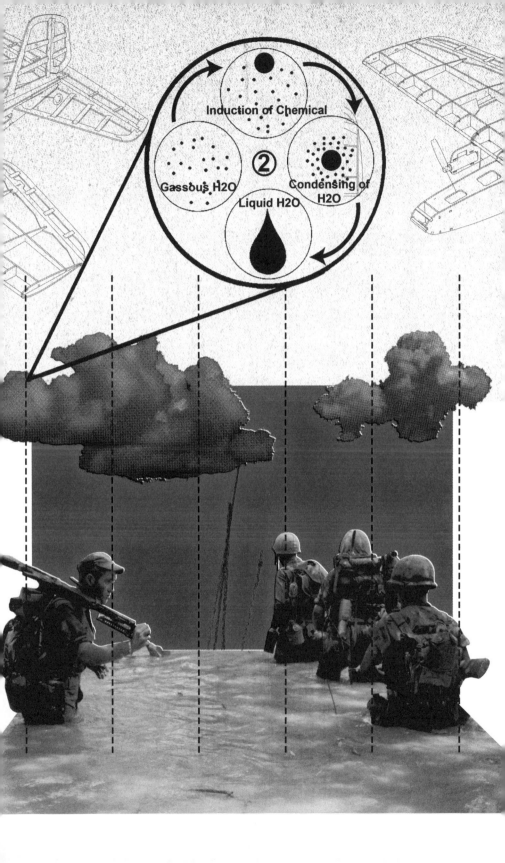

Induction of Chemical

Gassous H2O

② Condensing of H2O

Liquid H2O

you say, "Oh well, that's not so...," let me whip out my inflation calculator and multiply by the five years the project lasted. That is the equivalent of the project costing $156,906,405 if it were undertaken today. Doesn't seem so insignificant to me!

Just as the Blutos suspected, keeping Operation Popeye a secret proved challenging. Which should have been obvious to the Johnson administration and later the Nixon administration, which took office about halfway through Operation Popeye's run. Arguably, it was obvious to some members. In one effort to keep it out of the public eye, the name of the operation changed multiple times. In addition to Popeye, it also went by Operation Intermediary Compatriot and Operation Motorpool—because people who didn't have the appropriate security clearance kept finding out about it. I guess the best way to keep a secret if you work for the State Department is to make sure no one actually knows what you're talking about?

Ultimately, Operation Popeye continued for a little over five years, trying to stay under wraps and just barely squeaking by, thanks to swapping out pairs of nose-and-mustache glasses on the project. But it wouldn't stay a secret forever.

GOING PUBLIC

In March 1971, investigative reporter Jack Anderson was working at the *Washington Post* when he uncovered some crucial information. Anderson wrote a column called "Washington Merry-Go-Round" about the various dramas and corruption in the district. Once he uncovered proof of Operation Popeye, he put pen to paper and dramatically broke the story about the air force's top secret efforts to seed clouds over the Ho Chi Minh Trail.

Jack Anderson was not just any old reporter. He was the most famous and feared investigative reporter in the country at the time. He ate political scandal for breakfast, lunch, and dinner. And his favorite target was Richard Nixon. Anderson watched Tricky Dick rise through the ranks and took it upon himself to expose as many of his political and personal acts of corruption as he could. Atta boy, Anderson.

Nixon notoriously hated journalists. This was a man who ordered illegal wiretaps on reporters, and whose aides put together lists of "enemies" as targets for government retaliation. Plus, he filed antitrust charges against TV networks that criticized him. So Nixon was the type of politician who not only took notice of Anderson but who had an active vendetta against him. (The Nixon administration even allegedly aimed to have Anderson assassinated, but that's a SNAFU that would put me well over my word count.)

Still, Nixon's boys continued to do what they were best at: lying. In a 1972 Senate hearing, when he was asked about Operation Popeye, Nixon's secretary of defense, Melvin Laird, testified that they had never seeded clouds over North Vietnam. The denials were so consistent and adamant that some people now refer to the whole incident as the "Watergate of weather warfare." But the lying was catching up to them as more and more journalists were becoming interested in the story.

On July 3, 1972, Seymour Hersh wrote an article for the *New York Times* headlined "Rainmaking Is Used as Weapon by U.S." The cat was really out of the bag now.

Though Anderson had already outed the program, this article included some major new revelations. Not only did Hersh's sources confirm that US forces were cloud seeding over Vietnam, but they were doing more than trying to wash out the roads. Hersh's article reported that some of the rain they were causing was not your typical H_2O. The Attack Clouds were treated with chemicals that "produced an acidic rainfall." That's right, we may have been literally getting the sky itself to rain acid on our enemies. The anonymous officials who talked with Hersh told him it was "fouling the operation of North Vietnamese radar equipment" and shutting down their surface-to-air missiles. Hersh's article was actually the only source to report this acid rain, so it remains a bit of a mystery to us today whether this was some puffed-up official overselling the scope of the operation or if the exact details of how and why the acid rain was made are buried in a top secret file somewhere.

In the end, the pressure was too much. American sentiments toward the Vietnam War had soured, and Operation Popeye was just another on the stack of missteps by the US military. A few days after the *New York Times* story came out, Operation Popeye was officially shut down.

AFTERMATH

In 1974 the Senate Foreign Relations Committee had gathered in the Senate chambers to talk about the weather. Sure, it was the first day of spring, but they weren't there to remark on the sunshine and fresh blooms. Committee chairman Senator Claiborne Pell was tasked with understanding what the report before him termed "weather modification activity." After mulling over the decision to conduct a years-long wartime weather manipulation operation and keep the whole thing under wraps from Congress and the American people, Senator Pell said, "The thing that concerns me, is not rainmaking per se, but when you open Pandora's box, what comes out with it?"

Senator Pell wasn't the only one worried about trying to stuff acid rain back into its proverbial box. Two months after that meeting, he placed the formerly top secret hearing into the public record. In his estimation, the country—and the world—deserved to know.

Later that year, President Nixon met with the Soviet Union's general secretary, Leonid Brezhnev, to sign a joint statement intended to limit environmental warfare with effects that would be "wide-spread, long-lasting and severe"—words that the US National Security Council had advocated to include. This was hypothetically the first step toward eradicating future weather warfare.

The Soviet Union understood that the United States was using these words as loopholes to justify their own cloud seeding operations, which they bafflingly didn't view as long-lasting or severe. So in the wake of the Watergate scandal, they seized the opportunity to take diplomatic initiative. They brought the issue of weather modification as a weapon of war to the United Nations and called for an international convention to ban it. Their proposal did not include those pesky qualifiers, nor was it a bilateral agreement. They wanted a treaty holding all members of the UN to the same standard—no more using the weather or climate for military purposes or international security. Period.

The UN General Assembly was on board and everything was going swimmingly until President Gerald Ford's administration (Nixon having resigned by this point) had a flash of panic spurred on by fear of further embarrassment. The administration insisted that those qualifiers—*wide-spread, long-lasting and severe*—be added into the treaty before they agreed to sign it. And of course, they got their way.

With the loopholes worked in, it was clear to everyone how little the end result meant. As James Fleming writes in his book *Fixing the Sky: The Checkered History of Weather and Climate Control,* rather than banning weather weapons, the language of the treaty actually "legitimized the use of cloud seeding in warfare," including things like "the diversion of a hurricane and other, smaller-scale techniques." That's right—bafflingly, the US government had decided that cloud seeding was *not* long-lasting and severe, despite all proof to the contrary. The treaty said nothing about prohibiting the research and development of new weather weapons, either.

Three years and three massive qualifiers later, the treaty was signed into international law. Thanks to the loopholes, the US military's Air Weather Service emerged unaffected. All their cloud seeding tricks stayed right where they were, locked and loaded in the American arsenal.

The question remains: Was Operation Popeye a success? There's really no way to know. It's possible that the efforts of Operation Popeye did result in more rainfall over the Ho Chi Minh Trail. But to what extent did that influence fighting the war? In that 1974 Senate hearing, Senator Pell asked the assistant secretary of defense whether he thought Popeye was effective. The secretary responded, "It looks to me like when you are getting twenty-one inches of rain in a given area and we add two inches, if I was on the bottom, I do not think I would know the difference between twenty-one and twenty-three." I'll partially agree; the difference in two inches of rain may not feel like a lot, but if someone lopped off two inches from my two-foot game day hoagie, they'd be hearing from my attorney. Thank you very much!

The extra rain had little effect on the movement of North Vietnamese fighters, who could easily reroute to new paths when the trail was taken out and who were reportedly using bicycles to transport supplies. That rain barely mattered to them as they slogged through the mud atop their bikes like they had every other monsoon season.

In the end, the US government pulled the plug on federal funding for weather modification programs. In 1978, just a year after they had fought for a treaty to reserve their right to seed clouds, the military decided that weather manipulation technology was a watered-down stand-in for real weapons and no longer served a purpose in American national security.

Today, weather modification for non-military purposes is very common. The Chinese Meteorological Association runs a huge cloud seeding operation to create billions of tons of rain every year. And in the United States, private companies are using cloud seeding to address drought in Red Rock Canyon. These are projects that largely go unnoticed or heard about. Cloud seeding alone isn't necessarily cause for concern. It can be really useful when it comes to agriculture or attempting to make sure the powder is fresh on ski slopes. I've even heard of couples hiring someone to seed clouds in advance of their wedding to bust the rain before their big day. Alanis Morissette might find that ironic. I know I do! Who would have thought we'd come so far from the days of weaponizing the weather? It figures.

CATCHING FIRE ON THE CUYAHOGA

How a fiery SNAFU on an oil-slick river changed the face of American environmentalism forever.

We always talk about fifteen minutes of fame...but what about fifteen minutes of *flame*? That's approximately how long the polluted Cuyahoga River burned in 1969 when a flare tossed from a passing train hit oil and debris floating atop the river's surface, setting it ablaze. That's right. A flare from a passing train literally caught the surface of the river *on fire*. The fire burned hot and quick—so fast in fact that there was no time to snap a photo of the inferno.

Call me crazy, but it *seems* like catching fire is something a river shouldn't ever do. Imagine all those poor little river fish, bubbling in a sludgy fish stew... that is, if the Cuyahoga River hadn't been so polluted in 1969 that most of the fish were dead already. At the time it was even said that bloated rat corpses the size of small dogs would float down the river.

Dead fish and rat stew, a Cuyahoga delicacy!

PRIDE OF CLEVELAND

The Cuyahoga River hadn't always been a polluted cauldron of oil and debris. One of the biggest rivers in the country, it stretches for about 100 miles across what's now the city of Cleveland, Ohio, before it empties into Lake Erie. And there was a time—hundreds of years ago—when the Indigenous people of the region, like the Ottawa tribe, Ojibwa tribe, and Ohio Seneca people, relied on the river for some of their food supply. So how did pollution in the Cuyahoga get so bad that it blazed for longer than a lighter flicked during a song at the end of an arena concert?

Well, part of it was location, location, LOCATION. During the Civil War, Cleveland became a manufacturing hub almost overnight due to its location on Lake Erie and the Cuyahoga River, plus its access to steel, lumber, and coal. From the 1860s on, the banks of the Cuyahoga River were home to some of the biggest names in manufacturing. Standard Oil, American Ship Building, the Sherwin-Williams Paint Company, and Republic Steel *all* had factories lined up along the riverside. Along with that came more than 850,000 new residents between the beginning of the Civil War and the Great Depression.

But hand in hand with the economic and population boom came the toxic waste of manufacturing. By the 1870s, the Cuyahoga was basically used as a sludge dump. And by 1881, Cleveland's mayor was referring to it as an open sewer. The curdling river became so polluted that it even began to affect the city's water supply. Hence, the origin of dead fish and rat stew and...cue Billy's Joel's "We Didn't Start the Fire."

At this point in our tale you *might* think that the 1969 fire was the first time that the Cuyahoga had burned. But dear, sweet, naive reader...you would be very wrong. In fact, with all that toxic sludge swirling around for about *a hundred years*, the river had burned at least *nine* times before.

The first fire that caught the attention of the press was in August 1868, when a spark from the smokestack of a passing tugboat ignited an oil slick in the river (sound familiar?!). The blazes of 1883 and 1912 were *quite* dramatic, causing tugboat captains to speculate about when that cagey ol' river was going to catch fire again and singe everything in sight. Some of the fires killed people, and some, like a fire in 1952, caused millions of dollars in damage. That was the most severe, but not the last: There's still the fire of 1969, which burned for under thirty minutes, and damaged a railroad trestle, but left bystanders unscathed.

But the thing is...the people of Cleveland didn't really seem to care. The toxic, combustible river was more a badge of honor than a worrisome blight. The thinking was: "Sure, you can't swim in the water and the oil slicks burn from time to time like a deadly Slip 'N Slide, but who needs a clean river when what we *do* have in Cleveland are...jobs!"

But while the river was burning...the *jobs* were drying up.

By the time of the 1969 fire, manufacturing in Cleveland was slowing—the city was in the process of *losing* more than 125,000 residents. The

Scene along the Cuyahoga River.

How are you a getting long Marford,
I am having a Good time

Scene along the Cuyahoga River.

How are you a getting long Marford,
I am having a Good time

benefits of polluting the river no longer seemed to outweigh the negative (and flammable) side effects of all that bustling industry.

Enter Carl B. Stokes.

STOKING THE FLAMES

In 1967, Stokes was elected mayor of Cleveland, becoming the first-ever Black mayor of a major American city. Stokes, tall with close-cropped hair and a well-kept mustache, had grown up on Cleveland's East Side. As a progressive, forward-thinking politician, he'd already begun initiatives to scrub the Cuyahoga and clean up the urban environment. So, when the 1969 fire broke out, it seemed like the perfect opportunity to rally attention for his cause.

One other thing about Carl Stokes—he was a great speaker, and savvy with the media. So, the day after the fire, on June 23, 1969, he decided to hold what his team dubbed a "Pollution Tour" around the city of Cleveland. Stokes led the press through the greatest hits of the most spoiled, soiled, and stained spots in Cleveland: sewers, industrial sites, and the main attraction—the site of the recent fire.

In a sea of journalists, Stokes stood atop the very railroad trestle that had sent sparks flying the day before and addressed the press assembled around him. He lamented the sorry state of the river and reminded the journalists that as the mayor of the city of Cleveland, he actually had no power over how the surrounding suburbs—or the state of Ohio, for that matter—regulated pollution in the river. Stokes was not-so-subtly hinting that controlling pollution wasn't just a city government problem; rather, it was a state-level and perhaps even a *national* issue.

In the crowd that day was Betty Klaric, traipsing over that infamous railroad trestle with her notepad under her arm. Klaric, a small woman with short, light hair, stood out in a sea of suits as the only person in patent-leather heels on the trestle that day. She was one of the first environmental reporters in the nation—she'd been on the environmental beat for the *Cleveland Press* since 1965. When she returned to her desk, she wrote that during his pollution tour, the mayor wondered aloud how this kind of pollution in the Cuyahoga could be tolerated by the citizens of Cleveland. Little did Betty know, chomping on the end of her pencil as she wrote, that the story she was penning would catch the attention of national news outlets. Including *TIME* magazine.

In their August 1969 issue, *TIME* printed an article about the Cuyahoga River fire with the headline "The Cities: The Price of Optimism." The short article slammed the polluted river, saying, "Some river! Chocolate-brown, oily, bubbling with sub-surface gasses, it oozes rather than flows." They even quoted anonymous Clevelanders who evidently said, "Anyone who falls into the Cuyahoga does not drown. He decays." That's our Cuyahoga!

Below the article was an image of Mayor Stokes from his pollution tour, alongside a picture of the 1969 fire. The picture of the fire showed a steamboat caught in the enormous, long-burning conflagration...except...wait, do you happen to recall that the 1969 Cuyahoga fire burned so fast that there was no time to take a picture of it? You do? Well then dear, sweet, extremely savvy reader, you've proven yourself far more observant than the average editor at *TIME* magazine (it was the 1960s—maybe we can blame it on one-too-many lunchtime martinis).

Because the picture that *TIME* printed wasn't actually a picture from the 1969 fire. It was a picture from the fire in 1952 that had caused $1.5 million in damage. *TIME* didn't explicitly say that the picture was from the 1969 fire... but they didn't say it wasn't, either. Along with this dramatic image of a burning river, this particular issue of *TIME* also happened to include an exposé about the Chappaquiddick scandal, which meant that *a lot* of people bought it looking for a little Kennedy family gossip. But once they opened the magazine, they found not just the Teddy K. drama, but a jaw-dropping picture of a boat engulfed in flames on the Cuyahoga.

And with that image of a *different* Cuyahoga fire burned into the eyeballs of millions of Americans, the 1969 fire achieved mythic status. It became a symbol of what rivers *aren't* supposed to do, and how far pollution had allowed America's natural landscape to decline.

THAT EARTH DAY GLOW

The American people were primed to respond to the burning Cuyahoga. Environmentalism was beginning to take hold in the United States with the recent publication of Rachel Carson's *Silent Spring* in 1962, and this sensational image of a river burning sparked the imagination of the nation. Take Randy Newman's 1972 song "Burn On!" about the Cuyahoga fire. Or take the Great Lakes Brewing Company, who named their Burning River Pale Ale as an homage (which I may or may not have sampled many times in my college days at Oberlin, just a *scootch* west of Cleveland). Oh, right, and we were *also* inspired to dream up what Carl Stokes had hinted at on his pollution tour: legislation to curb urban pollution at the national level.

So the wheels started a-turning to get the river to stop a-burning: In January 1970, just a few months after the *TIME* article came out, the National Environmental Policy Act (NEPA) was passed. The act proclaimed that it would "establish a national policy which will encourage productive and enjoyable harmony between man and his environment." Basically, laying out the blanket on which the picnic of soon-to-be-enacted environmental legislation could be spread.

Then, on April 22, 1970, the city of Cleveland took part in the very first Earth Day celebration. The event had been in the works for a while, but Earth Day's founders used the hullabaloo around the fire to heat up interest around the country. It worked: Twenty million Americans, which was fully 10 percent of the population at the time, ended up marching in demonstrations through streets and parks all around the country.

On that first Earth Day, in Cleveland's elementary schools, children wrote letters to Mayor Stokes, expressing their disappointment in the sludgy Cuyahoga, and their fears about the air and water quality in their city. In their book *Where the River Burned*, David and Richard Strandling compiled a few choice quotes from the mouths of those letter-writing babes: One student—an aspiring dystopian novelist or something—wrote, "It is plain to see that our area is deteriorating at a rapid rate...by 1980 we may all be walking around wearing gas masks in order to breathe." Another kid put it more like, well, a kid: "Would you please tell me how any river could become a fire hazard because of the oil on it...That is really weird." Couldn't have said it better.

In the end, those pesky letter-writing children of Cleveland got what they wished for. About a week after Earth Day, on April 28, 1970, Mayor Stokes spoke to the US Senate about water pollution on behalf of the National League of Cities and the US Conference of Mayors. And the very next day, a council created by President Richard Nixon to review environmental policy recommended the creation of the federal Environmental Protection Agency (EPA), the very first federal agency dedicated to the preservation of the environment.

Thanks in part to the legislation that this fiery SNAFU inspired, today the Cuyahoga River is thriving. Once declared dead by the national media, the river now boasts more than sixty species of fish and is home to freshwater mussels. On March 20, 2019, fish caught in the Cuyahoga River were declared safe to eat by federal environmental regulators. Meaning that you can now eat *real* fish stew straight from the Cuyahoga—no rat seasoning required.

And the river never caught fire again, right?

...

Right?

Sadly, I must report that on August 25, 2020, a fuel tanker spilled its flaming contents into the river after a road accident, lighting the river on fire yet again. So you never know, you might still get a chance to flick those lighters open and join Randy Newman as he sings, "Burn on, big river, burn on!"

TOP FIVE...

FAILED PLOTS TO ASSASSINATE EL COMANDANTE

Cuban president Fidel Castro survived
634 assassination attempts by the CIA,
all of which were fumbled, thwarted,
or straight up abandoned.

Folks, it's no secret that the CIA had it out for our feisty friend Fidel Castro from the moment he took office. According to several credible sources, there were 634 (!) assassination attempts on his life by the CIA. You know what they say: If at first you don't succeed, try, try again...633 more times. But there are a few that particularly piqued my interest. Let's count 'em down!

5. PILL-POPPIN' MOBSTAH (1960)

In 1960, the CIA enlisted Fidel's fellow countrymen to help take him out. The enlistees were Cubans who also just happened to be gangsters involved with the Chicago Mob—some of whom were on the FBI's Ten Most Wanted list. After multiple failed hits, one of the gangsters suggested lethal poison pills. The CIA granted him (a *mobster on the FBI's top-ten wanted list, yeesh*) access to the poison pills and put him on the task.

Why didn't the plan work? The mobster got cold feet. I don't know about you, but that seems to me like low-rent mobstering.

Win $14,250
Journal American
AFTERNOON EDITION
Police on Alert
KILL CASTRO!

4. I SCREAM, YOU SCREAM (1961)

In case you were unaware, let me just get this fun fact out of the way: Fidel Castro loved ice cream. Don't we all? #relatable. And that's why the CIA gave even *more* poison pills to Cuban government official Tony Varona to plant in one of Fidel's mouthwatering milkshakes. But after Varona passed the pills to a restaurant worker in Havana, those pesky pastilles spilled into the freezer, rendering them useless. The worker, Varona, and the CIA all had to watch Castro walk out, slurping down his nontoxic creamy concoction.

That's cold, Comandante. Real cold.

3. SCUBA DYING (1963)

Knowing that Castro enjoyed scuba diving, the CIA plotted an underwater assassination that would catch the eye of any collector. You see, agents tried to plant explosives in a shiny seashell on the seabed floor, hoping it would lure Castro in, and *KERSPLOOSH!* explode upon contact. After the agents struggled to find a suitable location for the seashell, the plan was disregarded as "impractical" (you don't say...), and they went a different route: contaminating his diving suit with a fungus that would give him a toxic skin disease. This time, they put James Donovan, a lawyer regularly involved in hostage negotiations with Castro, on the job. (I suppose they were desperate to get to anyone close enough to him.) However, Donovan chickened out, providing Castro a clean diving suit.

I don't know about Fidel, but no matter the wetsuit, once I dip myself into salt water longer than a few minutes, I find I'm 94 percent more likely to leave with a horrible rash in the worst possible junctures of my body.

2. THE PEN IS NOT MIGHTIER (1963)

Like a gadget from a Bond film, an unassuming fountain pen was once chosen by the CIA as a potential death-dealing device. According to records, the pen was fitted with a stealth hypodermic needle, and filled with Black Leaf 40, a commercially available (and lethal) poison made from nicotine sulphate. It's widely available because, well, it was actually created as an insecticide.

The mysterious assassination agent known on record only as "AM / LASH" refused the needle after analyzing it, allegedly stating: "Come up with something more sophisticated than that." What were they expecting, a Q-Branch concoction of highly concentrated nitric and hydrochloric acids that could dissolve any metal? (Roger Moore knows what I'm talking about.)

*Honorable mentions:

Before we reveal the final assassination attempt, let's give it up for some honorable mentions.

- A bomb painted to appear like a softball was *supposed* to be thrown at Castro's limo (the bomb-maker's wife called the police before the first "pitch" could be tossed).
- Poisoning (they love their poisons at the CIA) his favorite box of cigars. And would you believe it? They got lost in the mail.

And now let's get a drum roll for the silliest assassination attempt of them all...

1. THE SOLE MAN (1960)

The CIA planned to sabotage another of Castro's speeches during his trip to New York in September 1960. They hoped he'd put his shoes in the hotel hallway while he slept, allowing an agent to sprinkle thallium salts into his soles. The plan was for the fumes from the thallium salts to, quite literally, make his beard fall out. It would ruin his image as a leader...or maybe just embarrass him a teensy bit. Okay, okay, this one's not even a fully developed assassination plot. It's just plain hilarious. But as it would happen, travel plans frequently change, and at the eleventh hour, Castro canceled the trip.

So the next time you're in the Big Apple, keep a nose out for any funky fumes, and *don't* leave your shoes in the hallway...The CIA and their salty shenanigans could be right around the corner!

PART THREE

THE
SEVENTIES

SPIES, LIES, AND MILITARY WISE GUYS

Just when you thought it was safe to go back in the water...up came the seventies! In many ways the seventies were a continuation of the sixties, and Tom Wolfe called the seventies "the Me Decade." As Americans grew disillusioned with the lack of global action in the sixties, some say that citizens became a bit...*ahem*...self-centered. But who could blame us? We'd been through a lot, after all.

But we weren't entirely out of the woods. 'Twas also an age of blockbusters, big personalities, and even *more* political upheaval. As films like *The Godfather* (Parts I and II) popularized characters like Fredo Corleone, accusations of bribery, fraud, and tax evasion would lead Vice President Spiro Agnew to resign. The following year brought us the infamous Watergate scandal. Not long after, President Gerald Ford even survived an attempted assassination. Meanwhile, dissent was happening all around: from anti-Vietnam protests to civil rights advocacy.

In the seventies, women's rights made major strides through the introduction of Title IX, the Supreme Court ruling on *Roe v. Wade*, and of course Billie Jean King's resounding victory over Bobby Riggs in the Battle of the Sexes tennis match. Advanced technology was also no longer exclusive to military forces as Bill Gates, Steve Jobs, and Steve Wozniak all began constructing personal computers, *and* creating the two largest personal tech brands to date.

But as rogue rockets and space debris fell from the sky, a web of covert operations and informants spread across international borders. Espionage became the name of the game, and I'm not just talking about Connery and Moore swapping shaken martinis. The errors of the seventies spanned far beyond the White House in this decade defined by spies, lies, and a handful of military wise guys.

SILENCIO:

THREE METEORS, TWO LIGHTNING STRIKES, AND A ROCKET FROM THE NEIGHBOR NEXT DOOR

How a massive accident put a
spooky Mexican town on the
international map.

In the early morning of July 11, 1970, the ATHENA V-123-D rocket was launched from a complex in Green River, Utah, bound for the missile range in White Sands, New Mexico. But as the rocket blazed a trail through the fresh, dim light of the morning, it became very clear that the rocket wasn't headed to its intended location. Few in attendance at the launch could have guessed where this rocket would lead them.

ATHENA started in the right direction, but quickly veered off course: toward Mexico. She came careening down out of the sky, landing in southern Chihuahua near the town of Ceballos, around 200 miles south of the US border. And, oh yeah, the test rocket was carrying two pellets of the *highly* radioactive element cobalt-57. This test flight had officially become a mess for the US government, and like a kid who left all their toys in the yard, they were going to have to clean it up themselves.

WHOOPS! OUR BALL WENT OVER THE FENCE

It was embarrassing, sure, but this also wasn't the first rocket the United States had lost on Mexican soil. In fact, it was the third. I mean, imagine how you'd feel if your neighbor kept accidentally hurling fireballs into your yard. Even if your swing set didn't catch on fire, I think you'd be...pretty pissed.

The ATHENA was launched as part of the Advanced Ballistic Reentry System program. The goal of the program was to study how missiles reenter the atmosphere from space in order to coordinate more precise landings. The program wasn't doing well (obviously). It had been shut down once already in July 1968 after three consecutive failures. But just like any unnecessary television reboot these days, the project was revived later that year, leading to a handful of successful launches. In spite of those successes, almost a third of the funding was dropped between 1966 and 1969—a serious challenge to a program that had already had its fair share of trials and tribulations. Maybe it's no surprise, then, considering the budget cuts, that the ATHENA landed where she did.

In a memo to President Richard Nixon, Secretary of State Henry Kissinger laid out the air force's massive faux pas, noting that Mexican authorities had already been contacted and agreed to help the United States locate the rocket and retrieve it. All that was left was an extraction plan: how to get the rocket, or should I say rocket *pieces*, back to the United States. For that task, the military brought in NASA rocket scientist Wernher von Braun. To say von Braun was an interesting choice would be an understatement. He was a former member of the Nazi Party whom the United States relocated from Germany along with 1,600 other scientists as a part of Operation Paperclip. But that's a story for another book.

The point is that in 1970, NASA threw von Braun on a plane to Mexico with one directive: Bring the ATHENA back.

LA ZONA DEL SILENCIO

To an outsider, it appeared that the ATHENA landed in an unremarkable, unpopulated area in southern Chihuahua. But for a small group of locals, this was not their first rodeo. The area, known as the Mapimí Zone, had seen more than its fair share of celestial bodies falling from the heavens. Three separate meteorites had hit the zone in 1938, 1954, and 1969. They struck pretty close to one another, with two landing on the same ranch sixteen years apart. That's uncanny if you ask me.

It wasn't just the chances of getting hit by a large rock that made this place special. In 1966, a group searching for oil struggled using their radio to communicate. They dubbed it the Zone of Silence.

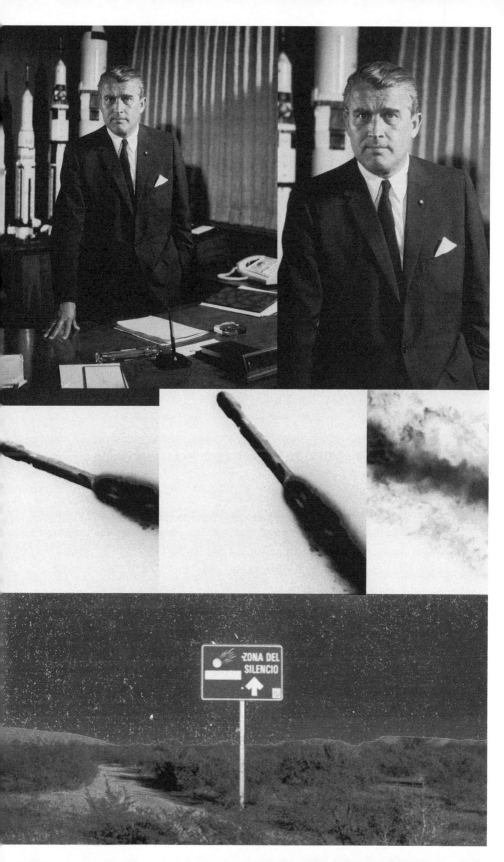

It was in this area that von Braun, the former Nazi rocketeer, showed up in 1970 with one objective: operation "Bring ATHENA Home." (And no, that's not the official title of the operation. Only I call it that. It was actually called Operation Sand Patch. Booooo.) To execute on "Bring ATHENA Home," they planned to build a sixteen-kilometer railroad extension to the crash site to transport all the pieces of the rocket back to the main rail line and into the United States. In order to accomplish this, they enlisted the help of 300 local workers.

Once the railroad was built, a US Army radar communications team came in to excavate the rocket. And when they came, they really set up shop. They brought dormitories, mobile labs, kitchens, and medical facilities. They even built an airstrip to send cargo back and forth from Houston.

All told, the team ended up staying twenty-eight days, at which point they packed up sixty drums of radioactive soil (thanks, cobalt-57!), plus another three containing anti-contamination clothing, boots, and gloves. And they hightailed it out of Chihuahua.

YOU CAN'T PUT THE COBALT BACK IN THE BAG

The US Army may have left the zone of silence, but their presence fed into a much larger narrative about the mystique of the zone. Fascinated gawkers across continents have been trying to get a look at the area ever since. Legends about the area have cropped up claiming that it's home to an electromagnetic vortex that serves as an interdimensional portal for UFOs. Today you can stay at UFO-themed ranches and go on UFO sighting tours in the area.

Some people even claim they've been lost in the desert nearby and encountered tall beings with light-colored hair whose only question is "¿Tienes agua?" or "Do you have any water?" Alien hunters call them "Nordics." You can explain that story a lot of ways. Real aliens? Locals *faking* aliens to bring in tourists? Personally, I'm not sold on the story that all the NASA workers left when all was said and done. "Nordics" asking for water in Spanish sounds a little suss to me: especially when I think about the kind of team a former—*ahem*—"Nordic" like von Braun might put together.

The oddities of the region aren't relegated only to the otherworldly, though. In 1977, seven years after the ATHENA rocket crashed, the Mexican government designated the land around the zone as the Mapimí Biosphere

Reserve with the intention to preserve the area for research. Today researchers travel to the reserve from around the world to study the unusual flora and fauna in the area. Mostly, it's the *Gopherus* tortoise, North America's biggest reptile.

As for the Advanced Ballistic Reentry System program, it's still around today in spite of the significant budget cuts. It's evolved into a program called the Rocket System Launch Program, which does pretty much the same thing. Maybe the new name is part of a rebranding effort after their handful of mistakes?

No evidence remains of the ATHENA rocket crash. Of course, some would argue that the incident and surrounding secrecy left a legacy that won't fade anytime soon. If you're ever in the area, make sure to keep an eye on the sky.

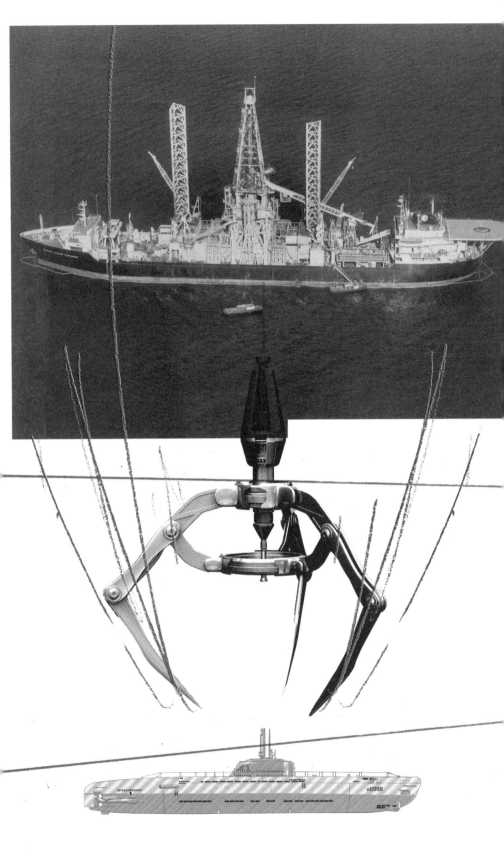

PROJECT AZORIAN:

A SUB ABOVE

How the CIA tried to win the world's most
expensive and difficult claw machine.

In the early hours of June 5, 1974, security guard Mike Davis stood outside the building at 7020 Romaine Street in Hollywood. As he enjoyed the balmy sixty-degree weather, the light of the full moon shining through the cloudy sky, Mike suddenly felt something pressing into his back.

A gun.

A group of four burglars grabbed poor Mike and forced him to unlock the door. Why did these thieves want to get inside so badly? Because the building Mike was guarding was the corporate headquarters of Howard Hughes, the reclusive billionaire aviator, film producer, philanthropist, and all-around all-American weirdo rich guy. Think Jeff Bezos, but with a pencil-thin mustache and actually, ya know, adventurous.

After the burglars forced Mike to let them in, they wheeled in a heavy tank filled with highly flammable acetylene gas. They mazed their way through the Art Deco–style, two-story building before finally marching into an office that contained a safe and a large vault. Jackpot.

Wait a second, you might be asking, the burglars just *waltzed* right in there? Shouldn't this famously secretive guy have some sort of security or alarm system for this building that houses his sensitive, top secret shit?

Well, reader, there *was* an alarm system. It just wasn't working. Actually, it had been out of order for some time. And Mike was the only guard on duty. Seriously, this place had worse security than the gas station where my friends and I used to steal packs of gum as kids.

The burglars turned on the acetylene tank and grabbed their torches. You know the big heist scene in *Thief* where James Caan puts on a welding suit, lights a long-ass torch, and drives it straight into a locked metal door as sparks fly everywhere? Just imagine that. And after hours of slowly melting the door off its hinges, one of the burglars took off his suit, wiped his brow, and smirked as he said: "We're in."

The burglars stormed into the vault and grabbed everything they could. Four hours after first arriving, the burglars escaped, hauling the acetylene tank with them and all their stolen loot. They ended up with quite the grab bag: $68,000 in cash, two Wedgwood vases, a ceramic samovar, two butterfly collections, three digital watches, and an antique Mongolian eating bowl. Again, Hughes was a rich weirdo. Maybe he was planning on sitting down to a delicious meal of pickled butterflies, perfectly arranged in his Mongolian bowl.

But even *more* valuable than those preserved critters and antiques were two footlockers full of files—documents that would soon cause an international diplomatic scandal. These documents revealed Hughes's participation in a secret CIA plot that involved a sunken Soviet submarine, underwater nukes, and the most difficult claw game in the world.

THE SUB

It all began six years earlier on March 1, 1968, when a Soviet submarine named K-129 sailed out from a naval base in Petropavlovsk, way out in the Russian Far East and over 4,000 miles from Moscow. K-129 was equipped with three nuclear warheads; each single warhead was nearly seventy times more powerful than the bomb dropped by the United States on Hiroshima. In the case of nuclear war, the sub would fire off its nukes to targets on the West Coast of the United States.

The sub began its standard peacetime patrol in the North Pacific. But at some point in the middle of March, the Soviets lost communication with K-129. The sub went radio silent. We still don't know exactly what happened.

A declassified, heavily redacted CIA report published in 1985 simply says that "the submarine suffered an accident—cause unknown—and sank 1,560 miles northwest of Hawai'i." The report is also mum about how the CIA came to ascertain the location of the sub's sinking. According to military historian Matthew Aid, archival documents have suggested that the US Navy's underwater sonar, the Sound Surveillance System, might have discovered the location of the sunken sub.

Whatever the case, the Soviets had lost a nuke-equipped submarine. They fruitlessly searched for it for two months, then gave up. And that whole time, the CIA knew exactly where it was.

Why was the CIA so interested in the sub? Because inside was potentially valuable intelligence that could reveal the inner workings of the Soviet Navy: codebooks, decoding machines, and burst transmitters—not to mention the nukes themselves, which would still be functional.

There was just one problem. K-129 lay 16,500 feet beneath the surface of the ocean. How the hell do you get down there in the first place? And once you're three miles deep, how do you then bring the sub back up to the surface? These questions might have left a recovery effort dead in the water, but with such a tantalizing prize on the ocean floor, the CIA couldn't resist.

To consider their options, longtime CIA agent John Parangosky convened a task force in an anonymous office near, of all places, Tysons Corner, the largest shopping mall in the DC area. Today if you showed up there for a meeting, you could browse the racks at Urban Outfitters and grab a pretzel from Auntie Anne's, but there isn't a secret meeting room anymore. At least Parangosky got in ahead of Auntie Anne, though. According to the book *The Taking of K-129*, he "was a fair boss, occasionally even friendly, but no one was immune from his temper." I assume Parangosky wasn't very forgiving if you came back late from lunch at the food court.

Anyway, Parangosky assembled a team of scientists, engineers, and submarine experts to brainstorm ideas for the sub rescue mission. Imagine a bunch of suits scribbling ideas on a whiteboard. Maybe they could place "buoyant material" (kind of like a really sophisticated pool noodle) under the sub, and then hope the material was floaty enough to carry the sub all the way up. Maybe instead of a pool noodle, they could simply generate a buoyant gas like hydrogen or nitrogen through electrolysis, causing the sub to float back up without even touching it.

All of these ideas were 100 percent real and actually considered by the CIA. And yeah, if they sounded harebrained and doomed to fail, you'd be right. But believe it or not, the solution Parangosky and company finally landed on was even *more* harebrained: the doomedest to fail of them all.

That's right, folks. Parangosky and Co. decided to use a literal claw to pick up K-129 from the bottom of the ocean and lift it back up through brute force.

THE CLAW

The claw would consist of five separate grasping claws, connected to heavy-duty winches that would be mounted onto a specially built ship. The ship had to be able to withstand the weight of the 1,750-ton Soviet sub. The plan was for the claw to descend to the seafloor, slip a sort of metal hammock beneath the sub, and then gingerly lift it back up.

You're probably picturing one of those arcade claw games at Chuck E. Cheese right now. And yeah, that's exactly what I want you to imagine. Because think about how hard it is to even pick up a stuffed animal from the bottom of the machine. Those things are impossible to win! Now think about trying to pick up a submarine that's more than three miles underwater and has the weight of about 875 passenger cars. What could possibly go wrong?

As it turns out, just about everything. And they knew it, too. Senior intelligence officers gave the project a 10 percent success rate. If you were a civil engineer and designed a bridge that had a 90 percent chance of collapsing, what do you think your boss would say? Would they be like, "Great idea! Here's an ungodly amount of money to build this bridge that, nine times out of ten, will catastrophically fail!"?

Well, that's exactly what the CIA decided to do. On October 30, 1970, two years after K-129 sank, the agency authorized Project Azorian, the official name for the mission to recover the Soviet sub.

There were definitely concerns about the mission, especially the constantly ballooning cost. Suspiciously, the declassified CIA report redacts any and all specific dollar figures. What it does mention is how, like the making of *Apocalypse Now*, the project kept getting delayed and going over budget. For example, Project Azorian "was first costed at [REDACTED] in 1970. In less than a year it had jumped more than 50 percent to some [REDACTED]."

We'll probably never know the exact cost, but Matthew Aid estimates it at half a *billion* with a *b* dollars at the time. That's over $3 billion in today's money. How much is $3 billion? It's more than the individual GDP of thirty-five sovereign nations. In other words, this CIA floating claw machine was more expensive than entire economies. Which, damn, that makes paying a quarter to play a claw game at Chuck E. Cheese seem like a bargain.

THE VOYAGE

The CIA had one last problem with Project Azorian: How do we keep this thing a secret? We can't exactly tell everyone we're building a giant claw ship to retrieve a Soviet nuclear submarine. By 1971, the United States and the USSR were in a period of détente—the two countries had signed the Nuclear Nonproliferation Treaty in 1968—and a mission to essentially steal a Soviet sub wouldn't be great for diplomatic relations.

So the CIA needed a cover story and decided to reach out to Howard Hughes. Could Hughes pretend to be constructing a research vessel equipped with a giant claw for the purpose of mining deep-sea metals? Hughes was in many ways a perfect choice: He already had a reputation as a secretive, eccentric billionaire who invested in all sorts of expensive projects, and already had a stated interest in deep-sea mining. He had also previously collaborated with the government to develop satellites for classified intelligence purposes.

And sure enough, Hughes was more than happy to help. Construction on the *Hughes Glomar Explorer*—Hughes also agreed to let the claw ship be named after him—began in 1971 in a shipyard in Chester, Pennsylvania, a half hour south of Philadelphia. In November 1972, the ship was christened in the usual way—smashing a bottle of champagne on the hull. Not that things exactly went to plan. The person who was supposed to smash the bottle missed *twice*, and had to throw a third bottle at the ship as it cast off. Not everything is an omen, but...sometimes such occurrences are a little on the nose.

The CIA was able to maintain this cover for quite some time. When the *HGE* (let's call it the *HGE* so I don't have to keep saying "Glomar") finally set sail in 1973, the *Los Angeles Times* noted, "Newsmen were not permitted to view the launch, and details of the ship's destination and mission were not released." The press chalked up the secrecy surrounding the ship and its mission to Hughes's own propensity for privacy.

The *HGE* first sailed from Pennsylvania to Bermuda. Because it was too big to pass through the Panama Canal, it had to sail all the way around the southern tip of South America.

After making a brief pit stop in Chile, the *HGE* sailed on and reached its destination of Long Beach, California, at the end of September, where it stayed at harbor for several months in preparation for the recovery mission. It also kept experiencing mechanical failures. Literal cracks started showing in the hull, which divers had to seal up. This thing was pretty much held together by duct tape and a prayer. The crew couldn't fix everything and eventually just gave up: "One small but persistent seal leak was never corrected, and the seepage of a few gallons per hour was accepted. Thus, the *HGE* lived with a small puddle in the starboard wing well."

Kind of embarrassing. Imagine a real estate agent trying to sell you a house and explaining that there's a permanent puddle on the top floor because the roof isn't fully sealed.

But! The CIA had already invested too much time and too many resources into this over-budget, creaky-ass claw ship. I guess you could say that they'd fallen into the (sorry) sunk cost fallacy (so sorry). On June 7, 1974, President Nixon personally gave the official and final green light to recover the sub.

It was showtime.

THE MOMENT OF TRUTH

On Independence Day, as fireworks exploded over cities across the country in celebration of America's 198th birthday, the *HGE* traveled to a spot 1,560 miles northeast of Hawai'i, where K-129 lay at the bottom of the ocean. John Parangosky, the CIA agent who had come up with the whole claw idea, was closely monitoring the mission back at headquarters.

But when the *HGE* arrived at the site, the mission was very nearly thwarted. The crew noticed Soviet helicopters flying overhead, taking photos. Plus, Soviet Navy ships kept surveilling the *HGE*. One vessel named *Chazhma* came within a mile of the *HGE* and sent a radio transmission: "What are you doing here?"

The Americans replied, "We are conducting ocean mining tests—deep-ocean mining tests."

After a few more tense back-and-forths, *Chazhma* signed off with, "I wish you all the best," and went on its merry way to Petropavlovsk—the port city that K-129 originally set out from. The Soviets were none the wiser about the *HGE*'s true purpose.

But even with the Soviets off their backs, the crew still had to worry about maintenance issues, which just kept getting worse. One mechanical failure caused "a display of noise, fire (sparks and smoke primarily) and spastic shaking of the derrick." And as I always say: Whenever there's spastic shaking of the derrick, things aren't looking good. The crew in general weren't confident about their chances for success. In fact, they had nicknamed the claw "Clementine," since they figured the sub was "lost and gone forever."

But it was too late to back out now. Just after midnight on July 21, the world's most expensive and difficult claw game began. The ship's onboard computers flashed with real-time info and photos as the massive winch slowly unspooled miles and miles of piping, with Clementine descending into the deepest reaches of the Pacific. According to the book *Blind Man's Bluff,* one man who recruited sailors for the crew later compared the mission to "lifting a 25-foot-long steel tube off the ground with a cable lowered from the top of the 110-story World Trade Center, on a pitch-black night haunted by swirling winds." So, you know, everyone was set up for success.

Down Clementine went. Not much lives 16,500 feet beneath the surface of the ocean. That depth is considered the "abyssal zone," where there's no sunlight and the temperature is just above freezing. The water pressure can reach up to 600 times the pressure of the atmosphere. The only things swimming around are freaky-looking sea creatures with creepy names like "faceless fish" and "fangtooths."

It took eleven days for Clementine to reach the bottom of the ocean. Using the built-in cameras, the crew carefully maneuvered the claw to grasp the sub... only for them to miscalculate and slam the claw into the seabed. Whoops. But Clementine, faithful ol' girl, was still intact. They went in for another attempt, and this time were right on target. Clementine latched on to the sub and gingerly began lifting it up, at an agonizingly slow rate of six feet per minute. It took another eight days for the claw to rise from the crash site. Imagine the crew's excitement when, after waiting for more than a week, the claw finally returned to the surface. To quote another American military vessel: Mission accomplished!

And then imagine their disappointment when the claw emerged...with only a thirty-eight-foot-long section of the front hull. About two-thirds of the sub had broken off. On Clementine's way up, three of the five grasping claws had cracked and sunk. With only two claws still holding the highly fragile sub, the sub then split off and sank as well, along with the nuclear missile, codebooks, decoding machines, and the burst transmitters. Essentially, they lost everything the CIA was dying to reclaim.

What the claw *did* recover were the bodies of six of the sub's crew members who were trapped in the front 10 percent of the sub. Parangosky had ordered that any recovered bodies would be given a proper funeral. The Soviet crew members were buried at sea with full military honors; the funeral was filmed, and the recording was given to the Russian government a year after the Soviet Union's collapse. There's honestly something touching about that—the crew of K-129 may have been working for America's sworn enemy, but they certainly didn't deserve to die in the depths of the Pacific, thousands of miles from home. At least after their deaths, they were treated with a little humanity.

And so it was that on August 8, 1974, with most of K-129 *still* at the bottom of the ocean, the *Hughes Glomar Explorer* began its voyage home.

THE BLOWBACK

Well, the CIA told itself, *at least we were able to maintain our cover story and no one's the wiser that our mission failed.* Some in the government even believed Project Azorian to be a success—in a post-mission White House meeting, Secretary of Defense James Schlesinger declared that "the operation is a marvel." The CIA figured that even if they didn't recover the entire sub, they'd proved that it was at least possible. John Parangosky pushed for a second attempt, which was scheduled for July 1975. Hopefully they could keep the nosy press from catching on one more time.

But alas, back on June 5, 1974—while the *HGE* was docked thirty-three miles south in Long Beach waiting to launch out into the Pacific—a group of four burglars broke into the Hughes corporate headquarters and stole top secret documents that revealed the true purpose of the ship. The press discovered these documents, and Azorian's cover story was finally blown in February 1975, when the *Los Angeles Times* published the first article revealing the actual mission of the *HGE*. The following month, our good ol' pal, Pulitzer Prize–winning columnist Jack Anderson—you'll remember him from Operation Popeye—broke the story of Azorian on national TV.

And—surprise, surprise—our other legendary journalist Seymour Hersh also wrote about the failed mission for the *New York Times*. (Anyone else miss the glory days of gumshoe reporters like Anderson and Hersch?) Hersh spoke to an anonymous navy admiral who pointed out that even if the CIA *did* recover the secret Soviet codebooks (which would've been seven years out of date by that point), the codes wouldn't mean much because they were automatically, randomly scrambled every twenty-four hours.

By June 1975, all this bad press forced the CIA to cancel the planned second recovery attempt. John Parangosky, the agent who had spearheaded

Project Azorian, had retired by then. And naturally, the Soviets weren't happy about the news, either. The USSR ambassador to the United States pressed for more details about Project Azorian—perhaps the Soviets were embarrassed that despite heavily surveilling the *HGE*, they'd failed to ascertain its true purpose.

American journalists also kept digging. A journalist named Harriet Ann Phillippi filed a Freedom of Information Act request for more info. Walking a diplomatic tightrope, the CIA stated that they could "neither confirm nor deny" the agency's connection to the *Hughes Glomar Explorer*'s true mission. It's the perfect non-denial denial: Maybe this thing isn't true. But if it *is* true, we can't tell you about it! A court case the following year upheld the CIA's "refusal to confirm or deny existence of records," and Phillippi's FOIA request was thrown out.

You've probably heard this phrase, of course. It became so widespread and infamous that today it's known as the "Glomar response." In perhaps the worst example of branded accounts on Twitter (now X), @CIA's first ever tweet in 2014 was, "We can neither confirm nor deny that this is our first tweet."

Hilarious.

As for the *Hughes Glomar Explorer* itself, in 1976 the US government tried to auction it off to the public. The maximum offer they received was $2 million, which was nothing compared to the estimated total mission cost of $500 million (again, the *actual* mission cost is still classified info). The *HGE* was put into storage, and over the decades was leased to various private interests to drill for oil and to actually mine for deep-sea metals, before finally being completely scrapped in 2015—all 51,000 tons of it.

In an ironic twist, there's probably more of K-129 left than the massive claw machine that was built to recover it. Maybe James Cameron can build another deep-sea explorer and try to recover the sunken Soviet submarine himself—but on the other hand, perhaps it's best to let sleeping subs lie.

PIGEON PALS:

OUR NEW EYE IN THE SKY

A bird's-eye view of the CIA's
absurd avian spy program.

In many ways, a well-trained actor has all the makings of an excellent spy. I should know. Actors are well *accustomed* to donning disguises, memorizing critical details, and following directions (usually). Take Do Da: a fellow actor turned spy in training for the US government...who also happened to be a raven. We'll come back to his story, but he wasn't the only one.

In fact, the US government ran a sweeping, secret project called TACANA wherein birds were trained to be deployed on surveillance missions around the world. After all, what could give the United States an edge in the Cold War if not an eye in the sky?

A LITTLE ISLAND GETAWAY

Yes. Birds are real and also were, at least briefly, spies. At this point it should come as no surprise to you that in the sixties and seventies, the CIA had a thing for animal experiments. (RIP, Acoustic Kitty.) But the seventies saw a push for a less invasive training process for animal spies. The general concept was to get a bird's-eye view of a restricted area from something that could already fly and was fairly commonplace. You know, like a bird.

So the US spy agencies wanted to get a camera in the air. But how would they capture the footage? If you're familiar with Project Acoustic Kitty, you might think perhaps a nifty bionic eye or some other surgical attachment. For once, the CIA's Office of Research and Development opted for something straightforward—a tiny camera affixed to a tiny, bird-sized harness. So then came the big question: What kind of bird was best suited to the task at hand?

This is where the Avian Training Program came into play. They set up shop on a craggy island off the California coast called San Clemente, populated now primarily by military personnel (and local non-spy birds). But back in 1974, the island saw an influx of thirty avian spy hopefuls. The main muscle of the Avian Training Program was a motley crew of raptors, ranging from falcons and eagles to hawks and owls. Except for one clever black bird: a raven. These birds were chosen for their spy-worthy skill sets like vision, speed, endurance, or command recall—and evaluated by a small team of official US intelligence officers and bird trainers. The ultimate goal was to ascertain which type of bird was best suited for use in the field.

Would they be able to fly five miles from their release point with a camera, over a targeted site for surveillance, and then back to their base approximately fifty miles away? Of all the candidates, one plucky little raven stood out.

CANARY IN THE COLD WAR

Do Da took everyone by surprise, even the handler who had raised him since he was a fledgling. Earlier in his career, Do Da had been an actor on both camera and stage, and as an actor myself, I can confirm that remembering blocking is a veritable skill. He was chosen to participate in the program on the basis of his superb flying, but his handler admits to having had modest expectations. When the time came to show what he could do, Do Da blew them all away. He quickly became a beloved favorite of the project on San Clemente Island.

His four-month stint on the island showed continuous improvement, with only two breaks, one of which lists him as "At studio" and the other for an ambiguous "Texas trip." (There's always time to brush up on your two-step.)

In just over three months, he was outpacing the presumed stronger candidates. In the third progress report of the Avian Training Program, he was championed for flying five miles from land to the target boat, exceeding by one mile the previous record for distance flown over water. Mind you, these weren't leisurely cruises through the balmy ocean air over a California coast. Think less David Attenborough and more Michael Bay. Do Da and the others had to contend with blustery winds that averaged around forty miles an hour in the winter and fiercely territorial native gulls and ravens who had been known to drive Do Da's fellow trainees into the sea.

In a cruel twist of fate and dramatic foreshadowing, Do Da's penultimate report noted how eager the handlers were to acquire a chase boat until a tracking device could be procured for their birds, who often flew beyond the range of visual contact. But neither would come soon enough. The native ravens who were always trying to take Do Da out of the sky had become accustomed to the training schedule. They could now time their ambushes. And they seemed to have it out for our unlikely hero.

On June 19, 1974, Do Da flew out over the blue and was set upon by the usual pair of local ravens, but this time his evasive maneuvers weren't working. The shore operator watched in horror as the local birds pecked at the back of his head. Within seconds, the three birds disappeared behind a cliff.

Despite a full week of searching on land and along the coast, Do Da would never be found. In an uncharacteristically tender sentence for a government report, Do Da's tragic fate is conveyed with a "deep sense of loss." Yeah, losing a cast member in a local bar fight is always gonna be a blow to morale.

THE SHOW MUST GO ON

With their prime candidate out of the picture, the Avian Training Program did their best to press on with understudies, testing the flight capabilities of other species. Several of the remaining birds would come close to being spy-ready. When the TACANA camera system was finally ready for use in September 1976, the CIA's first fleet of avian spies would be—drumroll, please—pigeons.

That's right. Rats with wings. But, boy, can they fly.

Unlikely as it may seem, the humble homing pigeon can fly for hundreds of miles and have an inexplicably good sense of direction. They're also literally everywhere, making them the perfect candidate for an incognito aerial photography mission.

The details of Project TACANA are frankly hilarious. In an almost 200-page internal report called "Feasibility Research on a System to Provide High Resolution Photography Over Denied Areas" (1978), every conceivable minute detail of pigeon use is discussed, including methods for their release where the CIA cites *magic tricks* for inspiration. The three methods outlined in the report include smuggling a pigeon (or several) in the bottom of an overcoat to be released when an agent knelt down, cutting a hole into the floor of a parked car to drop pigeons onto the pavement below, and my favorite, shopping bags and briefcases with trick bottoms. They say a magician never tells their secrets, but I can't help but wonder if they might've reconsidered for a lucrative government contract.

A series of test flights over Andrews Air Force Base and the Washington Navy Yard showed promise, but for all its funding and multiple years of research and development, Project TACANA had trouble taking off. In 1976, there was talk of taking the birds to Leningrad, but an internal memo from the director of scientific intelligence determined that the specific conditions necessary for a successful pigeon flight were too restrictive to justify.

Here's where we hit our own failure to launch: Whether the birds ever took flight, we don't actually know. The CIA has only *partially* declassified the documents surrounding Project TACANA through April 1978.

The Avian Training Program and the subsequent Project TACANA were just a few of the many animal experiments conducted by the CIA. Our poor friend Do Da and a few other unnamed pigeons were unfortunate casualties in just another series of projects that would be shelved for logistical or budgetary reasons—but notably *not* for animal endangerment. And these are just the projects we know about! One has to wonder why a project from almost fifty years ago that supposedly never took flight still remains classified.

Could there be darker developments in Project TACANA—ones that would offend PETA and the public—hidden away somewhere in a government archive? What other creatures have been subjected to the CIA's pursuit of an animal spy? For the sake of everyone involved, let's hope that from now on we let ravens be ravens.

While it's unlikely that the CIA would still feel the need to deploy pigeons when we now have drones and CCTV, I know I'll be keeping an eye out for any particularly observant feathered friends.

OPERATION SNOW WHITE:

A FAIR GAME OF ESPIONAGE

How one woman's bullshit detector
exposed the largest-ever infiltration
of the US government.

On the evening of June 11, 1976, Christine Hansen went to the library—her request had arrived. This was a slightly unusual request, though: She had asked the librarian to call her...if two men from the IRS showed up.

That night, they had. So unbeknownst to them, Christine threw on her sensible shoes, clicked her briefcase closed, and stepped out her door. She was on her way to meet them—and she wasn't going alone. She picked up her partner on the way. Because Christine was an FBI agent. And she was following a lead.

Word had reached her that a couple of IRS agents had been snooping around the US Courthouse Library on Capitol Hill. More specifically, they had been snooping around the assistant US attorney's office around the back. And they'd been acting...kind of shifty, ya know? Not the straitlaced sort of behavior you would expect from two IRS men with horn-rimmed glasses and the *big* clipboards. Now that they'd been spotted again, Christine was determined to find out what those guys were *really* up to.

When she and her partner arrived at the US attorney's office, they found the two IRS agents pacing outside the front door, waiting for the cleaners who were still inside to finish tidying up. So the four of them had a little chat.

I picture these guys being a little fidgety as they swap badges and IDs with the two FBI agents. Can't you feel the interagency tension tingling? The IRS pair claimed they were just in the law library copying some legal

texts for a case they were working on. It's also exactly what you would say if you were caught *skulking around* in a law library. But the excuse was good enough that Christine and her partner took down their names and ID numbers and let them walk.

Except Christine had a perfectly tuned bullshit detector, and this conversation had set it off like fireworks on the Fourth of July. She went digging for records of every time these two IDs had been used to enter a government building.

And when Christine Hansen went to the home address of one of the IRS fellas, just to check the box, no one there knew who the guy was—or at least, not the name he'd given her. Then, she showed them his picture.

Oh, yeah, they knew that guy. His real address was just a couple of houses down. And his real name...led Agent Hansen to expose history's biggest-ever infiltration of the US government.

MIRROR, MIRROR

It's true that the IRS flunkies were suspicious characters. But they were *also* being honest: They really were working for the IRS, and their primary mission was copying documents.

But that mission didn't come *from* the IRS. It came from a *secret organization*—one that wanted to infiltrate the IRS from within. And the guy Agent Hansen sniffed out? His name was Michael Meisner. He was a spy, and in fact, he was leading a whole team of spies to infiltrate US government agencies across Washington.

Christine Hansen was now hot on his trail. Like Christine, he also had good instincts. He knew he'd been rumbled. So he dashed off a report to his handlers, and then ducked into a safe house, out of sight.

That was the smart move. His partner, using the secret code name Agent Silver, went back to his job at the IRS. That's where Christine's boys nabbed him. And they put a warrant out for Meisner, too.

Christine was determined to figure out who these men were, where they came from, and how they had managed to infiltrate a government agency.

As the FBI questioned Agent Silver and spread out their dragnet for Meisner, they began to find the answers. And, dear reader, this is where our story starts to get weird.

Because, yes, Agent Silver and Michael Meisner were spies. But despite all of this happening in the depths of the Cold War, they weren't agents from the Soviet Union. They weren't agents of *any* foreign government.

In fact, they were part of an intelligence agency based on home soil. This secret American intelligence agency was like a funhouse mirror version of the FBI: They were dedicated to gathering intelligence on their foes, spreading misinformation to cover their activities, and finding vulnerabilities and angles of attack on their enemies. They were called "the Guardian's Office."

The secret organization was run by a literal Mary Sue—Mary Sue Hubbard, that is. She controlled their operations and sent out orders to agents like Meisner and Silver from her headquarters in Culver City, California. And all of this spying, burgling, and espionage was done in the service of her husband's brainchild:

The Church of Scientology.

WHO AUDITS THE AUDITORS?

Scientologists—heard of 'em?

They're the group started by science fiction writer L. Ron Hubbard, who put together this story that...um...well, basically, there's an alien in your body—the real you. It's buried under a pile of dirty laundry, which is all the bad stuff that's happened in your life. The way to free your inner alien is to sit in a room interrogation-style, with a Scientology muckety-muck called an *auditor* who can help you put it all through the wash and hang you up to dry.

That's, you know, what I could piece together. I also took a peek at the Scientology website, which says, "Scientologists hold no such beliefs" about the alien thing. I guess that's what you get when your founder is a sci-fi writer. I definitely wouldn't hold it against any Scientologist who says, *Yeah, I don't buy the whole aliens thing.* (Me neither!)

Rather than snip into the thread count of Scientology's tightly woven theology, let's get back to the story at hand. Because when Christine Hansen caught Meisner in the library, she was about to drag Hubbard's dirty laundry into the light.

You see, back in 1956, Hubbard had registered this whole *banish-your-personal-aliens-by-brain-audit* thing as a religion. And here in the good old US of A, religions are *tax-exempt*. That meant that any money passing through

Hubbard's hands was now safe from the sticky fingers of the government tax-man. Ah, dodging taxes, an American tradition.

Until, that is, the IRS yoinked back that special status. Ten years after giving Scientology the stamp of approval, they told Hubbard that this "church" he was building operated a lot more like a *commercial enterprise*. Tax-exempt status: revoked. *Retroactively*. Meaning, uh, yeah, they were supposed to pay *back taxes*.

Well, this made L. Ron furious. But fortunately for him, he'd already built a doctrine into the bedrock of Scientology that entitled him to turn the full might of his growing global following against the government. It was called the "fair game" doctrine. He declared that if anyone attacked the church, they were fair game for retaliation—using any means necessary. As Hubbard had written in 1959, in the confidential booklet for his followers he grandiosely called *The Manual of Justice*: "People attack Scientology; I never forget it, always even the score."

Now, in many cases, "any means necessary" meant that the Guardian's Office took part in another American tradition: filing lawsuits. That's how they battled groups who called them a cult, journalists who wrote critical stories about them, and comedians who made fun of them in books. (Gulp.) And when I say lawsuits, I mean an *extreme* number of lawsuits, like, *thousands*.

But with the IRS, their litigation game went even further. In an attempt to regain that sweet, sweet tax-exempt status, the Guardian's Office launched a program of international espionage they called Operation Snow White. And their vendetta wasn't *just* against the IRS, either. They launched missions against organizations ranging from the American Medical Association and the Better Business Bureau to the Department of Justice, the Treasury Department, and even the Federal Trade Commission.

Over the course of a decade, they infiltrated at least 136 government agencies in the United States and around the world. Their goal was to place Scientologists into low-ranking positions in government agencies, where they could duck under scrutiny but also get access to important documents about the church.

That's what Agent Silver was up to. He had landed a job with the IRS as a clerk-typist. During the day he was clackity-clacking away on his typewriter and filing this and that—all bureaucratic paperwork. But when supervisors looked away, he slipped into confidential files, created copies, and made off with a stash of secrets. Once he was caught, it was alleged that he had stolen something like *30,000 pages* of documents. Pile that up and you'd get a stack ten feet high.

Beyond that, the Guardian's Office was up to all the traditional intelligence agency shenanigans, including bugging the offices of officials like the IRS chief counsel, so they could stay ahead of any IRS audits that came their way. Yeah, *we* do the audits around here, buddy.

Michael Meisner was accused of being at the center of it all. He was the one on the ground in Washington, carrying out orders from Mary Sue Hubbard. On the night that Meisner and Agent Silver were caught in the law library, they were actually on a mission to break into that backroom US attorney's office. They meant to loot it, to keep the church ahead of prosecution.

Since the two spies landed in Christine Hansen's crosshairs, the end of 1976 saw Meisner hiding out from the FBI, trying to keep all of that under wraps. And it was working. The search for him was coming up empty.

But his friends in the Guardian's Office cooked up a plan that wasn't exactly to his taste. Mary Sue decided she could best protect Scientology by pinning the whole operation on Meisner—and turning him in.

However, Meisner got the jump on his boss. Fall guy? No thanks. In June 1977, he—as usual—slipped through the locked doors of the safe house where he'd been holed up, dodged the lookouts, ran into a *bowling alley* of all places, and hopped on the phone. Only now he was calling the FBI.

He was ready to cooperate.

FAIREST OF THEM ALL

It turns out that committing a whole raft of crimes makes you...*fair game* for FBI raids.

On July 8, 1977, two teams of FBI agents raided Scientology offices. One was in Los Angeles, the other in Washington, DC. They scooped up almost 50,000 documents, and the secret spying apparatus of the Guardian's Office was exposed.

While the Church of Scientology squawked that its freedom of religion was being violated—and followed up with a lawsuit, *duh*—government prosecutors, with Michael Meisner's help, put all the pieces together.

The trial that followed two years later convicted all the leaders of the Guardian's Office of "brazen, systematic and persistent burglaries," and "a vast spying operation."

When the evidence was laid out in court, the judge wasn't impressed by freedom-of-religion arguments. They ruled that Hubbard's crew were abusing America's sacred principles to hide their misdeeds.

The leaders of the Guardian's Office were convicted for their massive list of felonies, as were their agents. It wasn't quite Snow White's 300 years, but their work was put to sleep for a long, long time.

HAPPILY EVER AFTER?

Done and dusted, right? IRS: 1, Scientology: 0.

Well, not quite. Despite their spy agency getting caught and crushed in court, Scientologists continued their fight for—emphasis on the scare quotes—"religious freedom." In fact, despite Mary Sue Hubbard being thrown in prison, and despite L. Ron Hubbard going on the run—and then dying in hiding in 1986—the Church of Scientology *escalated* their battle...to a field where they knew how to win.

That's right, time for—*ding ding ding*—MORE lawsuits! By 1993, the Church of Scientology had filed a mind-melting 2,400 lawsuits against the IRS alone. And that litigious barrage eventually brought the federal government to its knees. In a closed-door meeting between the new leader of Scientology and the commissioner of the IRS, they struck a deal to make Scientology tax-exempt once again.

Chalk up a win for the Brain Alien Spy Guys.

But Scientologists weren't the only ones wrapped up in Operation Snow White who later sued the government—so did FBI agent Christine Hansen.

Like Michael Meisner, Agent Christine Hansen found out that her own team was undermining her on every side. For instance, when Michael Meisner came in for questioning, naturally Christine expected she would lead the interrogation, and of course, the case itself. But when the day came, she was reassigned, while her case was given to other agents—agents who hadn't, I don't know, blown the whole case open by confronting two potentially dangerous spies on a dark evening at the US courthouse library.

It was pretty clear why. You see, Christine Hansen was one of the first dozen women ever hired as agents by the FBI. She joined the agency hoping to do real police work. It turns out that for the most part, the agency used her for a publicity stunt.

But Christine already had a law degree and a career as a veteran reporter before the agency decided to jerk her around. She quit the bureau in disgust in 1977. And then she turned around, organized other women who'd quit the bureau, and put together a class-action lawsuit against the FBI for gender discrimination. "Women presently in the FBI are all tokens," was what she told the press. Her bullshit detector worked in *every* direction.

And the courts agreed. She compiled the evidence. She made the case. She got the win. The women she pulled together received back pay, landed better jobs, and, with the power of the courts, busted up the discriminatory boys' club in the FBI hierarchy.

So, if there's one major takeaway from the case of Operation Snow White, it's this: Don't try to bullshit Christine Hansen. She can put you to sleep for a long, long time.

It would be only fair.

SKYLAB:

THE LITTLE SPACE STATION THAT COULDN'T

The story of how one space station
went up . . . and came down in hundreds of
teeny-tiny, flaming pieces.

In July 1979, you could almost feel the utopian energy emanating from the Earth's core and seeping out through the cracks in the sidewalk. McDonald's Happy Meals had just hit the streets, and the Sony Walkman had debuted just in time for The Youth™ to start pumping AC/DC and Donna Summer directly into their eardrums. But a dark cloud hung over that sense of possibility... actually, it wasn't a cloud at all. It was a massive *space station*. It was called Skylab, and as it threatened to fall out of orbit and hurtle toward Earth, it kind of took the shine out of a Grimace-shaped eraser.

A COMET-Y OF ERRORS

In a way, Skylab was a battleship on the most frigid front of the Cold War—the vast expanse of space. After the United States claimed the euphoric victory of being the first nation to land humans on the moon, NASA wanted to place a star-spangled spaceship in the final frontier long term. That space station of stars and stripes was Skylab.

And so, the unmanned Skylab launched from Kennedy Space Center on May 14, 1973. And for sixty-three seconds, NASA could relax into a job well done; their ship—which looked like a massive version of those little handheld, battery-powered fans with flashing LED messages—had reached the heavens.

But about a minute after launch, the micrometeoroid shield prematurely deployed...and then tore. You're probably asking, what the heck is a micrometeoroid shield? Well, it was designed to regulate the ship's temperature and to protect the ship from debris. Instead, the failed micrometeoroid shield *became the debris* that damaged the ship's solar panels—which were the power source for the whole ship. The ship was underpowered and overheated. And that post-launch SNAFU only marked the beginning of Skylab's troubles. (Side note: How fun is it to say micrometeoroid shield??)

Fortunately, Skylab's first crew featured an all-star lineup. The mission, confusingly named SYKLAB 2 (because the space station itself was called SKYLAB 1), featured Mission Commander Charles "Pete" Conrad Jr.—the third person to walk on the moon and the first person to yell "Whoopee!" when he did so. They also had the first medical doctor in space in Science Pilot Joseph P. Kerwin, or as I like to call him, "Doctor Astronaut." And rounding out the team was Paul J. Weitz, a be-buzz-cutted pilot who had flown in Vietnam. And for extra credit, all three crew members were bona fide handyman husbands.

They raced against the clock to repair the damaged micrometeoroid shield before their space food spoiled, along with their $2.5 billion mission.

With all that extra time from not having to save the space station, the next crew—SKYLAB 3—got busy. In fact, they conducted 300 more hours of research than planned, which gave NASA some false expectations about just how much science an astronaut could get done while rattling around inside a tin can in space.

Finally, SKYLAB 4, the crew of the third and final mission, brought NASA's expectations back down to earth. Urban legend has it that the crew went on strike because NASA overloaded them with tasks based on the last crew's speedy work, though NASA's official record denies the claim. Whatever happened, those astronauts on SKYLAB 4 returned home on February 8, 1974, and never flew into space again.

DON'T LET THE SKYLAB GO DOWN ON ME

As these crews performed their experiments and ate turkey and gravy in a can, the space station was working to stay afloat against a constant drag: Earth's atmosphere. Now, the Earth's atmosphere isn't like a gate or fence—it doesn't abruptly stop so much as...fade away. Even at Skylab heights—270-plus miles above solid ground—a few scattered air molecules flit about. Those small air molecules dipping their metaphorical toes into outer space create enough drag to, eventually, pull an orbiting object right out of the sky.

So basically, Skylab was the 170,000-pound ball in NASA's game of "Don't Let It Touch the Ground." But Icarus and Skylab's stewards had something in common: Both underestimated the destructive power of the sun.

During the 1970s, the sun radiated more solar energy than NASA predicted. That extra energy heated the outer layers of Earth's atmosphere and made those few air molecules hanging out up there a bit more energetic, increasing drag on Skylab, and hastening its descent back to Earth. Before this solar snag, they had hoped that Skylab would remain in orbit *at least* until November 1979, but optimistically until March 1983. NASA floated a few ideas to keep Skylab in the sky. But amid delays and budget cuts, the agency shut down Skylab operations in December 1978, leaving the space station hanging...but not for long.

THE SKY(LAB) IS FALLING

After taking destruction-by-missile off the table, NASA scientists decided to just let the natural forces of gravity run their course. *Apparently*, using missiles to pulverize the space station into a bajillion pieces and then controlling where those bajillion pieces landed was a bit too unwieldy of a proposition. Sure, *fine*. But even without an assist from a well-aimed warhead, this massive space station was expected to break into about 500 pieces upon reentry. And the splash zone where those pieces might land? It was so wide that it encompassed 90 percent of the world's population. Yikes.

In an effort to step away from the cliff of catastrophizing, I should mention that any *one person's* chance of getting hit was 600 billion to one. But those infinitesimal odds didn't stop the world's denizens from jumping right off that very cliff-o'-catastrophe, Hands Across America–style.

British tourists took cover in caves. The city of Brussels established an air horn emergency warning system. A contingent from the Psychoenergetics Institute in Brookline, Massachusetts, attempted to prevent Skylab's demise through coordinated telekinetic meditation sessions.

Others took a more flippant approach. Some suggested Skylab Splatdown picnics (real name—nice alliteration), and some baked crashing-Skylab-themed cakes. In one Nebraska neighborhood, residents painted a target in the center of their cul-de-sac, daring the space station to hit them.

Alongside the Skylab psychics and picnickers lurked the profiteers. In Washington, DC, two computer specialists established Chicken Little

Associates, offering personalized up-to-the-minute danger estimates, for a fee. Montgomery storefronts sold "Skylab Repellant" with a money-back guarantee and "Skylab Impact Balm" for anyone actually hit (probably because they forgot to buy their Skylab Repellant—rookie mistake).

Among the money-grubbers trying to get in on the action was the Bay-area newspaper the *San Francisco Examiner*. Especially columnist Jeff Jarvis, svelte and bespectacled, with a beard that put him in the company of heavy hitters like Gandalf and James Harden.

Jarvis had a nemesis: Herb Caen at the *San Francisco Chronicle*. Anything Jeff could do, Herb could do better. In fact, by Jeff's own admission, "Herb Caen was the God of San Francisco" and he himself "the 87th sacrificial lamb."

So when Jarvis learned that the *Chronicle* would pay $200,000 "injury insurance" to anybody struck by Skylab, he figured out a way to one-up them: The *Examiner* would pay $10,000 to anyone who could produce bona fide pieces of Skylab within seventy-two hours of its crash.

Finally, Jarvis would score against Caen, and it wouldn't cost his publication a single cent—Jarvis called up NASA, and they told him there was no chance Skylab would hit land. But he hadn't counted on NASA's faulty math or the determination of one plucky Australian teenager.

PAYDAY

Esperance, Western Australia, is a sleepy town with a beach that looks like it was ripped straight from a Sandals Resorts commercial—the kind of place where you might set a Hallmark movie about a city slicker who learns to slow down after falling in love with the proprietor of a seaside bed-and-breakfast. One of the extras in that film? A seventeen-year-old beer hauler by the name of Stan Thornton, a real-life Norville "Shaggy" Rogers of Scooby-Doo fame.

And when a handful of Skylab debris bounced off his mom's garden shed, Thornton went from background extra to leading man.

America's first and only space station began its final voyage back to Earth on July 11, 1979. The scientists at NASA calculated that Skylab's remains would trade the skies for the seas. But you should know by now that "plans that go off without a hitch" aren't what we do here.

So while much of Skylab *did* end up in the ocean, a 4 percent miscalculation of Skylab's reentry path caused about a thousand chunks of junk to hit a sparsely populated swath of western Australia, and at least a few of those chunks to land in Thornton's yard.

Reasonably confused by the UFOs—unidentified falling objects—among his mother's petunias, Thornton took the blackened chunks to Esperance's head of Emergency Services. Turns out, that guy was a real homie; he told Thornton about the competition in San Francisco *and* a radio station in Perth that was conveniently offering free flights to anyone who could claim the cash.

Because he'd never left Australia before and hadn't needed a passport, he'd...misplaced his birth certificate. But Thornton was determined to get to America and claim that *Examiner* cash, so with an assist from an Australian radio station to get his passport expedited, Thornton *casually* made his way halfway around the world, rolling up to the offices of the *San Francisco Examiner* in a limo, with little more than his bag of space junk and the clothes on his back.

He should have packed more, because it took a week to authenticate the prized space debris. At first, NASA scientists found that Stan had filled his sack of miscellaneous space stuff with organic matter—not exactly what you'd expect to find when a heap of metal falls to Earth. Was Stan full of shit? Or had Stan played ferryman to literal space shit—years-old feces left behind by previous Skylab crews?

Turns out it was balsa, a high buoyancy wood from a tropical American tree, which NASA had used to insulate the ship; the space stuff was certified. Stan was the man—he had won the ten grand—and not a moment too soon. While waiting for a layover in Melbourne, before he had even left the continent of Australia, Thornton said, "I won't be staying long...I'm homesick already and missing my girlfriend." A true Hallmark romantic lead.

While only Thornton cashed in with the *San Francisco Examiner*, other folks got prizes of their own. Skylab chunks showered the only hotel in the teeny-tiny town of Balladonia—population nine. And good ol' rural-peanut-farmer-turned-president Jimmy Carter felt so bad about it that he personally called the owners to apologize for the inconvenience.

As for Jeff, things were a little...rocky at work. By Jarvis's account, the newspaper's publisher was pressed—partly because the paper had to shell out all that cash, and partly because he was jealous of all the publicity that was coming Jarvis's way. In any case, the office was prettyyyyy frigid until Jarvis eventually left the *San Francisco Examiner* in 1981.

WHEN AT FIRST YOU DON'T SUCCEED . . .

Skylab's influence on the zeitgeist didn't abruptly end with the *San Francisco Examiner* forking over that money—the literal remnants of Skylab linger on dry land, even to this day.

Take, for instance, the Australian rancher who came across his cattle drinking from the end cap of a Skylab oxygen tank in the early 1990s.

Or NASA's Skylab-induced littering fine. Shortly after Skylab fell to Earth, Esperance fined NASA $400 for the cosmonautical litter, well, *littered* across the landscape. The fine went unpaid for decades, but lucky for NASA, Scott Barley of Highway Radio in Barstow, California, crowdfunded and paid the fine in 2009.

But the grandest piece of Skylab's legacy is its successor: the International Space Station. In 1993, the United States abandoned plans for a solo effort at replacing Skylab, and instead joined a coalition of nations to construct the ISS between 1998 and 2011, and it hasn't been empty since November 2, 2000. And unlike Skylab, a space project rooted in American individualism, the ISS is an international effort; space travelers from more than twenty countries have visited the station. The success of the ISS is a testament to what is possible when humanity prioritizes international collaboration and community.

And hopefully, it won't be falling out of the sky any time soon.

SWINGING SPIES:

THE KOECHERS

The naked truth of how a swinging
Soviet spy penetrated the CIA.

It was a cold February 11, 1986. All eyes followed Karl and Hana Koecher as they crossed Germany's Glienicke Bridge. Karl sported his signature dark hair and glasses. His tall and lanky frame was dressed in...well, few remember what he wore.

But Hana! Her blue eyes sparkled brightly, and a mink hat was pulled tight over her shoulder-length blond hair. She tugged her coat, also mink, closer to her supermodel body.

The scene on the drab green bridge could have come straight out of Hollywood. Except the Koechers weren't actors. They were spies. The pair were two of nine people changing hands in the last Cold War prisoner exchange, all of whom had been accused of spying.

Reporters and camera crews, bundled up in warm winter coats, jockeyed for the best positions along the snow-covered roadside for the historic moment.

The swap was hardly a first for the Koechers. Oh, no. You could say they were swapping connoisseurs. You see, the husband-wife team were regulars in the swinging scene of the seventies and eighties. In fact, it's how they got their intel. In other words, spycraft with a side of orgasms.

Cozy up, friends. This story of trysts and twists is anything but plain vanilla.

MEET THE KOECHERS

It all started with rules. Nothing bothered Karl Koecher more. In 1948, the Communist Party took control of Prague, Karl's hometown. And in communist Czechoslovakia, there were a *lot* of rules.

Anyone who didn't dance to the socialist tune found themselves in serious trouble. The Czechoslovak secret police, aka the StB, not only worked covert government assignments but also searched homes looking for anything offensive—you know, like banned literature. Those who spoke out against the powers-that-be got a lovely staycation inside a communist prison.

It was 1950, and teen Karl and his friends had a rebellious streak. While their peers abided by curfews, Karl and his pals stockpiled guns and told authority figures just what they could do with themselves, all of which earned them the unwavering attention of the StB.

Despite his rebellious nature, Karl was actually pretty darn sharp—he aced his studies and could converse fluently in English, Russian, and French. Impressive! His smarts didn't keep him out of trouble, though. In 1958, he was sentenced to probation for snogging in public.

Karl applied for overseas gigs, but his request for a passport was denied. He tried his hand at teaching and reporting, but thanks to his run-ins with the StB, they didn't last. He eventually found his calling as a comedy writer for radio, until the StB accused him of partying with underage girls.

Karl didn't see himself as a rebel. No, sir! He was an "extreme individualist," thank you very much. Finally, in 1963, Karl decided that if the Communist Party wanted to hand him lemons, he might as well make lemon-flavored Molotov cocktails and applied for a job with the StB. In his mind, it was the only way to stop the harassment.

Of course, as part of the hiring process, he had to pass a psych eval first.

The report wasn't flattering. It stated Karl was "over-confident, hypersensitive, money-driven, emotionally unstable, touchy, and intolerant of authoritarianism." The eval also found him "hostile toward people," antisocial, and exhibiting a personality bordering on psychopathic.

Which meant that Karl was perfect for the job.

Of course, evaluators also found him highly intelligent and a cunning linguist. Additionally, he had previous experience working as a tour guide. In the eyes of the StB, this suggested he had plenty of connections to the West. You know what they say...never trust a nice man who takes you on a breezy walking tour of Prague!

With the new job as a spy came an obvious warning from his superiors—tell no one what he did for a living.

For the next two years, he trained in counterintelligence, because nothing says keep your friends close and your enemies closer than working for the people already spying on you. It would be a phrase Karl took to heart.

By 1963, the Beach Boys were Surfin' in the USA, freeze-dried instant coffee had made its way into mugs around the world, and Castro had just made his first visit to the USSR, dapping up Khrushchev with their specialty Communist handshake like pro athletes on the sidelines of the Super Bowl.

One evening, Karl attended a party in Prague, where he met Hana Pardamcová, the daughter of a prominent Communist Party official. She was just nineteen and packed a lot of personality into her five-foot, two-inch frame. Her smile, big blue eyes, and outgoing nature charmed everyone, including Karl. He was officially smitten.

Three short months after Karl and Hana met, they exchanged wedding vows—and secrets. Karl had no problem breaking the StB's golden rule and told Hana that he was a spy.

So far, Karl's work mainly consisted of spying on West Germans in Prague. But in 1965, the StB handed him a truly ballsy assignment—to penetrate the CIA. Intrigued, he asked how, exactly, he was supposed to do that. No one had *ever* infiltrated the CIA. His handler's response was short and sweet: Figure it out.

And Karl did, in the most inventive way possible.

THE UNITED STATES OF KARL

With his marching orders in hand, Karl and his young wife set off on their new adventure.

First, they moved to Austria, claiming to be defectors escaping communism. From there, they headed to New York City in 1965. America offered them freedoms they didn't have when they lived behind the Iron Curtain. In the United States, snogging in public was perfectly acceptable. After all, it was the sixties—the sexy, sexy sixties, full of free love and plenty of swinging.

Karl's language skills and his persona as a defector quickly landed him a job at the CIA-sponsored Radio Free Europe. The broadcasting station provided the communist bloc news from around the world, helping to discredit communist regimes.

Life was good in the lap of Lady Liberty, and Karl made the whole infiltration thing look easy. The pair created the perfect cover. The Koechers readily discussed their escape from communism, making friends and coworkers alike think the pair was devoutly anti-communist.

Meanwhile, Karl met with StB handlers operating in the States, casually passing along whatever bits and pieces of information he overheard. It wasn't much, but he didn't have a true insider's view and hardly had secret clearance. But underneath the cover story, Karl began to question the ethics of it all. Sure, the StB had given him considerable freedom, but the Soviets had fully invaded Czechoslovakia in 1968, forcing communists everywhere to confront the methods of their Russian overlords. The ranks of the StB's counterintelligence unit were no different. And he *liked* living in the United States.

The discontent was mutual. Karl's 1969 state report claimed he hadn't provided a single tip. Karl might have been socially active, but in the eyes of his handlers, he lacked performance.

Like any disgruntled employee who thinks they have an unreasonable boss, Karl began looking for a way out. He contemplated changing sides and tried to turn himself in to the FBI. But the bureau determined that his story sounded too far-fetched to be true. It was a stroke of pure absurdity. The FBI was more concerned with the *mafia* than with spies giving away government intel to foreign countries. They had their priorities, after all.

By 1969, Hana's can-do attitude and personality landed her a position with a prominent broker in New York's Diamond District, which required frequent trips to Europe. Meanwhile, Karl's love of learning—and his need for another way to get inside the CIA—brought him to Columbia University. As well as studying Soviet affairs, he graduated in 1971 with a PhD in philosophy. It was a good year for the Koechers—they also became naturalized citizens.

When they weren't working, the couple enjoyed spending time in fun-in-the-sun locations in the Caribbean, and hanging out with new friends. Like, literally—they visited a nudist colony. In family photos, the happy couple sport huge smiles for the camera *and* each other.

However, Karl's overlord handlers back home were less than impressed with his progress. More reports rolled in from the StB. In 1970 and 1971, they wrote that Karl rated below average in his newsfeed, which is something like the pre-1999 version of an *Office Space* TPS report. His bosses faulted him for not taking advantage of his contacts at Radio Free Europe.

Karl was fed up. The StB had been a thorn in his Calvin Kleins for far too long. Had he made a mistake in joining them? He wondered if he had sold his soul to the devil in exchange for freedom.

His handlers hadn't exactly given him a road map for how to get deep inside the CIA, and it wasn't like he could ask for top secrets around the watercooler. At last, Karl's doctorate and citizenship were enough to apply for a translator position at the CIA.

Suddenly the whole scheme clicked into place.

SWUNG INTO ACTION

While his wife traveled extensively in her business, Karl finally found himself in a position to gather valuable American intelligence. In 1972, the CIA hired him to intercept and translate sensitive Soviet documents. His StB handlers tasked him with supplying the names of Soviets whom the CIA recruited or had targeted.

The Koechers were doing very well financially. The couple bought a BMW and an apartment on New York's trendy Upper East Side, making them neighbors with Mel Brooks and Anne Bancroft, among others.

Karl and Hana enjoyed an active social life. But they didn't spend their time hitting up museums and plays. No, they took up *swinging*, and not the kind that involved a golf club or tennis racket. Nope! They fancied the kind that involved group sex and swapping partners.

The Koechers must have kept their BMW *very* busy on the northeast corridor, because it turns out that the seventies and eighties were also a real swinging time for diplomats and agency officials. So much so that the couple considered DC "as the sex capital of the world." And that suited the Koechers perfectly. Having lived behind the Iron Curtain and its strict rules, the couple enjoyed the sexual freedom they found in the United States.

Part of their social life centered around dinner parties. At least once a week, they invited other couples over for dinner. Afterward, instead of swapping recipes, they swapped partners.

They had quite the friends-with-benefits list, but they were particular about whom they had sex with, choosing to wine, dine, and delight those who *might* have juicy intel the KGB and StB could use. From dinner parties to orgies, there was always something spicy cooking at the Koechers'.

And it worked. Many of those couples were willing to share government secrets or drop names and leads over...*dessert*. The Koechers had successfully incorporated their favorite pastime of swinging with spying.

And no one knew better than they did that pillow talk can topple kingdoms. Who knew sex worked better than libations at extracting government top secrets?

It brings meaning to "Do what you love," right? Work, work, work! And boy, did Karl and Hana enjoy their job!

The pair claimed that they *passed the dessert tray* with a prolific number of partners. Hana's good looks and enthusiasm for multiple orgasms, er, I mean, orange tarts, made the couple very popular.

In addition to their weekly Bring-a-Side-Dish nights, Karl and Hana enjoyed visiting notorious DC and New York swingers' clubs like Plato's Retreat and the Capitol Couples Club. Every hookup was a chance to gather more information.

Though Karl had been the one to introduce the couple into the world of swinging, it was Hana who took to the lifestyle with vigor, often taking multiple men to bed at the same time. Her partners referred to her as exceptionally orgasmic. Yep, Hana was certainly an O-verachiever.

While Karl often joined in, other times he left, choosing to pursue conversation rather than play an extra *part* in his wife's fantasy fest. Pillow talk and general chitchat while distracted seemed to loosen lips as much as it did inhibitions.

For the Koechers, it was all sex and Cold War games. But, as they should have known, what goes up must come down.

CAUGHT RED-HANDED

By 1975, Karl's relationship with the StB had become strained. It might have had something to do with him missing meetings or telling them to "fuck off."

Whatever the reason, the response was warranted, Karl thought. They kept asking for stupid things like employee license plates. Besides, Karl felt they didn't pay him nearly enough.

Needless to say, neither the StB nor the KGB gave him the Spy of the Month award. In fact, officials in Prague hated Karl, while the KGB thought him invaluable—right up until 1976. They suspected Karl's loyalty had waned. Maybe they learned of Karl and Hana's parties and thought that they were losing themselves in American decadence. Sheesh. It's like no one trusts anyone in the counterintelligence business!

Karl's handlers demanded he fly in for a meeting. The KGB brought in one of their big guns for Karl's interrogation: Oleg Kalugin, the head of Soviet counterintelligence and one of their most feared generals. He ordered Karl to hold a press conference, drop his cover, and undermine the CIA's meddling around the world. Using his favorite four-letter word, Karl told him exactly what they could do with that request.

Did Karl refuse because he had fully switched loyalties? Rumors swirled in the KGB that *both* men worked with the United States, though Kalugin denied it. Given this, you'd think they'd be BFFs. But, by the end of the interrogation, it's safe to say they didn't exchange Christmas cards.

The KGB and StB had a difficult time deciding if Karl was a mole for the CIA or if he was still loyal to the Soviet Union. In the end, they landed on an interpretation that kept Karl working: They decided his defiance and insubordination were just a personality quirk.

Still, the KGB gave Karl a choice: Quit the CIA or face certain death. You know, something to think about. And with that little performance review, Karl returned to New York and put in his two-week notice in September 1976.

He was finally a free man. At least, Karl thought so. They hadn't demanded he return, after all. Or maybe it was just wishful thinking on his part. But come on! Spying is like a Roach Motel, right? You check in, but you never really check out.

Over the years, the political landscape had changed. By the early eighties, Reagan was in office and the Cold War had intensified, in no small part due to the president's anti-Soviet speeches. You might remember he once called the Soviet Union an "evil empire." Turns out that really honked them off.

Both sides eyed the other's penchant for increasing military might and growing arsenal of nuclear weapons as a potential threat. When the Soviet government became convinced the United States was about to attack, the StB began to rethink Karl's retirement from the CIA.

And so, one day in 1982, Hana found a letter in her office mailbox. It was a nice little note from a Czech agent named Jan Fila, asking for an appointment. When they met up, Karl got the surprising news: The StB had reinstated Karl. And this time, Hana was in on the gig. She would assist as a courier on her husband's behalf. For every message tucked away in a pack of cigarettes or gum, she earned at least $500.

Karl went back to ask the CIA if he could work for them again. They said yes. That's right. The Central *Intelligence* Agency rehired him without hesitation. And just like that, Karl and Hana were back in the sexpionage business. All too easy. But if it left Karl cackling behind the steering wheel, it turns out they were a little craftier than he realized. The CIA and the FBI were onto them, and the FBI bugged the Koechers' home, Karl's car, and Hana's office.

And once the FBI had eyes on the Koechers, they started to see a lot. They watched Hana carry out dead drops—passing information for pickup via packets of gum or cigarettes. She also made brush passes to exchange information with fellow Soviet agents. Even her travels in the diamond business were a front for passing along intel and retrieving payment.

Now, American agents listened in on parties where libidos and libations coaxed government officials to give up their secrets. While the CIA never released precisely *what* top-level secrets the Koechers took, they admit the couple supplied the Soviets with very damaging information. It's also unclear what sort of trade secrets, if any, the FBI overheard when the swinging couple entertained friends at their apartment, but agents cued in on one alarming detail—the Koechers were planning to move to Austria.

If they boarded a plane, they'd disappear into the wind. FBI agents decided it was time to turn their one-way surveillance into a little two-way talk.

So, when the Koechers were out running errands on November 15, 1984, an FBI agent approached Karl and asked if they could have a word. Karl agreed, and they ducked into an unmarked car. The car drove to the Barbizon Plaza Hotel, where the FBI had rented a couple of rooms to interrogate the swinging duo.

Agents offered the Koechers a deal—answer a few questions and return to the CIA as spies for the United States. In return, they'd receive full immunity. Karl readily agreed. He was tired of all the deception. He talked about his assignment and time as an agent for the StB and a KGB spy.

But on November 27, the FBI had a change of heart and apprehended the pair. Agents arrested Karl for espionage and took Hana into custody as a witness. New York set out to prosecute the pair, sending in lawyer Rudy Giuliani. Yes, *that* Giuliani.

Karl initially pleaded not guilty, but it didn't matter: The prosecution failed to make a solid case. The FBI had no jurisdiction to negotiate a deal with the Koechers in the first place. And *that* made prosecuting them difficult. Nothing they had given the FBI could be used in court.

Karl had been forthcoming, but Hana stayed tight-lipped, and her refusal to testify earned her a sentence for contempt of court. The American Civil Liberties Union took her case before the Supreme Court, and Hana's former sex partners contributed to her million-dollar bail. After four months in prison, Hana walked free. A karmic return of all those party favors, I guess.

Karl wasn't as lucky. He remained in prison with drug traffickers and murderers and faced the death penalty for espionage. He feared for his life, and with good reason. Once, a prisoner with a pair of scissors appeared from nowhere during lunch and tried to stab Karl. Luckily, he had made a friend— one of the Hells Angels. The biker tackled the assailant, saving Karl's life. No one saw the attacker again.

A KGB record claimed that Kalugin had sent the assailant. Another source believed that Czech agent Jan Fila, who had reactivated Karl, had something to do with the assassination attempt. That meant that a Czech-American spy working for the Soviets (Karl) was betrayed by...wait for it...a Czech-American spy working for the Americans. That's right, Fila was *also* a double agent. A swingers' orgy is truly the best metaphor for this whole mess. The fact that a Hells Angel jumped in to save the day is just the cherry on top.

Karl wrote to the Soviets, telling them of the attempt and that he feared for his life. He asked if they would consider swapping him in exchange for Natan Anatoly Sharansky, a Jewish dissident they insisted was a spy. The Soviets agreed, and they set up a swap.

Karl and Hana were headed home.

SPY SWAPPING

Fourteen months after his incarceration, Karl walked out of prison. The Koechers were escorted to the airport, and then to Germany for the trade.

And once more, the Glienicke Bridge became the location to exchange prisoners between two superpowers. With a host of onlookers and journalists present, Karl and Hana Koecher walked across the bridge together.

In contrast to Hana's movie-star outfit, the other prisoner wore baggy pants and a black overcoat. He crossed the bridge, heading in the opposite direction, from East Germany to West Berlin.

Their exchange for Sharansky was the last swap on the Glienicke Bridge, aptly named the Bridge of Spies. The Koechers slipped into a gold Mercedes, and as cameras flashed, the driver whisked them away.

It had been a harrowing two years for the couple. After the exchange, they celebrated their freedom with a glass of champagne and partied at what Karl recalled as "some Stasi Villa." The following day, they traveled to Karlovy Vary for the second part of their welcome home party: two months of KGB interrogation—most likely without cake and party hats. On their release, the Koechers moved in with Karl's mother, where they hopefully never threw a naked dinner party again.

In December 1989, Czech agent Jan Fila went missing. Some believe he may have taken on a new identity in the United States.

As for Oleg Kalugin, he currently resides in the United States. The Soviets had been right about their suspicions that he had cooperated with the Americans. He failed to turn over a single American agent during his time in counterintelligence. These days, he divides his time between his home in the DC suburbs and a beach resort in Ocean City, Maryland.

That doesn't mean the days of Soviet spies in the United States are over. In 2010, the FBI arrested *ten* Russian spies operating on US soil.

Presently, the FBI states the threat of Russian intelligence operating within the United States is something they are constantly battling.

In an interview at his home just outside of Prague, Karl Koecher used his favorite word to describe his sentiments on the subject. "The world is really fucked up, and intelligence services" are partly to blame.

At eighty-nine and seventy-nine, respectively, Karl and Hana are still alive and happily married. There's still one rule Karl must adhere to: Neither he nor Hana can ever step on US soil for the rest of their lives. It's probably one rule he doesn't mind following.

PART FOUR

THE
EIGHTIES

LAISSEZ-FAIRE AND
METAL HAIR

Walk through the newly introduced mall food courts of the eighties, and you would smell the metallic tang of hair spray, witness a mullet flip or two, and spot plenty of Lycra aerobic outfits. They were everywhere! The eighties were synonymous with colorful fashion and big hair blowouts. Self-expression had reached uncharted territory, and it was spearheaded by one cable TV channel: MTV. Madonna, Duran Duran, and Michael Jackson were now not only heard but also seen, as music videos aired 24/7. Media and pop culture dominated life. I mean, even the president was a former movie star!

With a lengthy film career, Ronald Reagan had starred in westerns and even alongside chimpanzees. His larger-than-life presence on the big screen resonated with millions of Americans as he dominated the political arena throughout the eighties. What with trickle-down economics, the War on Drugs, and a friendship with Margaret Thatcher, Reagan's presidency was polarizing, no doubt. (Can we at least all agree to forget the whole ketchup-as-vegetable in school lunches fiasco?) But during the decade, defeating the Soviet Union in the Cold War ranked supreme. Thanks to the likes of western VHS tapes, the glam rock of Slade, and a cool sip of Pepsi, the Soviet Union's power and prestige slowly began to fade until the Berlin Wall fell in 1989. From underground spy tunnels to Pepsi's surprising navy fleet, get ready for laissez-faire and metal hair.

OPERATION MONOPOLY:

DO NYET PASS GO

The road to hell is actually
a secret underground tunnel.

In 1969, the United States signed an agreement with the Soviet Union.

Not a peace treaty. We were still *deep* in the Cold War at this point. But a diplomatic gesture, at least: an eighty-five-year lease on the land located at 2650 Wisconsin Ave NW. We're talking Washington, DC. Yep, this agreement gave the Soviets land for a new embassy in our capital. (This same agreement also gave the United States a plot of land in Moscow. PS: Remember this!) In 1977, the Soviets started construction.

This was a goodwill gesture on the part of the Americans, right—the dawn of a new era of communication and cooperation?

Not a chance.

This was a rare and golden opportunity for the US of A to do some star-spangled spying. The FBI fashioned the house across the street from the new embassy into surveillance central. They outfitted the roof with an assemblage of antennae, carried in bags and bags of Kodak film, and even tinted the windows black—you know, for UV protection.

But the FBI didn't make even the most superficial attempts to pretend that actual people lived at 2619 Wisconsin Avenue. No fake family, no lights on a timer. Nothing. In fact, there was a revolving door of very official-looking visitors. One local even reported seeing a long, telescopic camera sticking out of a window.

And when neighbors swung by to borrow some sugar, all they would see was someone peeking through the blinds before promptly disappearing, and refusing to open the door. Tsk tsk, how rude.

But more than unneighborly, this house was super suspicious. So suspicious that Jim Popkin took it upon himself to do some digging of his own in the late aughts.

Popkin, then a journalist with NBC, eventually *created* the NBC News Investigative Unit and led the network's coverage of the 9/11 attacks. Today, Popkin's sitting pretty on four shiny gold Emmy Awards, not to mention being something of a silver fox himself. This was the intrepid reporter who was going to bring the FBI's house of cards tumbling down.

Fortunately for him, maybe unfortunately for the reputation of the FBI, Jim didn't have to dig very deep. He consulted public records and found that a resident of the house was listed as an employee of the Federal Bureau of Investigation. The resident's occupation? "Clerk really a spy." No joke: The house was on record as belonging to a spy from the FBI.

But ultimately, Popkin didn't do much besides confirm the weird vibes that neighbors had felt for decades. Plus, several senior US officials advised NBC to keep the house's address a secret in the interest of national security. Besides, "FBI Does Secret Spying in Washington, DC," doesn't exactly rise above the fray of expected government activities.

Nonetheless, getting caught in the spying was certainly not the most surreptitious behavior from the FBI. But maybe it was better that way; if people had believed that the *house* was a poorly kept government secret, then the *tunnels running under the house*—in the general direction of the Soviet embassy—would fly that much lower under the radar.

TUNNELS, TUNNELS, TUNNELS

Soon after the Soviets broke ground on their new embassy, the US government started digging tunnels underneath the barely-a-secret spy house, in order to spy on said embassy.

They called it Operation Monopoly—a joint project between the FBI and the NSA. I don't want to do too much armchair psychology about the name here—was it a send-up of the side-by-side real estate deals? a celebration of American capitalism?—but it does kind of seem like the FBI was treating this whole thing like a game. In theory, digging a secret tunnel under the enemy's position seemed like a good idea—such a good idea that the FBI eventually gave tours of the tunnels to senior officials. Reality was a lot messier.

See, when they set out, they found that unless you're Tim Robbins in *The Shawshank Redemption*, it's not that easy to dig a tunnel that actually goes where you want it to. Where they aimed to land, of course, was across the street and under the Soviet embassy. The FBI and the NSA did have access to a general floor plan of the Soviet complex. But in their defense, that floor plan didn't tell them the specifics of each room. So while the FBI was digging in the general direction of the property, they couldn't actually tell what part of the embassy they were digging toward.

So when the feds got down to the business of eavesdropping, it was unclear what they were actually hearing. They spent a lot of time wiretapping random storage closets. Maybe the janitors were swapping secrets of international importance?

And if it wasn't one thing, it was another.

The FBI was also building the tunnel in a city that was rainier than Seattle. All that atmospheric moisture wrecked a bunch of their high-tech equipment that the NSA had so thoughtfully provided. And what wasn't ruined by rain didn't always work as intended. When they couldn't figure out how to get their gear up and running, frustrated FBI technicians speculated that the Soviets had somehow already taken countermeasures to prevent American surveillance of their embassy.

If the tunnel had one thing going for it, it was that it was tall enough for a person to comfortably stand up in. But at the end of the day, if you didn't take a highly classified audio recording, did you even dig a secret tunnel under the Soviet embassy?

CALL THE EXTERMINATOR

In 1976, the year *before* the Soviets broke ground on their DC embassy, Robert Hanssen was sworn in as an FBI special agent. After years spent trying and failing to earn his father's respect, he promised to undertake one of the most important jobs possible—protecting America's secrets from foreign adversaries, secrets like a haphazard system of tunnels under the Soviet embassy.

He didn't protect them for long—it took only three years for Hanssen to flip. By 1985, the FBI was still fumbling around in the dark, Hanssen was hard at work trading government secrets to the Soviets, and the American embassy in Moscow was in serious need of some bug spray.

US intelligence had learned that their new embassy, sixteen years in the making, was so inundated with surveillance bugs that it was basically unusable. There were bugs in the walls. There were bugs in the halls. There were bugs in the loo, they'll hear you drop a *deux*.

And just to be thorough, the Soviets had thrown unconnected diodes, wrenches, pipes, and other assorted junk into the building's concrete to make it harder to detect these surveillance devices. To top it all off, the construction workers used darker bricks to spell the Cyrillic initials for USSR into the building's facade, a totally unnecessary *fuck you*—but almost admirable in its pettiness.

The Senate Committee on Intelligence wanted to tear the whole thing down. They settled on demolishing only the top few floors, and then importing good ol' American workers to rebuild them. American officials would have their spiciest conversations in the penthouse.

The agreement between the USSR and the United States technically stipulated that neither country could occupy their embassy until the other country did—and after this massive setback, America forced the issue. Even though the Soviets' embassy was completed in 1985, they didn't fully occupy it until 1994. And technically, "they" were now the Russian Federation. As far as Operation Monopoly was concerned, this was a bit of a "cut off your nose to spite your face" situation. If the Soviet embassy was un(der)inhabited, then the mole-people in the FBI tunnels didn't even have Soviet secrets to eavesdrop on.

SLOPPY, SLOPPY

February 18, 2001, in Vienna, Virginia, was the worst kind of winter day—really cold with no snow to show for it. Maybe that's why Robert Hanssen decided to drive to Foxstone Park, even though it was a short walk from his house. After parking his car on a nearby street, Hanssen clambered his way along a wooded path to a footbridge over Wolftrap Creek, where he deposited a bounty of government secrets in a black plastic bag. He wouldn't make it back to his car.

Instead, an arrest team took him into federal custody. To avoid trial, Hanssen pled guilty to thirteen counts of espionage, one count of attempted espionage, and one count of conspiracy to commit espionage. Basically, a boatload of espionage.

And among that boatload? The thimble, the top hat, and the rest of Operation Monopoly. Hanssen had handed the details of the tunnels over to the Soviets back in September 1989.

Meaning that after 1989, whatever blips of information the FBI managed to gather from the Soviets could have very well been disinformation. And had the USSR made it to the embassy's grand opening, they could have flooded the tunnels with fake intel, completely under*mining* the whole operation.

So why did Hanssen do it? Officially, the answer was money—$1.4 million in cash, bank funds, and diamonds. Money he could use to pay his children's school fees, or to take a stripper friend on platonic international vacations. Yeah, he did that.

Others think the truth is more complex. For instance, psychiatrist Alen Salerian, who spent thirty hours interviewing Hanssen in jail, believes that Hanssen was deeply traumatized by his past and fighting "psychological demons" his whole life.

Hanssen did a *bad* thing. This fact can't be overstated.

But it's not like the United States was doing a *good* job at keeping their secret project under wraps. A civilian was basically able to do the 2000s version of a Google search and find out that the FBI owned the shifty house across the street. If nosy neighbors could see the cameras peeking behind the curtains, certainly so could the Soviets.

And while the United States was doing a bad job of spying stateside, we were also doing a bad job avoiding spies in Moscow. Remember the poor American embassy that could(n't)? The rebuild of the top floors didn't begin until September 1997. The embassy finally opened in May 2000, and it only took thirty-one years and over $370 million. Since we're talking about money, those tunnels came with their own nine-figure price tag.

All those Benjamins behind a project that led only to supply closets, ruined tech, and misinformation.

The tunnels have been sealed off since the nineties, and today, the spy house where they started has been demolished to the foundations. But as the story goes, the tunnels haven't ever been filled in. Maybe in another twenty years, we'll hear about another misguided US surveillance scheme—extending those underground surveillance tunnels from Park Place to Pennsylvania Avenue in a second desperate bid to bankrupt the opposition.

Or maybe as the former Russian ambassador to the United States proposed, Operation Monopoly's tunnels will have a second life as a sauna.

OZONE:

A SPRAY TAN FOR THE WHOLE PLANET

The one where our hair spray almost
took out the ozone layer.

"That's weird," thought Jonathan Shanklin.

He was looking at the yearly measurements of atmospheric ozone levels for the British Antarctic Survey, and for the third year in a row, they were wonkily low.

Back in 1982, Jonathan Shanklin and his boss, Joseph Farman, chalked the funky figures up to machine malfunction. In 1983, those figures had perplexingly dropped even more—nothing to worry about, right?

But now it was 1984, and the Brits could no longer deny that our beloved ozone layer came, ironically, with an America-sized hole.

In the words of iconic Bond villain Auric Goldfinger, "Once is happenstance. Twice is coincidence. The third time it's enemy action." The enemy's choice item of cinematic supervillainy in this instance? Poisonous gas (in a manner of speaking).

The British Antarctic Survey sounded the alarm: Stratospheric ozone—you know, that thing that the Nobel Prize Committee says we need for animals and plants to exist—had been in decline since the 1960s.

It would have been shocking—positively shocking! Except for the fact that two atmospheric chemists predicted this very thing over a decade earlier. Where's Q Branch when you need 'em?

HOLEY OZONE, BATMAN!

First off, let's be clear: Without ozone, our eyes would fall out and our skin would melt right off our flesh. Well, not quite *that* gruesome. But without the Earth's sunscreen, skin cancer rates would skyrocket and we'd all be blinded by debilitating cataracts. The UV radiation would throw entire ecosystems out of whack. It would be like a cross between *The Day After Tomorrow* and *Radium Girls*.

After a scientific linkup between meteorologists and chemists in 1972, Dr. F. Sherwood Rowland became *really* interested in how certain chemicals impacted the atmosphere.

In particular, he was interested in chlorofluorocarbons (CFCs), a type of chemical that was originally created to replace much more toxic chemicals such as ammonia, methyl chloride, and sulfur dioxide, which people were— amazingly—using to cool the food they ate. Eventually, CFCs could be found in anything from Frigidaire fridges to Aqua Net hair spray.

Sherwood Rowland was a total overachiever. While other sixteen-year-olds were consumed by the pursuit of their driver's licenses, he was starting college at Ohio Wesleyan. He earned tenure at the University of Kansas in just two years. He even played on a semiprofessional baseball team in Ontario while earning his PhD. Even his height exceeded expectations—he stood at six foot five.

As Dr. Rowland founded UC Irvine's chemistry department, he needed a collaborator. Luckily for him, Mario J. Molina, a newly minted doctor himself, fell right out of the sky and into his research lab. Matching ambition with ambition, Molina chose to work on CFCs because the topic didn't exactly rank high on the list of all the super science-y things he already had expertise in— Molina didn't just want to "do"; he wanted to learn.

Rowland and Molina, a chemical-curious Batman and Robin, linked up in the smog capital of the world. And it took them only three months to discover something juicy.

The pair realized that while CFC molecules don't do much low to the ground, up in the stratosphere, they shed their chlorine atoms. This process could take anywhere from 40 to 150 years, but when the chlorine atoms are finally set loose, they destroy their victims in a way that teeters on the edge of absurdity—one chlorine atom can cleave that third oxygen atom off as many as 100,000 ozone molecules, leaving plain ol' molecular oxygen.

And the scariest part is that while CFCs were invented in 1928, they really hit their stride after the early 1960s. Meaning that, according to Molina's calculations, even if the world stopped all CFC production right at that very moment, humanity could still be living with the consequences in the *twenty-second century.*

In January 1974, the pair submitted their findings to the scientific journal *Nature*. Rowland and Molina's bombshell appeared in the June 28, 1974, issue.

At first, it seemed like their bid to literally save humanity...worked. In 1976, the National Academies of Science issued a report backing up Rowland and Molina's observations, and in 1977 the US government announced a timetable for phasing out CFCs in the aerosols of America—your whipped cream cans, your hair sprays, your spray paints. And we all lived happily ever after.

Well, not quite. By the early eighties, companies were churning out as much CFC as ever.

"THE MOST MARVELOUS CHEMICALS YOU COULD FIND"

The bigwigs whose profits relied on CFCs pounced on the fact that the Rowland-Molina Hypothesis sat on top of a bunch of other hypotheses; they couldn't prove it 100 percent in a lab. No proof meant no ban. Phew, finally somebody's thinking about the shareholders!

And to be fair, underneath the Scrooge McDuckery of it all, CFCs were a major part of people's lives—by 1980, basically everyone owned a fridge, and the coolest kids rocked the biggest hair.

The CFC industry tried all sorts of tactics to undermine Dr. Rowland and Dr. Molina's work. The chairman of DuPont was quoted in the July 16, 1975, edition of the industry publication *Chemical Week*, calling the ozone depletion theory "a science fiction tale...a load of rubbish...utter nonsense." The president of an aerosol manufacturing firm suggested that the KGB orchestrated the criticism of CFCs.

Another foot soldier in the fight: Dr. Richard Scorer. Sent out by CFC industry bigwigs, Scorer traveled the country for a month, sharing the good word of Rowland-Molina Hypothesis skepticism. He even went into the LA smog cloud—which was definitely *thick* at the time—and said that humans were too insignificant to impact the climate on a large scale. He called Rowland and Molina's work "pompous claptrap." Not what I would call a substantive critique, but when you're trying to get people to ignore the evidence right in front of their eyes...I guess insults are about the best you can do.

In *Ozone Crisis*, Sharon Roan writes that when Dr. Molina was asked about Dr. Scorer's mudslinging tour, he said, "The gentleman is good at attacking. But he has never published any scientific papers on the subject."

Dr. Scorer—you just got scorched.

But no number of sick burns could make up for the fact that while Big Chemical continued their brouhaha, the ozone hole over Antarctica only grew larger.

SWEET, SWEET VICTORY

Just when the world needed them most, another dynamic duo made a finding of their own. Remember Shanklin and Farman? They proved that the ozone layer was in danger—*we* were in danger. But they couldn't prove CFCs were responsible.

Enter Susan Solomon.

Solomon, who received her PhD at the age of twenty-six and got hooked on science by watching *The Undersea World of Jacques Cousteau*, led a research team to Antarctica in 1986. Over the course of two months, she and her team tried to make sense of decades of ozone-related hypotheses and findings, even when it meant fiddling with a spectrograph with one eye because the Antarctic chill had frozen the other one shut. (It's true. She's extremely badass.)

Their work found that the iridescent clouds that are super common in Antarctica and less so anywhere else were actually the first domino in the chain reaction that ended with ozone annihilation. Specifically, the clouds' teeny-tiny ice particles catalyzed chemical reactions that freed up the chlorine in CFCs for other stuff—namely, destroying ozone.

The evidence couldn't be denied. In 1987, fifty-six countries agreed to the Montreal Protocol, pledging to cut CFC use and production in half. The United Nations has since amended the Montreal Protocol to totally phase out CFCs and is one of the only treaties to be ratified by every member state in the UN.

After more than a decade of haranguing from the chemical industry, it was vindication at last for Dr. Rowland and Dr. Molina. As a bonus, they shared the 1995 Nobel Prize in chemistry. And in the years since—with CFCs no longer running amok—the ozone in the atmosphere has been steadily rising. The hole beaming in flesh-melting levels of radiation should be completely closed by 2066.

So yay! We did it! Nature is (literally) healing. Are we done here? Not quite.

Well for one, the danger to the ozone layer isn't the only climate threat we face. The emission of greenhouse gases—particularly carbon dioxide—will continue to cause temperatures to rise, causing droughts in some places, and floods in others.

And just like how fridges in Philly helped put a hole over Antarctica, our actions today continue to have global ramifications. The island nation of Tuvalu is literally sinking into oblivion in the South Pacific while rich countries emit far more than their fair share of CO_2.

You would think that with such high stakes—literally nation-ending consequences—world leaders would have sprung into action. But while the global scientific community is unified behind the reality of human-caused climate change, there are, let's say...scientifically disinclined voices in powerful places that insist our straits aren't that dire (tell that to Tuvalu). And these voices have the advantage; it's easier to maintain the status quo than to incite change.

But there's good news: We know what to do. A whole web of folks, all invested in the greater good, contributed to a scientific exchange that caused real, humanity-saving change.

It was hard work. But we've done it before. We can do it again.

THE COLA COLD WAR

That time Pepsi briefly held the
sixth-largest navy in the world.

It was the 1989 Super Bowl. Halftime. The Cincinnati Bengals and the San
Francisco 49ers were tied, with a whopping three points each. And after what
I can only imagine was a riveting first half, Americans across the country set-
tled in for the real showdown. Pepsi versus Coca-Cola.

You see, while the Bengals and the 49ers were trading tackles on the field, the
two cola giants were waging an all-out war. And, frankly, Coca-Cola was winning.

In the United States, the soft drink company controlled more than 40 percent of the market, slightly more than Pepsi's 31 percent market share. But
abroad, it was a bloodbath. Coke was scoring major sales in Japan and Europe,
where Pepsi was barely on the board. And, as far as the Super Bowl was concerned, it was looking like a blowout.

Diet Coke was the title sponsor of the halftime show, and in the months
leading up to the game, they'd snuck around 20 million 3-D glasses into Diet
Coke packs around the country so that fans could take in the lasers and pyro-
technics in all their glory from the living room couch. Pepsi, meanwhile, had
planned a plain old two-dimensional commercial.

But—back at the Super Bowl watch party—when Pepsi's ad came on, there
was something different about it. Coke brought fireworks, an Elvis imperson-
ator, and magic tricks, but that's all run-of-the-mill halftime stuff. Pepsi did
something completely unexpected.

The first twenty seconds were all in Russian. Against the backdrop of
Red Square, teenagers in leather jackets hung out on motorcycles. A kid with
rolled-up jeans and a radio slung over his shoulder skateboarded past a group
of old women wearing babushkas. A worker in a Pepsi kiosk passed four glass
bottles through the window of a station wagon with drums strapped to the
roof. And a narrator said, in English, "Not very long ago, America introduced

Pepsi to the Soviet Union. And while it may be just a coincidence, a lot of refreshing changes have taken place ever since."

Pepsi had brought the Cold War to the cola war. And the company meant business. Because within four months, Pepsi would seal one of the biggest deals ever negotiated with the Soviet Union. A deal that, quite literally, had the potential to blow Coca-Cola out of the water.

HAVE A PEPSI, KHRUSHCHEV!

Pepsi's quest to sell cola to the Soviets started decades earlier, when a young PepsiCo executive set his sights on the USSR. The executive in question was the newly promoted Donald M. Kendall, vice president of PepsiCo International. And in July 1959, Don boarded a plane for Moscow with a trunk full of Pepsi concentrate and a plan.

The higher-ups at PepsiCo weren't thrilled about this cockamamie Cold War deceit, but Don had convinced them to let him man a booth at the American National Exhibition, which was basically a big PR event masquerading as international relations. The point was to show off how great life in the United States was to the Soviets.

The USSR had hosted a similar exhibition in New York a few months earlier and had blown the ascots off American crowds with Sputnik memorabilia and nods to Moscow's sophisticated music and theater scene. So the United States wanted to put its best foot forward. Time to showcase the shiniest cars and sleekest new vacuum cleaners as gleaming ambassadors of the American way. But the organizers were having a tough time recruiting major US companies. Coca-Cola, for example, had been issued an invitation. Mindful of the optics of handing out their product to Soviet leaders in the middle of the Cold War (and just a couple of years removed from the McCarthy era), the company said no. Too risky.

Don Kendall, on the other hand, had less to lose. His job was to challenge Coca-Cola's iron grip on the international market, and as far as he was concerned, the USSR was up for grabs. Of course, Don knew he had to do more than just show up if he was going to bring Pepsi to the Soviet Union. Fortunately, he had a secret weapon: Vice President Richard Nixon.

Don and Nixon were buddies. They had met in American business circles and became good friends over the years—Nixon would one day play piano at

Don's wedding. So, the night before the exhibition opened, Don pulled the vice president aside and leveled with him. He reenacted this moment in a speech to the Foreign Policy Association years later, saying: "I've gotta get a Pepsi in Khrushchev's hands or I'm in trouble."

On the morning of July 24, 1959—the opening day of the exhibition—Don set his Pepsi stand up on the pavilion. And then, he waited. Meanwhile, Nixon and Soviet leader Nikita Khrushchev were walking past a set of color TV sets, and getting into an argument that would make history.

You may have heard of the "kitchen debate"—the legendary verbal wrestling match where two major world leaders let it fly on everything from atomic warfare, to ultimatums, to the merits of communism versus capitalism. Like all truly good blowups, it went down in a kitchen. In this case, a model kitchen at the American National Exhibition in Moscow. (Fully stocked, Nixon might add, with a brand spanking new, top-of-the-line American dishwasher. Ah, cultural exchange!)

Accounts vary about what order everything happened in next. But with the world watching, Nixon led Khrushchev out to the exhibition pavilion—TV cameras, photographers, and giddy reporters in tow—and straight to Don Kendall. Don was waiting with his hands outstretched, offering the world leaders two delightfully refreshing cups of Pepsi.

Don had the foresight to prepare the cola by mixing Pepsi concentrate with water from Moscow, and Khrushchev insisted that it tasted better than American soda. After downing his cup (and six or seven more after that, according to some accounts), he poured glasses for all the other dignitaries in attendance.

The next morning, news of Nixon and Khrushchev's "kitchen debate" was plastered across papers around the world. And accompanying many of those reports was a photo…of the Soviet leader smiling jovially as he handed out bottles of Pepsi.

Don Kendall had won his first battle. But the cola war was only just starting.

WHAT WILL YOU GIVE ME FOR A PEPSI?

In Don Kendall's perfect world, he would have started selling Pepsi in the USSR back in 1959. After all, Khrushchev seemed ready to sign up as a brand ambassador himself. But Don did not live in a perfect world. At that time, he lived in a world on the precipice of the Cuban Missile Crisis, the construction of the Berlin Wall, and the start of the Vietnam War. Not a great time to start inking business deals with the Soviets.

But more than a decade later, in 1971, things were finally starting to calm down. And Don Kendall—now the CEO of PepsiCo—found himself sitting opposite the Soviet minister of foreign trade, trying to strike a deal to bring Pepsi into the country.

The problem was, Soviet currency was worthless outside of the USSR. Unless Pepsi wanted to just give its soda away, Don and the Soviet minister of foreign trade had to find another way.

So, in the spirit of two third graders striking a hard bargain at the lunch table—*two Fruit Roll-Ups for the Dunkaroos*—the CEO and the Soviet official made a *barter* deal.

Pepsi would give the USSR factories, bottling machinery, and cola concentrate—everything the country needed to produce Pepsi. And in exchange, the Soviets would pay them in (drumroll, please) vodka! Pepsi would become the exclusive distributor of Russian vodka in the United States.

But that wasn't all. Don made sure one more important clause made it into that contract. Pepsi had to be the only cola brand on sale in the USSR. The Soviets weren't allowed to bring in Coca-Cola.

SHOTS FIRED

In the decade that followed, Pepsi struck ground on bottling plants in Moscow, Siberia, Estonia, Kiev, Tashkent, Kazakhstan, and Georgia. A veritable six-, er, seven-pack of soda production powerhouses.

Don, ever the team player (as long as your brand didn't rhyme with *Shmoca-Shmola*), ultimately assisted other American companies in making business deals with the Soviets.

But when Coca-Cola approached Soviet officials in 1973—one year after the USSR struck its vodka deal with Pepsi—the Soviets shot them down. Coca-Cola tried again in 1976, but...nyet.

Pepsi, meanwhile, was amassing more Stolichnaya vodka than it could realistically sell. And when Americans started boycotting Russian goods following the start of the Soviet war in Afghanistan, getting vodka off shelves in the United States became even harder. Meanwhile, the cola market in the USSR was still growing. So, in the spring of 1989, just a few months after Pepsi touted its success in the Soviet Union in a Super Bowl ad, the company went back to the USSR in search of something else they could turn into cold, hard American cash. They asked the Soviets, "What else you got?"

And that's how, in May 1989, Pepsi came into possession of seventeen submarines, a cruiser, a frigate, and a destroyer. In that very moment, Pepsi would take possession of the sixth-largest naval fleet in the world.

Before you get too excited, Pepsi immediately sold it all off for scrap. To whom? Great question. At least some of it went to a Norwegian scrapyard. The rest could have been sold to Cap'n Crunch for all we know. So even if Pepsi had held on to its new fleet, it wouldn't have looked nearly as impressive as it sounded. The ships were old and rusty; they probably wouldn't have survived the voyage back to America.

But! A couple of shiny new Soviet oil tankers were also included in the deal, and Pepsi wound up leasing those to a company run by one of Don Kendall's friends in Norway, so the company did at least maintain some kind of presence on the high seas.

The *New York Times* reported that in a meeting with the US's national security adviser, Don Kendall joked, "We're disarming the Soviet Union faster than you are!"

POUR ONE OUT FOR THE PEPSKI GENERATION

Don and the Soviets planned to strike another deal in 1990, for more oil tankers and some freighter ships. The agreement would also double PepsiCo sales in the Soviet Union, and introduce Pizza Hut restaurants (that's right, PepsiCo didn't just sell cola and retired submarines; it made delicious personal pan pizza, too!) to some of the USSR's biggest cities. The deal would have been worth more than $3 billion.

But the astute historians among you will have clocked a problem: The USSR would not be around to fulfill its end of the bargain.

This was the culmination of years of democratic protests sweeping through Eastern Europe. The Berlin Wall fell in 1989. One by one, the states on the periphery of the Soviet Union rebelled, demanding independence. And on December 25, 1991, Mikhail Gorbachev, the president of the Soviet Union, announced he was stepping down. Within hours, officials lowered the red Soviet flag, hammer and sickle emblazoned in the corner, from its perch over the Kremlin. The Soviet Union was no more.

So, after decades of Cold War, the Soviet Union fell, and Pepsi's business aspirations in the USSR fell right along with it.

Suddenly, the delicate chain of agreements Don Kendall had painstakingly negotiated with Soviet officials was split between just over a dozen fragmented countries. The chemical plants churning out empty plastic bottles were on the other side of the border from the bottling plants that were supposed to fill them with Pepsi.

"All of a sudden, the whole thing was in pieces—hundreds of pieces," Don told a *Los Angeles Times* reporter. "We had a multibillion-dollar contract with a non-existing entity—the Soviet Union."

But worse news was still to come. Because the collapse of the USSR also meant that suddenly Coca-Cola had a way in. Within a decade, Coca-Cola invested hundreds of millions of dollars into expanding their business in Eastern Europe. And today, the company sells more soda in Russia than Pepsi.

Some might say that last fact leaves Coca-Cola with the upper hand in this episode of the cola wars. But if I were Coca-Cola, I'd check to see whether Pepsi definitely scrapped all those warships before I declared victory in a Super Bowl commercial.

TOP FIVE...

BODACIOUS VIRUSES THAT BUGGED US IN THE EIGHTIES

The decade that introduced enough malware to make us squirm.

In the eighties, we were introduced to some of the most iconic athletes to ever grace a gridiron or arrive in an arena. From the Miracle on Ice to Jerry Rice, there were plenty of reasons to don your favorite team's colors and tune in for a spectacle or two. And they were always full of characters. I mean, we had guys named Magic, the Great One, and the Fridge!

But around that same time, some folks were enthralled with a different competitive arena. One that was set in the burgeoning world of computer coding. These "Happy Hackers," as they were called, were scoring points with some of the first, and most tenacious, viruses of all time. That's right, the decade that brought us Air Jordans (and Cool Ranch Doritos) also brought us some of the first-ever bugs, malware, and viruses that would be replicated, mimicked, and meme-ified for decades to come.

So what is a virus, after all? Well, the term "computer virus" as we know it was first coined in 1984 by computer scientist Fred Cohen. And to his credit, it's a hell of a lot more elegant than calling the viruses "complicated self-reproducing automata." America's Cyber Defense Agency defines *computer virus* in simple terms: a program that infects certain files or a network router's hard drive and then replicates itself. Some are considered harmless, some do some light damage, and some, like Larry Bird's jump shot, exist to simply destroy.

If you're reading this on paper, then please enjoy the satisfaction of being a safe distance from my top five favorite computer bugs of the eighties:

5. THE POETIC PRANK
(THE ELK CLONER VIRUS, 1982)

Would you believe me if I told you the first-ever widespread virus was actually developed as a high school prank? In 1982, fifteen-year-old Rich Skrenta decided he'd pull a fast one on some of his computer club pals in Pittsburgh, Pennsylvania. They would exchange pirated copies of games via floppy disk, and Rich, the programming wiz, was able to alter a few with his self-made "booby traps." When his unsuspecting cohort would pop a disk into their Apple II home computer, a goofy message would appear.

But it got him thinking. Could he fudge with floppies without even touching them? The result: a program that would hop from disk to disk, lurking in the background from machine to machine, replicating and waiting for a certain code to awaken it from its slumber. It was called the "Elk Cloner." And while it spread like wildfire across the United States, it was relatively harmless. On every fiftieth boot of a system, the prank poem that Skrenta wrote would appear:

Elk Cloner: The program with a personality
It will get on all your disks
It will infiltrate your chips
Yes it's Cloner!
It will stick to you like glue
It will modify ram too
Send in the Cloner!

A lovely sestain! But maybe leave the poetry to the professionals, Rich.

4. IL TENNIS DA TAVOLO
(THE PING- PONG VIRUS, 1988)

Turin, Italy. Best known for its baroque architecture, the Parco del Valentino, the Juventus and Torino football clubs, and...Ping-Pong? In 1988, a rather playful bug dubbed the "Ping-Pong Virus" was first discovered at the University of Turin. A tiny white ball would appear and bounce all over your screen, touching all four corners (kind of like those classic DVD menus). Technically, rebooting the computer would get the ball to disappear, but eventually it would pong right back out again, simultaneously pinging your nerves. Its two variants are suspected to be active to this day, but only MS-DOS (Microsoft Disk Operating Systems) machines are susceptible. So unless you haven't upgraded since 1995, you're probably fine.

3. PARASKEVIDEKATRIAPHOBIA (THE "FRIDAY THE 13TH" VIRUS, 1987)

*Chh chh chh, ah ah ah...*Did you get chills just reading the visual version of that vocal percussion? If so, you probably suffer from paraskevidekatriaphobia, or the fear of Friday the thirteenth. Not the movie franchise necessarily, but the superstition-fueled day that pops up one to three times per year. And, in 1987, a virus originated in Israel (at the time called the Jerusalem Virus) that would give any paraskevidekatriaphobe the heebie-jeebies. It would infiltrate your system via floppies, CDs, and even email attachments. Once it had its slasher sights set on you and your standard MS-DOS files, all was lost when the clock struck, you guessed it, midnight on Friday the thirteenth. All files and programs that were in use would be effectively destroyed. No reboots or sequels for those files, either. They were as dead as counselor Kevin Bacon at Camp Crystal Lake. One way those infected could subvert the attack: Simply switch your system's clock to bypass the thirteenth altogether, going straight to the fourteenth. If only Kevin Bacon could have pulled that move on ol' Mama Voorhees.

2. MIXED MESSAGES (THE MACMAG VIRUS, 1988)

Sometimes our best intentions go awry. That's what happened to Richard Brandow in 1988. Richard was a magazine editor in Montreal. The mag covered computers, succinctly titled *MacMag*. With assistance from a mysterious coder named Drew Davidson, Richard intended to send a "universal message of peace to all Macintosh users around the world," after which the message would then disappear. Unfortunately, a bug within this bug led to Macintosh computers crashing and some reported files being completely deleted. The little mishap was made even worse when it was uncovered that the MacMag virus somehow ended up on iterations of Freehand, a vector drawing program

ELK CLONER:

     THE PROGRAM WITH A PERSONALI

IT WILL GET ON ALL YOUR DISKS
IT WILL INFILTRATE YOUR CHIPS
YES IT'S CLONER!

IT WILL STICK TO YOU LIKE GLUE
IT WILL MODIFY RAM TOO
SEND IN THE CLONER!

```
isplacement                  Hex codes                      ASCII u
000(0000)  FA E9 4A 01 34 12 00 07 14 00 01 00 00 00 00 20   -0J04‡●
0016(0010)  20 20 20 20 20 20 57 65 6C 63 6F 6D 65 20 74 6F        Wel
0032(0020)  20 74 68 65 20 44 75 6E 67 65 6F 6E 20 20 20 20    the Dun
0048(0030)  20 20 20 20 20 20 20 20 20 20 20 20 20 20 20 20
0064(0040)  20 20 20 20 20 20 20 20 20 20 20 20 20 20 20 20
0080(0050)  20 28 63 29 20 31 39 38 36 20 42 61 73 69 74 20   (c) 1986
0096(0060)  26 20 41 6D 6A 61 64 20 28 70 76 74 29 20 4C 74   & Amjad (
0112(0070)  64 2E 20 20 20 20 20 20 20 20 20 20 20 20 20 20   d.
0128(0080)  20 42 52 41 49 4E 20 43 4F 4D 50 55 54 45 52 20   BRAIN COM
0144(0090)  53 45 52 56 49 43 45 53 2E 2E 37 33 30 20 4E 49   SERVICES.
0160(00A0)  5A 41 4D 20 42 4C 4F 43 4B 20 41 4C 4C 41 4D 41   ZAM BLOCK
0176(00B0)  20 49 51 42 41 4C 20 54 4F 57 4E 20 20 20 20 20   .IQBAL TO
0192(00C0)  20 20 20 20 20 20 20 20 20 20 20 4C 41 48 4F 52
0208(0BD0)  45 2D 50 41 4B 49 53 54 41 4E 2E 2E 50 48 4F 4E   E-PAKISTA
0224(00E0)  45 20 3A 34 33 30 37 39 31 2C 34 34 33 32 34 3B   E :430791
0240(00F0)  2C 32 38 30 35 33 30 2E 20 20 20 20 20 20 20 20   ,280530.
```

that was being commercially sold and shipped out to customers. Thus, it became the first known "off-the-shelf" virus.

*Honorable Mention:

Before our top bug is busted, I'd like to share a bonus offering...and I hope you're not squeamish, because it's a worm.

- **Breaking the Internet (the Morris Worm, 1988)**
  Shortly before the World Wide Web came into existence, the internet was mostly a connected network of universities, research institutes, and government agencies. But on November 2, 1988, roughly 10 percent of the connected computers went dark. Folks were frantically searching for the cause, and some major players were affected: Johns Hopkins, Stanford, Harvard, and NASA, to name a few. The event was so impactful that several days later, after the dust settled and coverage was widespread in the news, the *New York Times* actually used the term "Internet" for the first time in mass newsprint. After some slick cyber-sleuthing, the FBI uncovered that the culprit was a *worm*. This worm had been created by Cornell grad student Robert Tappan Morris. He immediately felt regret and attempted to have a friend send an anonymous message apologizing to the masses. But the damage was done and Morris became the first-ever person convicted under the Computer Fraud and Abuse Act. The "Morris Worm," as it would come to be known, had dug its way into history.

At last, I give you my number one complicated self-reproducing automata of the decade...

1. THE BENEVOLENT BUG (THE BRAIN VIRUS, 1986)

Is there such a thing as "friendly" malware? Well, in 1986, the world's first-ever official PC virus was developed as a way to notify users in a friendly manner that they were, in fact, utilizing stolen software. Two brothers from Pakistan—Basit and Amjad Farooq Alvi—developed and sold medical software, but they were continuously bootlegged and pirated. Saying enough was enough, and understanding that their IP was being exchanged through floppy disks, they created a function that would secretly spread from floppy to floppy and calculate the amount of piracy occurring. When booted up, the non-malicious malware program would essentially fill up the floppy, slowing its speed to a halt and rendering it useless. Then, the user would be greeted with a jovial message alerting them to the illegally pirated program, and even provide the names, phone numbers, and store location of the Alvi brothers, so they could help the user fix the software. Congenial coders, that's what we like to see here at SNAFU!

People like Skrenta, Brandow, and the Alvi brothers? They were the happy hackers of the eighties generation. Those bugs were created with positive intent. Sadly, they also opened up Pandora's box. Cyber criminals began developing malicious malware that would become sticky sap in our machines forevermore. In February 1991, the Michelangelo virus began to spread through USB drives, hard drives, and (yes—people were still using them!) floppy disks.

As the internet and email evolved and widened to mainstream use, so, too, did the number of viruses and worms. In 2000, the email worm ILOVEYOU infected 10 million Windows computers. And in 2004, MyDoom became the fastest-spreading worm ever, infecting 50 million computers through email attachments and causing an estimated $38 billion in damages. (It's still active to this day.) All of this is to say, cybersecurity dangers are all around us and growing exponentially worse.

So be careful out there, and don't click that invoice for the membership you never ordered to the Wayne Gretzky Fan Club. Let's hope the next cybersecurity SNAFU doesn't infect you, my friend.

NORIEGA'S NIFTY PACKAGE

How the US military exploited the
dark side of "rock around the clock"
to take down a dictator—who was
once on their own payroll.

Ever been told that your singing is a form of torture? Speaking from experience, let me tell you, it really stings. Maybe the world just wasn't ready for a banjo-only cover of "Don't Stop Believin'"...but the thing is, music really *has* been used as a form of torture in the past!

In fact, the good old US Army pioneered the technique in 1989, when soldiers assaulted the hideout of a nefarious Central American dictator not with guns, but with Guns N' Roses. How did turning it up to eleven help the army depose a military strongman? And why, exactly, had this particular strongman been on the payroll of the CIA? Crank up the Van Halen, because we're going down to Panama...

A MAN, A PLAN, A CARTEL

Like so many future enemies of America, Manuel Noriega would never have reached his position as de facto dictator without America's help. Noriega was in his early twenties—bright-eyed, fresh-faced, looking a bit like an ever-glowering Peter Lorre—when he first became an informant for the United States. It started with the US Army. They paid Noriega for information about the Panamanian Socialist Party, of which he and his brother were both active members. He must have shown a real knack for informing, because the Central Intelligence Agency soon recruited him and began paying him for information as well. Officially, Noriega became an officer in the Panamanian military, but for the next twenty years, he was in regular contact with American intelligence agencies, receiving payment in exchange for information.

Next, it was on to the US Army School of the Americas, an American-run facility located in Panama whose graduates numbered among the most notorious figures in twentieth-century Latin American history. Coup plotters, death squad leaders, and the future military dictators of Argentina, Bolivia, Ecuador, Guatemala, Haiti, Peru, *and* Panama all passed through the School of the Americas at some point in the 1950s, sixties, and seventies. Noriega's future looked bright!

In 1968, a coup overthrew the populist president of Panama and installed Noriega's friend and patron, Omar Torrijos, as the country's leader. Within two years, Torrijos had named Noriega chief of military intelligence. Then, in 1981, Torrijos died in a plane crash, making Noriega the de facto leader of Panama. As he consolidated military and political power, Noriega developed deep ties with many of the drug cartels operating in the region, including the infamous Medellín Cartel of Pablo Escobar. Noriega rigged elections, sold weapons to Colombian rebels, let Escobar and other drug lords launder their money through Panamanian banks, and used his military to facilitate the flow of cocaine from South America into North America.

The CIA and the Defense Intelligence Agency were well aware that, as one classified report stated, "nothing moves in Panama without the instructions, order and consent of Noriega." Does that mean the American intelligence community *wanted* all this illegal activity to continue? Far be it from me to suggest such a thing...until we get to our chapter on CIA drug trafficking later in this book...but for a period in the mid-eighties, Noriega was receiving $10,000 a month for his services to Uncle Sam.

Central America was a hotbed of revolutionary fervor at the time, and a growing number of left-wing radicals had somehow gotten the idea that US involvement in the region was making things worse. Crazy, I know. Regardless, the United States needed all the regional allies it could get as it played Whac-A-Mole with rogue drug lords and communist insurgents. So when the left-wing Sandinistas overthrew a right-wing, United States–backed dictator in neighboring Nicaragua, Noriega's value to the United States only increased. Nothing could ever tear Noriega and his American friends apart! Right?

WITH FRIENDS LIKE THESE . . .

In the early to mid-eighties, Noriega was sitting pretty—even though he'd become noticeably pockmarked as he aged, earning the nickname "Cara de Piña" or "Pineapple Face." He was trafficking in cocaine, weapons, information, and political favors, expertly playing both sides of the War on Drugs *and* the Cold War. But this subtle dance between Noriega and the Western Hemisphere's power players was thrown ever so slightly off-kilter in 1985, when his soldiers abducted, tortured, and beheaded one of his political critics. When the headless body was found in a post office bag, bearing signs of brutal torture techniques suspiciously similar to those taught at the School of the Americas, Noriega's alma mater...Well, let's just say it generated some bad press for the Panamanian strongman.

Noriega's excuse that he'd been on a trip to London at the time, and therefore could not *possibly* have been involved in the murder, was even less effective than his skincare regimen. And yet he *still* might have gotten away with it, if only his American friends had managed to get away with some other crimes they were committing nearby.

You see, beginning in 1985, members of the Reagan administration had been secretly selling weapons to Iran, in violation of their own government's embargo. Not content with propping up just *one* authoritarian regime, those same officials passed some of the money Iran paid them along to the Contras, a right-wing counterrevolutionary force operating in Nicaragua. Today, we know this convoluted, illegal plot as the Iran-Contra Scandal. Never one to miss out on an illicit deal, Noriega jumped right into the middle of it.

Trying to make amends for that whole beheading incident, Noriega called up his American buddies and offered to help them out. Not only would he allow the Contras to operate inside of Panama, he said, but as a friendly gesture, he'd even go to the trouble of assassinating a left-wing Nicaraguan leader. What a thoughtful gesture! Unfortunately for Noriega, almost as soon as he involved himself in this affair, the American press found out about it.

Noriega was already known worldwide as a dictator, murderer, torturer, and drug trafficker. But if the history of Latin America has taught us anything, it's that you can be *all* of those things and continue to rule your country quite comfortably *as long as the United States is still your friend.* The thing is, after Iran-Contra became public, that was no longer the case for Noriega. Many of his strongest allies in the US government had been implicated in the scandal. As they resigned or were removed from their positions, longtime CIA asset Noriega suddenly found himself with no more friends left in Washington.

So in 1989, when Noriega overturned the result of a Panamanian election that his party had lost, newly elected US president George H. W. Bush decided it was time for a regime change. Bush declared that the United States would not negotiate with drug traffickers—a flagrantly hypocritical claim, given that Noriega had not only been on the American payroll for decades, but *he had personally met with then–CIA Director Bush in 1976, and again in 1983 when Bush was vice president.* Regardless, as Christmas 1989 approached, Bush plotted to give Noriega a lump of coal, and then some.

GOT TO GIVE IT UP

The invasion of Nicaragua began on December 20, 1989. Perhaps as a subtle nod to the decades of morally questionable American interference in the region, the US military code-named the invasion "Operation Just Cause." As in, "Just 'cause we worked closely with this guy for twenty years, that doesn't mean we don't have a just cause for arresting him now!"

The American attack began under cover of night, with troops seizing the country's main airport and Noriega's military headquarters. Within *hours*, the United States had sworn in a new Panamanian president...but the old one still remained at large.

Deposing Noriega had been a breeze, but arresting him was trickier. A sub-mission, code-named Operation Nifty Package—possibly the greatest name ever invented for a military operation?—focused exclusively on tracking Noriega down. In the initial assault, Navy SEALs destroyed Noriega's plane and his boat, leaving him without an easy means of escape. Backed into a corner, the dictator knew it was time for a Hail Mary. Emphasis on the Holy Mother.

On Christmas Eve, Monsignor Jose Sebastian Laboa, the pope's ambassador to Panama, answered the door of the Vatican's embassy in Panama City to find Noriega and four of his gun-toting lieutenants. They asked for shelter, knowing that it would be against international law for the United States to attack any embassy, and that attacking the papal embassy would be a particularly bad look. The Vatican had long promised sanctuary to anyone fleeing

persecution, so even though Laboa felt strongly that Noriega *deserved* persecution, his hands were tied. Unable to turn Noriega away but unenthused about his new houseguest, Laboa offered him a ten-by-six-foot room with an opaque window, no air-conditioning, and no sources of entertainment, aside from a crucifix and a Bible. It's unclear if he read much of that Bible, but if he was hoping for a quiet place to read it, Noriega was out of luck.

The American military had been operating a radio station, the Southern Command Network (SCN), in Panama for decades, and during Operation Just Cause, SCN's mission became to (1) broadcast important messages to military personnel across the embattled nation; and (2) keep the troops' spirits up with some kickin' rock tunes. Helpfully, the newly arrived American invasion force also brought a number of high-powered loudspeakers to Panama. These speakers were intended to broadcast messages to Panamanian soldiers—something along the lines of "Do you really want to sacrifice your life for the sake of a pineapple-faced crook? Yeah, we thought not." But they took on a new role once the troops realized that SCN took requests.

"We played a lot of songs with the word 'jungle' in it," noted an official report from one of the military DJs running SCN. "As well as 'God Bless the U.S.A.' by Lee Greenwood and 'We're Not Gonna Take It' by Twisted Sister."

Requests had been rolling in for a while before SCN's operators realized that their broadcast was being used as a form of torture, or "psychological warfare," if you'd rather. On December 27, someone identifying themselves as "a member of the PSYOPS team from Fort Bragg"—PSYOPS being short for "psychological operations"—called in to inform the radio station that soldiers had strapped their loudspeakers to Humvees, surrounded the Vatican embassy, and began blasting it with music in an attempt to force Noriega out.

Noriega was known to be a fan of opera, but over the next three days, he received a crash course in hard rock. Once the American troops got wise to what was going on, soldiers were calling SCN with requests day and night. For good measure, the soldiers picked songs that carried a "musical message" for the embattled dictator. Luckily for them, in recent years rock musicians had produced a wealth of tunes that were surprisingly appropriate for this unique occasion. Songs like "Refugee" by Tom Petty, "(You've Got) Another Thing Coming" by Judas Priest, "All I Want Is You" by U2, "Got to Give It Up" by KC and the Sunshine Band, and—of course—"Panama" by Van Halen were all beamed directly at Noriega, 24/7, interrupted only by news reports announcing the surrender of Panamanian troops and the freezing of Noriega's foreign assets (and, occasionally, a few cacophonous recordings of chickens). Crowds of Panamanian citizens gathered outside the embassy to jeer Noriega and demand his surrender, hurling insults that ranged from "Hitler" to "Pineapple Face." It was certainly not Noriega's jolliest Christmas.

Nor was it the Yuletide that Laboa and his fellow embassy residents had envisioned. Laboa complained to the American military, and reportedly even convinced the pope to intercede with President Bush to make the GIs turn down their music. After three days of thoroughly rocking Noriega's last-ditch casbah, the musical torture ceased with the dictator still holed up inside.

We'll never know exactly how pivotal Judas Priest was in forcing Noriega to surrender, but other priests ended up taking the credit. On January 3, Vatican emissaries informed Noriega they were considering moving to the school across the street and declaring *that* the new embassy, allowing the Americans to swoop into the old one and arrest him. That evening, after consulting both his wife *and* his mistress, the former CIA asset turned himself over to American troops. He was immediately arrested and flown to Florida.

Laboa later claimed the victory for himself in an interview with *TIME* magazine: "I'm better at psychology," he gloated. "Without his pistol, he is manageable by anyone." But the concept of using audio as torture caught on. Four years later, law enforcement surrounded the compound of David Koresh's Branch Davidians cult and blasted everything from experimental electro to Nancy Sinatra's "These Boots Are Made for Walkin'." Marines also reportedly blasted Metallica and Thin Lizzy at the Taliban during the war in Afghanistan.

Meanwhile, Noriega was convicted on drug and money laundering charges in a US court. He spent seventeen years in an American prison before being extradited to France, where he was convicted of similar crimes. He was finally extradited to his homeland in 2011, having already been convicted in absentia of several murders, including the 1985 beheading. Always eager to cash in, he unsuccessfully sued the makers of the *Call of Duty* video game franchise from prison in 2012, seeking damages after they used his likeness in *Call of Duty: Black Ops II*. He died in prison in Panama City in 2017, quite possibly with his ears still ringing. Is Noriega's story a cautionary tale about American intelligence agencies playing God in Latin America, or proof that music really can save the world? I'll leave that up to the reader to decide...But the next time Uncle Sam needs to smoke a dictator out of his hidey-hole, my banjo and I will be standing by.

```
15
16   const LOCALE = globalThis.navigator.language
17
18   const div = document.body.appendChild(document.createE
19   const list = div.appendChild(document.createElement('o
20
21   const dayNames = new Map()
22
23   for (let i = 0; i < 7; ++i) {
24       const d = Temporal.PlainDate.from({
25           year: Temporal.Now.plainDateISO().year,
26           month: 1,
27           day: i + 1,
28       })
29
30       dayNames.set(d.dayOfWeek, d.toLocaleString(LOCALE,
31   }
32
33   for (const num of [...dayNames.keys()].sort((a, b) => a
34       list.appendChild(Object.assign(
35           document.createElement('li'),
36           { textContent: dayNames.get(num) },
```

DARK DANTE:

BANNED FROM THE INTERNET

All it took to hack into a classified government database was a high school dropout.

On the morning of June 1, 1990, the on-air light flashed in the studio at KIIS-FM. An account published by the *Los Angeles Times* years later described how Rick Dees, the station's top disc jockey, adjusted his headphones and leaned into the mic. Every Friday for the past few weeks, he'd done the same thing...cued up three carefully selected songs, and announced to the entire city of Los Angeles, "Today is the day! You could be caller number 102 and win a brand-new $50,000 Porsche!"

The Porsche 944 S2 was a thing of beauty. A sports car with pop-up headlights, flared wheel arches, and leather seats. And as "Escapade" by Janet Jackson played over the radio, all twenty-five phone lines at KIIS-FM started buzzing with calls. Dees counted them live on the air..."Caller number one... number ten...number fifty."

"Love Shack" by the B-52s played next. And the calls kept coming in. "Sixty-three...Seventy-two...Eighty..." But suddenly, after caller number 101, with song number three—Prince's "Kiss"—starting up in the background, something very strange happened.

All of the calls stopped. Until one solitary line rang out in the station. It was caller number 102. "Michael B. Peters." And he'd just won himself a Porsche.

Only Michael B. Peters wasn't his real name. And he wasn't just some lucky caller. He was a twenty-four-year-old high school dropout on the run from the FBI for stealing government secrets.

VESTIBULE OF HELL

Kevin Poulsen was sixteen years old when his parents gave him his first computer. It was 1981, and to the two of them—a teacher and an auto mechanic who weren't interested in tech—the TRS-80 must have seemed like a bit of a mystery. But their quiet and brooding son took the computer up to his room. And out of their sight, like a real-life David Lightman, Matthew Broderick's iconic character from the 1983 cult classic *WarGames*, Kevin began tapping away at the chunky keyboard, opening door after door into the new world unfolding in front of him. The ARPANET.

In 1981, the internet was just a fledgling thing. It had started a little over a decade earlier, in 1969, when the Pentagon created a network to allow computers to communicate over long distances. The initiative was called Advanced Research Project Agency (ARPA), and the network it created: ARPANET.

The ARPANET would one day evolve into the internet we know and love today—a magical place overflowing with dance challenges, memes, and scammers trying to steal our data. But back then, it was pretty primitive. A team of computer scientists at UCLA sent the first-ever internet message over the ARPANET in October 1969. They were trying to transmit the word "LOGIN" to the Stanford Research Institute, hundreds of miles north. But the system crashed after just two letters: "LO."

The professor leading the project, Dr. Leonard Kleinrock, put a good spin on it. He told the press it was a poetic accident—LO, as in "Lo and behold!" But let's be honest, the ARPANET still had a *LO*ng way to go.

When Kevin Poulsen powered up his boxy monitor a decade later in 1981, the ARPANET had moved beyond two-letter messages. But it still wasn't a place you'd go to, like, hang out. It was basically a web of universities, research centers, and government offices all hooked up to one another using phone modems.

And, for those of you who missed out on the formative life experience of waiting for your big sister to hang up the landline so you could log back on to the internet and finish doing your geography homework, let me explain: The early internet was built on existing telephone infrastructure. And that system was fairly unsecured; if you had the right tools and understood how phone switches worked, you could hack into it.

For Kevin, our *WarGames* protégé, it was like sneaking into a virtual library, full of private—and sometimes classified—information.

FIRST CIRCLE (LIMBO)

It was 1979 when Kevin met Ronald Austin. They ran into each other—virtually—when both attempted to illegally tap into a long-distance phone system at the same time. A meet cute of sorts, for a couple of teenage hackers.

Kevin and Ronald were what people used to call "phone phreaks." They knew how to hack into telephone systems using stolen test sets, black boxes, and manipulated dial tones. Sometimes "phreaks" would just game the system to make calls for free.

But Kevin and Ronald would also hang out on gigantic conference calls, where they might brainstorm bigger hacks, skill-share, or even trade stolen bank and phone company credit card numbers.

By 1983, Ronald was a freshman at UCLA, Kevin had dropped out of high school, and both of them had graduated from "phreaking" around on phone lines to exploring the shadowy halls of the ARPANET.

Kevin would later tell a United Press International reporter that it all started when the movie *WarGames* came out in theaters that June. He and Ronald both saw it, and the idea of advanced research computer systems (and teenagers hacking into them) was interesting to them.

So they spent their summer vacation glued to their computers, their faces lit by screens as they probed their way into buzzing computer labs at universities and research firms. Kevin adopted an alter ego online: "Dark Dante." And as Dante, he raced against Ronald to dive deeper into the web of information at his fingertips, peeling back the Inferno, layer by layer.

In July, they managed to hack into UCLA's computer science department. The next month, they snuck into Rand Corporation, the government think tank based down the street in Santa Monica. As the summer wore on, the litany of their misdeeds grew more impressive: a couple of defense contractor plants, major research firms, and the Naval Research Laboratory in Washington, DC.

As playful as our budding Brodericks were trying to be, all of these breaches were still quite illegal. But in August 1983, Kevin and Ronald dialed it up a notch and did something *really* illegal. They hacked into the Stanford Research Institute (SRI). Which, if you didn't know (and you're not supposed to), conducted a *lot* of classified work for the US military. Unfortunately for Kevin and Ronald, SRI was pretty unwelcoming to surprise visitors.

Within a month an FBI agent and a couple of police officers showed up in Los Angeles to arrest Ronald Austin. He was eventually charged with theft, receiving stolen property, and a whopping fourteen counts of accessing information protected by the Pentagon. Not bad for a summer vacation! Though Ronald admitted to the charges above, he also maintained that he hadn't done any damage.

Across town, in North Hollywood, Kevin's parents answered the front door to find a similar array of visitors. But unlike Ronald, Kevin was only seventeen years old—meaning, he couldn't be charged as an adult. So, before giving Kevin a ride down to the police station, the FBI weighed its options.

It could slap this kid on the wrist. Have some guys in fancy uniforms give him a real good talking-to and scare him back onto the straight and narrow. Nip this prankster in the bud before he grew up into a real criminal.

Or—and stay with me here—the FBI could offer this ne'er-do-well teenager a job at one of the most prestigious and highly classified government research institutions in the country.

Suspend your disbelief, folks, because the FBI went with option number two. Kevin's "punishment" was $35,000 a year ($109,000 in today's money!) and the keys to databases containing some of the American government's most sensitive and highly classified information. The youngster had been hired to work at SRI, to protect the very classified systems he'd just hacked. What could possibly go wrong?

(It's worth mentioning here that the US government still works with "white hats"—or "good faith" hackers, who purportedly use their skills for good—to build and test our country's cybersecurity systems. Although they still won't hire anyone who's smoked weed within a year of applying for a job at the FBI. I'm guessing that Venn diagram overlap is not real promising.)

FOURTH CIRCLE (GREED)

Our story picks back up in early 1988, when a detective named James Neal pulled up to a storage facility in Menlo Park, California. The owner greeted him out front, and the two of them walked to a locker the size of a small room. When the owner turned his key in the lock and lifted the container door, Detective Neal's eyes widened. Years later, a reporter from the *Los Angeles Times* would paint this picture: The locker was full of stolen equipment, tools, and even lock picks. But that wasn't all.

Bewilderingly, whoever assembled all this contraband had also left behind a set of photographs, seemingly showing the culprit in action. A skinny guy with long, straight hair picking the lock of a phone company trailer and sitting in front of a computer terminal.

That guy, it would turn out, worked down the road at SRI. And he was *not* supposed to be breaking into phone companies and stealing their stuff.

Detective Neal brought Kevin Poulsen down to the station, where they spent a couple of hours debating the legality of wandering into Pacific Bell Telephone Company's offices with the help of a stolen ID card. But by the time Detective Neal saw what was in Kevin's apartment, the debate was over.

Kevin—while still an employee of SRI—had, in his spare time, once again inhabited his Dark Dante persona to break into and rifle through several Pacific Bell offices, making off with any proprietary information he could get his hands on, including manuals and computer passwords. After bringing it home, he'd used that information—and a host of computer terminals and related gadgets—to hack into Pacific Bell's computer systems. He dug up phone numbers for the Soviet consulate in San Francisco. He figured out who the federal government was wiretapping (for example, an alleged mobster and his restaurant in Malibu). He even listened in on phone conversations—including those of the security personnel who were investigating his break-ins.

Kevin didn't appear to publish any of the information he gathered. He certainly wasn't participating in espionage on behalf of a foreign entity. Behind the mask of Dark Dante was a smart and somewhat lonely kid, driven by his own ego, who collected digital breaches like trophies.

But by the time a San Jose federal grand jury had issued an indictment and the FBI showed up to arrest Kevin, he was gone. The twenty-four-year-old had fled back to his parents' house in Southern California. And when a team of agents showed up *there,* they were surprised to find the phone ringing. It was Kevin on the line, sounding like a kid in a game of tag, singing over his shoulder, "You can't catch me."

Obviously, the FBI agents traced the call. They hoped it would point to a phone booth, or a landline—somewhere they could go to nab Kevin in the act. But, according to the *Los Angeles Times,* when they discovered the source of the call, it was not a phone at all. Kevin was "calling" from a circuit at Pacific Bell.

EIGHTH CIRCLE (FRAUD)

Over the course of the next year and a half, Kevin kept himself afloat financially by "winning" radio call-in competitions. Sometimes with the help of old friends—like Ronald Austin, who'd since been released from prison—he would block all the calls coming into the station except for his own. By April 1991, Kevin had "won" $22,000, a free trip to Hawai'i, and two Porsches.

But all good things must come to an end. And in Kevin's case, the end came in the form of a body slam, capably delivered by two grocery store clerks one night in 1991.

Let me rewind a little bit...Back in October 1990, the NBC show *Unsolved Mysteries* aired a segment about Kevin. As his mugshot flashed on-screen, the host rattled off Kevin's litany of crimes. "If you have any information regarding Poulsen," he concluded, "please contact the FBI or call our toll-free number..."

Six months later, in April 1991, a grocery store manager in Sherman Oaks saw Kevin Poulsen walk into his store. He followed Robert Stack's televised advice and called the FBI. The next time Kevin stopped by for groceries, two clerks tackled him to the ground, and an FBI agent put him in handcuffs.

I can only presume they played rock-paper-scissors to determine who was going to drive his Porsche to the station.

It took the district attorney a long time to read out all the charges against Kevin Poulsen. There was computer and mail fraud...money laundering... interception of wire communications for all those phone conversations he'd eavesdropped on...obstruction of justice...Oh, and espionage. That was a new one, tacked on because of the military documents he'd stolen.

Kevin pleaded guilty to all of it. When a reporter outside the courthouse asked him why, he just said, "Because I am guilty."

His sentence was grim: $56,000 in restitution, and fifty-one months in prison. At the time, it was the longest sentence ever handed down for a cyber-crime. Kevin was one of the first hackers to be caught and tried for his misdeeds, and the feds wanted to make an example out of him. This time around, they did *not* offer him a prestigious job with a cushy salary.

When Kevin Poulsen was released from prison in June 1996, he emerged to find a changed world. Suddenly, it seemed like everyone—including his mother!—knew what words like "modem" and "ISP" meant. People were sending one another emails. You could even type "Kevin Poulsen" into a search bar, and the internet would spit back thousands of results (compared to about 2,120,000 today). Everyone was on the internet. Everyone, except Kevin.

"I was released from prison as the first American to be banned from the Internet," he would write in a blog post years later. But, at the time, Kevin wasn't allowed to so much as open a Word document without the express permission of his probation officer.

DANTE'S ESCAPE FROM HELL

Kevin set out to learn the new internet vicariously, by talking to other people who were online. In 1998, the technology magazine *Wired* hired him to write a feature about survivalists and the Y2K bug. They also published an op-ed he'd written about his experience in internet exile.

When Kevin was finally allowed back online in 2000, more opportunities followed. He started reporting on security and hacking news, breaking stories about everything from computer viruses taking out safety systems at nuclear power plants to hackers fleecing confidential files from Secret Service agents' phones. He helped newsrooms to design an online portal that allowed sources to submit anonymous tips to journalists while remaining truly untraceable.

In 2006, Kevin levied both his coding and research skills to produce his biggest investigation yet. He wrote a script that ran MySpace's 100 million-plus users against names in the National Sex Offender Registry. Kevin's query turned up several hundred sex offenders with profiles, and 500 who had committed crimes against children. Kevin identified at least one man who was using MySpace to contact underage boys. Talk about crossing the circles of hell and meeting all its denizens.

Wired published Kevin's code under an open-source license so anyone could use it, MySpace agreed to make significant policy changes, and the man Poulsen's code had identified was arrested.

It's been more than thirty years since Dark Dante made his debut on the ARPANET, scribbling coded messages to his friends in the shadows of hacked networks. Like his namesake, he's become a prolific writer. And, at least for now, he appears intent upon using his powers for good.

PART FIVE

THE NINETIES

SCIENCE AND TECHNOLOGY: THE NEW FRONTIER

When you reminisce about the nineties, what comes to mind? Leo DiCaprio's self-proclamation as world-king on the bow of the *Titanic*? Clinton's saxophone high notes on *The Arsenio Hall Show*? Or maybe you miss the simplicity of life before social media. Love me some modern nineties nostalgia! Everyone felt they were an observational humorist just like Jerry, or that they were the next Monica of fashion thanks to an onslaught of trendy magazines like *People* or *Cosmopolitan*. Heck, I still get chills thinking about Princess Diana's "revenge dress"—iconic.

In a ten-year period, America seemed to be developing and globalizing (for better or worse) faster than ever before. In fact, the entire world would recalibrate due to the conclusion of the Cold War, as the Soviet Union collapsed and Eastern Europe was restructured. Despite the constant chatter about peace and prosperity, what's *any* American decade without some controversy? Clinton's impeachment dominated political discussion, but we were also gifted the phrase "irrational exuberance" thanks to Federal Reserve Board chairman Alan Greenspan.

Technology had come a long way since the beginning of the Cold War, and America's innovations would *hopefully* be used for good from here on out. Email, pagers, and the iMac became status quo in middle-class homes. Likewise, hackers began targeting personal data and privacy.

Scientific discovery was also prevalent throughout the nineties: Americans aimed for Mars and replicated the Earth's environment in a big glass dome in the desert. However, these innovations wouldn't flow as smoothly as Clinton's saxophone licks might have entranced you to believe, and the nineties soon became a new frontier of their own SNAFUs.

SNOW WAY!

THE CIA'S ACCIDENTAL DRUG SHIPMENT

A little cocaine whoopsie by your
favorite neighborhood dealer:
the Central Intelligence Agency.

In late 1990, US Customs officials discovered a large shipment of drugs trying to pass through Miami International Airport. About 1,000 pounds of cocaine, worth, reportedly, hundreds of millions of dollars at the time. Now, US officials needed to find out: Where the hell had the drugs come from?

Customs officials soon traced the shipment to the Venezuelan National Guard, the militarized police that control the country's highways and borders. Now, if it sounds completely crazy that the police who were supposed to *control* the border were the ones giving the stamp of approval to shipments of illegal drugs, consider this: DEA investigators spoke to a source at the CIA, who indicated that the shipment had been approved by...the *US government. What?!*

Let's rewind for a moment. Throughout the seventies and eighties, America had been engaged in the War on Drugs, which seemed to have no end. In 1971, President Richard Nixon called drug abuse "public enemy number one" and oversaw the creation of the Drug Enforcement Administration, a new government arm whose sole job was to help fight this war.

In the eighties, President Ronald Reagan took a hard-line stance on drugs, emphasizing criminal punishment. At the same time, Nancy Reagan launched the "Just Say No" educational campaign aimed at schoolchildren, and Ronny built enough support so that Congress allocated $1.7 billion to help the fight.

But that wasn't enough for Reagan. He wanted to get to the heart of the issue. He directed the CIA to establish anti-drug programs in Central and South America, in the hot-zone areas where these drugs were trafficked. Around this time, more than half of the Colombian cartel's cocaine crossed the border into Venezuela as it was heading to the United States and around the world.

Little did Reagan know: Programs like these would, inadvertently, bring millions of dollars' worth of cocaine to the country's doorstep.

(SUPPLY) CHAIN OF COMMAND

In the mid-eighties, following Reagan's orders, the CIA began collaborating with the Venezuelan National Guard to form a joint anti-drug force in the country. They tabbed Ramon Guillen Davila, a Venezuelan general, to lead the effort and work alongside Mark McFarlin, the CIA's ranking officer.

I'd like to imagine the two men tasked with winning the War on Drugs as swaggering Schwarzenegger and Stallone types, covered in bullet belts and chomping cigars under highly reflective aviators—but nope. Not even close. Guillen was a slight, bookish-looking man, with a receding hairline and thick glasses. And McFarlin? Clean-cut, average build, and dark features. And their goal was to infiltrate the drug cartels in neighboring Colombia—the most powerful of which was run by Pablo Escobar—and learn more about how their businesses operated.

Under Guillen's leadership, the CIA-Venezuelan anti-drug force started an undercover drug smuggling operation. Maybe this started out as an effort to gain the cartel's confidence, but pretty soon it started to slip into *If you can't beat 'em, join 'em*. Why did anyone think this was a good idea? Perhaps they thought the cartel was dumb enough that, with the partnership in place, it wouldn't take much to wrap up the kingpins and call it a day. But if they thought that partnering with the cartels was going to be an advantage for the anti-drug forces, they were getting it completely backward.

Guillen's agents started handling cocaine deliveries from Colombian traffickers, and storing the drugs in a counter-narcotics center located in Caracas—funded by the CIA. Soon, Guillen's team was handling thousands of pounds of cocaine. It was like that kid who ordered 918 SpongeBob Popsicles on his mom's Amazon Prime account: Where could you even put it all without getting caught? But Guillen and his team were apparently working with the Colombian drug lords to gain intelligence from the inside. Straight to the Popsicle production line, if you will.

To keep up appearances, Guillen and the CIA decided to take things a step further. In December 1989, McFarlin met with Annabelle Grimm, the DEA attaché based in Venezuela. And he approached her with an audacious request: The CIA wanted the DEA to allow cocaine into the United States.

He asked her, in so many words, to "let the dope walk." Or put another way: allow it to come into America, make it into distributors' hands, and be sold on the streets. The CIA believed this would help them gain the cartel's confidence—and lead to bigger drug busts.

"They thought they were going to get Pablo Escobar at the scene of the crime or something," Grimm later told *60 Minutes*. "Which I found personally ludicrous."

Grimm and the DEA emphatically refused the request. "I told them what the US law was," Grimm said. "And the fact that we could not do this."

So what did Guillen, McFarlin, and the CIA decide to do?

LIVE, LAUGH, LOVE, CRY, COLLAPSE, ADMIT CONSPIRACY

About a year later, US Customs found a large shipment of cocaine at Miami International Airport. DEA investigators soon linked it to the CIA's counter-narcotics center in Venezuela. After some more digging, the DEA had two prime suspects in its investigation: McFarlin and the leader of the CIA-Venezuelan joint anti-drug operation, Ramon Guillen Davila. Our guys!

As the US investigation picked up, officials zeroed in on Guillen. They offered him immunity—meaning his words couldn't be used against him—if he cooperated. Guillen came to the United States, testified, and, according to one DEA agent, "cried, collapsed, admitted everything he had done."

Defying the wishes of the DEA, Guillen had quietly begun shipping cocaine into the United States. Throughout 1990, his agents flew several separate loads into the country, reportedly more than one ton of cocaine in all—right under everyone's noses. Not only did he admit to smuggling drugs into the United States, he said he'd *profited* from the operation, too.

The same DEA agent compared Guillen to Manuel Noriega, whom we met last decade—the Panamanian military leader who worked with the CIA and was also convicted of drug smuggling. The DEA agent told *TIME* magazine in 1993 that Guillen "was trying to do exactly what Noriega did—no worse, no better." Which makes this whole thing feel less one-of-a-kind, and more run-of-the-mill when it comes to the United States meddling south of our border.

All of this stayed relatively under wraps until November 1993, when *60 Minutes* ran an exposé on the scandal. The title? "The CIA's Cocaine." During the segment, Mike Wallace interviewed Robert C. Bonner, the former head of the DEA, who pointed the finger squarely at the CIA. He suggested the CIA had at least approved or condoned the drug smuggling.

Mike Wallace wondered aloud: Was it possible General Guillen acted on his own, without the CIA knowing? "[The CIA] built, they ran, they controlled that [counter-narcotics] center," Annabelle Grimm said on the program. "General Guillen and his officers didn't go to the bathroom without telling Mark McFarlin, [or] the CIA, what they were going to do."

The CIA conducted an internal investigation, and a spokesperson said it found no evidence of "criminal wrongdoing" on its part. Naturally. But the organization did admit that some of its officers had shown "instances of bad judgment."

And whatever became of Mark McFarlin, the CIA operative in Venezuela? He was never indicted. Instead, he resigned under pressure. Serving as a useful idiot for General Guillen didn't exactly pay off for him. And his boss, according to *60 Minutes*, was brought back to the United States and given a *promotion*, before he retired as well.

Until that *60 Minutes* piece, the CIA had kept all of this quiet. No wrongdoing. Nothing to see here. Just a couple of high-ranking agents stepping offstage into the dark.

COCAINE FOLLIES

For that same *60 Minutes* episode, General Guillen sat for an interview. He said that his past confession was false. With the cameras on him, he claimed the CIA approved the cocaine shipment to the United States, and that the operation had helped stop multiple trucks from bringing drugs into Venezuela. He painted himself as a victim, caught in a CIA-DEA squabble. He suggested they were trying to paint him as the fall guy.

Asked if he was clean, Guillen responded: "Clean until the last day God has for me." I'm not sure exactly what that means, but it has the beautiful quality of sounding extremely virtuous while being extremely meaningless. I'll say this for the guy, he's a wordsmith.

Despite his verbal prowess—and in English, no less—in 1996, a federal grand jury indicted Guillen on drug-trafficking charges. The indictment claimed that Guillen's drug operation had been larger than previously known.

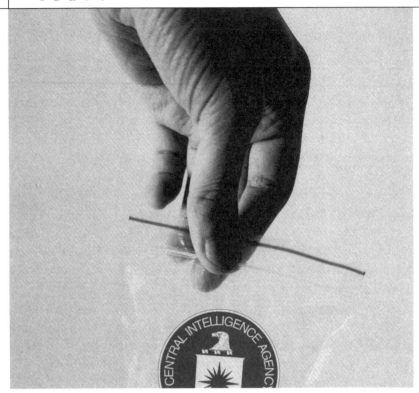

It said that Guillen had smuggled as much as *twenty-two tons* of cocaine into the United States over a four-year period when he ran the CIA-Venezuelan joint anti-drug force.

But by that time, Guillen was in Venezuela, and his country refused to extradite him to Miami. In fact, his country *pardoned* him for any crimes he may have committed. Guillen had always maintained that he only upheld his end of a bad bargain: He had shipped the drugs to the United States with approval from the CIA.

More than a decade later, in 2007, Guillen was arrested in Venezuela *by* Venezuela, for allegedly planning to kill President Hugo Chavez. Venezuelan authorities alleged that Guillen's own son had been caught discussing the plan on a recorded telephone line. However, he was never implicated or charged with any wrongdoing.

The CIA-Venezuelan anti-drug partnership never did catch Pablo Escobar. Remember those trucks that Guillen bragged about stopping at the border? In the end, the handful of vehicles was the sum total of his wins. For all this trouble, that's all Reagan's boys could muster.

BIOSPHERE 2:

TOO GOOD TO BE TRUE

The tourist trap/science experiment
that went awry...twice.

Jane Poynter had given up a lot.

She had left behind her life, her family, and everything she knew. And she had joined the project called Biosphere 2: a years-long experiment to see if human beings could re-create in miniature the ecosystems of the planet Earth—all inside a glass pyramid in the American Southwest. The subjects would be self-sufficient: They would grind the grain they used to make the dough they used to make the pizza, et cetera et cetera. Their goal? To create a closed system that could sustain life. It would be a model for the future of humanity—to be copied in future settlements on Earth, and maybe even...on Mars.

And there's another little detail about all this that brings us back to Jane Poynter. The members of the crew who went into Biosphere 2: They weren't allowed to leave.

So in service of this mission, Jane had given up the last year of her twenties—not to mention the grand opening of the Mall of America (yes, this is a subtle clue that we are back in the early nineties). She was about to give up a little more. Namely, the tip of her left middle finger.

See, all the "biospherians" had chores, and on this day, only their twelfth on the inside, Jane's job was to work the thresher, a machine for processing grain. Which was going well enough, until four of her five fingers got sucked in—she might have gotten off lucky, all things considered.

Ironically, though, she lost the precise fingertip she needed to fully express the shittiness of her situation.

The resident doctor did his best to reattach it, but it wasn't enough. She needed a hospital, which was kinda, sorta not allowed in their grand, *two-year* experiment. Theoretically, she would have to wait for any other medical professional to take a look until the biospherians rejoined the rest of the world...in 719 days.

What's a biospherian to do?

To understand exactly why Jane was trapped in a giant glass bubble with a two-year wait time on her next doctor's appointment, let's go back to where this whole thing started: when a little eco-cult got a big infusion of cash.

THEATER KID SHENANIGANS

Welcome to Synergia Ranch: a small ecovillage in the hinterlands of Santa Fe, New Mexico. In the 1970s, it was a charming little enclave of theater artists/farmers/furniture-makers. And at the helm? Actor/poet/playwright/film producer John P. Allen.

Allen was a big dreamer. In fact, he dreamed a lot bigger than his ecovillage. Time after time, he swept up his neighbors into his little projects. After a while, he started to attract "cult leader" allegations from critical outsiders. But if you asked him to describe himself, he'd probably say he was just a guy who loved to see the world. He had circled the globe on research journeys, and he loved what he saw so much that he cooked up a plan to stuff it all into a miniature glass city: Biosphere 2. (Earth, of course, being Biosphere Numero Uno.)

Allen didn't have the coin to turn Biosphere 2 into a reality. Luckily for him, billionaire Ed Bass did. And Ed fancied himself a patron of the arts (or at least of Synergia Ranch).

In 1984, they formed a partnership: Space Biosphere Ventures. Together, they bought a plot of land in Oracle, Arizona. And they shipped out a *lot* of glass. Seven years later, they finished constructing Biosphere 2, and boy, was she a beaut.

On one side of the new campus sat a giant glass pyramid, drinking in daylight for all the plants growing inside. Sprawling out from there were a network of glass corridors that led to a smaller pyramid and three long greenhouses divided into three segments, each like a set of sideways wedding cakes. Of course, across the campus from the main pyramid were a couple of glorious geodesic domes. Buckminster Fuller, eat your heart out.

In the middle of everything was a central hall in gleaming white. Its central chamber and wide wings gave off extremely *churchy* vibes, under the shadow of a bulbous tower in the shape of a giant mushroom.

On a more ecological note, Biosphere 2 contained a 3.15-acre sample plat-ter of Earth's biodiversity. Five ecosystems; 3,800 species. Even a frankincense plant from the Sultan of Oman. It was so idyllic, one participant described it in a later TED Talk as a "Garden of Eden on top of an aircraft carrier." And just like the first such-named garden, all that was left to add were the people. Cue the party music.

In the middle of the various gardens and ecosystems was a dormitory with ten bedrooms—one for each of the crew members who signed up for the proj-ect, plus a couple left over. And because this *wasn't* an interior design project, Biosphere 2 sported both a purple-carpeted spiral staircase and a black-and-white kitchen.

This crew was going to be physically sequestered, but not completely cut off from the world. After all, this was a project that was meant to show the world just how good their life could be. So even as they locked themselves away, the biospherians made plans to call, email, and even video-call folks on the outside. If they wanted to talk with loved ones face-to-face, they could pull up to the "visitors' window" and chat via telephone through the glass. If this sounds like the halfway point between a zoo and a prison...I'd say you're getting the idea.

Extremely weird vibes notwithstanding, the biospherians were sent off with a massive party. It was a 2,000-strong going-away shindig, attended by Woody Harrelson, "a fire juggler, an Indian chanter, and costumed dancers on stilts." They danced the night away on the lawn right outside the dome.

What can I say? Biosphere 2 got the people going. *Discover* magazine sug-gested that the project was "the most exciting venture to be undertaken in the U.S." since the moon landing. And *ABC News' Prime Time Live* proposed that Biosphere 2 might "save the world."

Yup. Humanity would be saved in this new "Garden of Eden."

What could go wrong?

LOCKED IN

On September 26, 1991, eight brave biospherians entered Biosphere 2 to the tune of "Fanfare for the Common Man," wearing identical red jumpsuits like a sports team headed for the field. And they were in for the game of their lives.

You know how the air we breathe is only part oxygen, and the rest is a bunch of other gases? Well, by month seventeen, the biospherians were

breathing air that was a little light on the O_2. It took them awhile to realize that the culprit wasn't quite as cartoonish as someone accidentally standing on an all-important oxygen-pumping hose, but was in fact due to an overgrowth of oxygen-munching bacteria. In the meantime, the oxygen shortage was giving everyone sleep apnea. Imagine waking up on the wrong side of the bed, every single day.

Add "hangry" to the list of grievances. The plants of Biosphere 2 never grew to their full potential. We should also pour one out for the hummingbirds and honeybees that dropped like flies. Soon, the biospherians were knee-deep in nematodes and chasing down cockroaches to feed to the chickens.

Back to our pal Jane Poynter, who sliced her fingers only *twelve days* after getting locked in. Fortunately, the powers that be deduced proper Biosphere 1 medical attention was a good idea, and they pointed her toward a local hospital. Once she came back from her brief intraterrestrial visit—fingertip reattached, thank goodness—she brought with her a duffel bag of desperately needed supplies.

The head honchos, fearful their experiment would come to a premature close, would end up sending bimonthly supply drops—complete with seeds, vitamins, and mousetraps. Not exactly how things might go on Mars, but hey, we've all snuck supplies from Mom's cupboard once in a while, right?

Sure, a sliced-off fingertip feels like a good reason to put the experiment on pause. But a bimonthly care package seems to totally undermine it. To get supplies, or not to get supplies, that is the question—that caused the biospherians to split into factions.

Space Biosphere Ventures played both sides. They sent in the supplies, but they also recognized the bad optics of doing so. Which is why reporters only found out about that first supply drop months after the fact, and the subscribe-and-save regular deliveries even later.

While the biospherians scrounged and scrambled, the general public in the Outside World was having the time of their lives. Biosphere 2 became the most popular attraction in Arizona, the Grand Canyon notwithstanding, as thousands of tourists—650,000 in the first couple of weeks alone—came to observe the biospherians in their (un)natural habitat. And if they got peckish from marching through the Arizona desert, they could go to an eatery next door to nosh on a biomeburger or a habitat hot dog.

Like I said: paradise.

LUCKY NUMBER SEVEN

If the two-year mission began with literal fanfare, it ended with a resounding "eh." At least one employee had quit in disgust, and Lynn Margulis, an actual biospherics expert, told the *Washington Post*: "It's a venture capitalist project which is intrinsically fascinating, but it's not scientific in any way whatsoever."

She wasn't wrong. Space Biosphere Ventures definitely had money on their mind, namely because they didn't have any left by the time they wrapped the mission on September 26, 1993. On the two-year anniversary of her "bubble-boy"-ification, Jane Poynter went home in a stylish blue jumpsuit. Thanks to getting actual medical attention, she was only a little worse for wear.

At least this was the end of it, right? For Jane, yes. But not for Space Biosphere Ventures. Rather than quit while they were behind, they said, "Double or nothing."

Strap in, kids, we're going back into the bubble.

On March 6, 1994, after an upgrade here and a new species there, a fresh-faced crew of seven entered Biosphere 2. According to a Biosphere spokesperson, this mission was supposed to be "more low-key and casual." The next month would be anything but.

Remember how Space Biosphere Ventures was hemorrhaging money? Allen didn't much seem to mind. But he wasn't the moneybags, after all. Ed Bass decided he wanted someone to come in and take control. Well, guess who he hired as his fixer: Steve Bannon. Yeah. *That* Steve Bannon. And long before he was convicted of contempt of Congress, he was pulling silly little April Fools' pranks.

On April 1, 1994, billionaire Ed Bass sent Bannon and a gaggle of US marshals to impose a regime change on Biosphere 2. Their mission? Cut out the expensive "science" shit that researchers were trying to do inside. Get the spending under control.

They swept onto the Biosphere campus and took over. Biosphere 2's mastermind, John P. Allen, and his team of spendthrift researchers were pushed off the controls. And in true deposed-leader fashion, Allen said what amounted to "Well, you can't fire me, because I quit!" After all, he wasn't in the Biosphere. He was in Tokyo. He sent his resignation by transpacific letter.

A few days later, in the wee hours of April 4, previous participants Abigail Alling and Mark Van Thillo staged an uprising of their own. After all, they

were still holding on to John Allen's dreams for the research that could be done in Biosphere 2—a dream they believed was lost once Ed Bass and Steve Bannon took control. So they snuck onto the Biosphere property, popped open the sealed doors, and smashed several panes of glass.

Alling and Van Thillo were members of the first Biosphere crew who had, to borrow a theater term, committed to the bit (the "bit" being science). Alling later claimed that they were trying to save the current crew from the dangers of bad management, lest Biosphere become another *Challenger* disaster. After all, during their first run at the Biosphere, they had nearly suffocated, and it was only careful monitoring of the atmosphere in their glass house that kept them alive. But however noble that explanation might have been, it wouldn't save them from charges of wrongdoing.

After all this rigmarole, even the inflation of the Biosphere tour price from $9.95 to $12.95 wasn't enough to save the project from ruin.

The research was shut down. The second Biosphere 2 crew exited the facility on September 6, 1994, after a measly six months, and just in time to witness the cancellation of the 1994 World Series. Talk about striking out.

ALL'S WELL THAT ENDS WELL

In the years since, Biosphere's public image has gotten a real facelift. After a couple of decades of ownership hot potato, Biosphere landed with the University of Arizona in 2011, which continues to use the compound as a quite reputable research facility. Science: back on the menu.

It's easy to say that those early Biosphere 2 years were a failure. After all, what might you call a $200 million project that couldn't sustain eight people? Not to mention the free-range cockroaches.

But we shouldn't throw Biosphere 2 out with the bathwater. For Jane Poynter, Biosphere 2 showed her how completely we in the Outside World obscure humanity's relationship to the planet and its processes.

If we take anything from Biosphere 2, it could be that humans are in fact living creatures on this massive rock hurtling through space, just like the moss or the hummingbirds or the nematodes. Or that the Earth doesn't belong to us; we belong to it. Or maybe, *just maybe*, we don't have to accept the planet's doom as inevitable and preemptively workshop humanity's escape.

Instead, we can put on some jumpsuits (metaphorically speaking) and figure out how to live and thrive on the planet we all call home.

KEYBOARD COWBOYS:

PARTNERS IN CYBERCRIME

That time two hackers dumped the Mentos of classified data stolen from Korea into the Coke of an American secret server.

May 12, 1994, started out as a typical Thursday for Richard Pryce, a sixteen-year-old British kid with a penchant for playing double bass. That afternoon he was doing what he normally did: sitting with his angular face awash in the glow of his computer screen, reading an internet forum up in his attic room at his parents' home in North London.

Out the corner of his eye, he saw lights flashing outside his window. Then the sound of heavy footsteps racing up the stairs. When the cops busted in, Richard's fingers were still on his keyboard. They lifted his fingers away from the keys and warned him not to move another metacarpal. As he later told a reporter for the *Guardian*, at that moment Richard thought simply, "Oh shit."

It turned out the cops had been monitoring Richard's internet activity for a while. Ever since March, when he'd hacked into a US Air Force system and then *casually* dropped in data from a Korean atomic research facility. The US government wasn't sure *which* Korea the data belonged to: North or South. If it was the North, well, Richard's hack was *maybe* a *teeny-tiny*...act of war.

But teenage Richard hadn't executed this hack alone. He had a partner in cybercrime.

And now that the cops had ripped up all the floorboards in his room and seized his computer, they were hot on his partner's trail, too.

RIDE 'EM, COWBOY

Now, if there's one thing I know from all the beautiful, sunny days I've spent inside my house with the shades drawn watching Western movie marathons on TCM, it's that cowboys come in pairs: Butch Cassidy and the Sundance Kid, Buffalo Bill and Annie Oakley, Doc Brown and Marty McFly (in *Back to the Future III*, the Western one, duh). All that frontier-style law-bending is just a little more fun with a friend by your side. Well, ain't that just rootin' tootin' *heartwarming*.

So let's fast-forward that TCM marathon, and zoom past the black-and-white gunslingers kicking their boot heels on the dusty frontier...to a pair of teenage boys, each staring at their chunky computer monitors and wearing matching pairs of wraparound sunglasses. *These* were the outlaws of the 1990s, making trouble on a new frontier: the early internet.

Our internet-era version of Wild Bill and Calamity Jane? The aforementioned sixteen-year-old Richard Pryce and his partner, twenty-one-year-old Mathew Bevan. The hacking duo even had outlaw-style nicknames: "Datastream Cowboy" for Richard, and "Kuji" for Mathew. They were what the 1994 movie *Hackers* termed *keyboard cowboys*: pardners on the cyber-hacking frontier.

TWO HACKERS ON THE OL' DUSTY TRAIL

Although Richard and Mathew had both grown up in the UK—Richard in the London suburb of Colindale and Mathew in Cardiff, Wales—the siren song of the World Wide Web is what brought them together.

Richard acquired his first computer at the age of fifteen to help with his schoolwork. And after his double bass was stolen, that computer became his primary creative outlet.

Mathew—a self-described nerd and big fan of all things *X-Files*, alien, and UFO—was beaten up and bullied mercilessly in school. He got a computer at the tender age of twelve as a means of escape. Eventually the two stumbled onto the same hacking forum, and from there, the young outlaws upped their game.

One of their favorite early pastimes? A hack known as "phone phreaking"—the title of a nineties rave jam if I've ever heard one...*oom chicka oom chicka oom chicka*...*cough*—the two would break into telephone systems to make calls for free. Manipulating a computer system made Mathew in particular

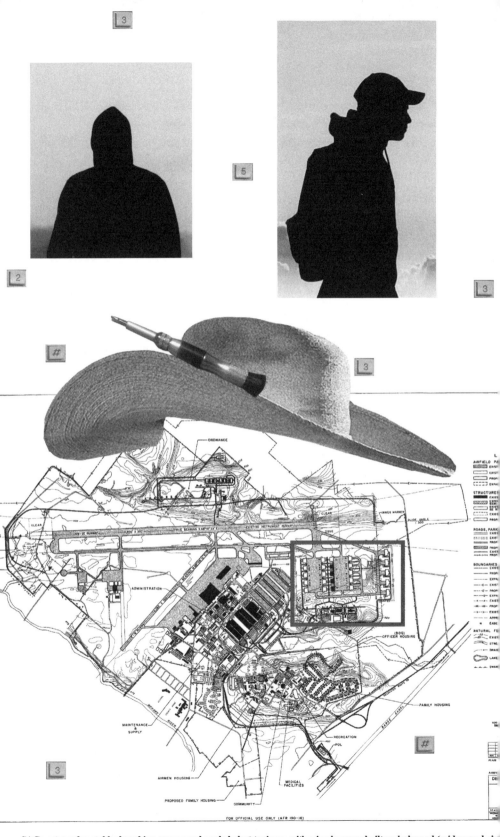

SAC rectangular stubbed parking aprons and angled alert taxiway, with wing hangars built and planned (midground rig~
Force Base, Directorate of Installations, Master Plan of October 1957. Collection of K. J. Weitze.

feel powerful in the face of all those school bullies. In the real world he was a nobody. But online, he was king of the cyber frontier.

As their hacking knowledge grew, Richard and Mathew shared tips to gain access to bigger and more elaborate computer systems—though, more often than not, it was Richard asking Mathew for help. Mathew was the older and more experienced hacker, after all. And it didn't hurt that Mathew's newest hacking obsession—uncovering government files about UFOs and other conspiracy theories—gave him a lot of experience breaking into government computer systems that were, to put it kindly, a lot *easier* to crack into than you'd think.

Like the outlaws of the Wild West before them, our boys were addicted to the thrill of the chase: the adrenaline rush of gaming the system and bending the law. As Mathew eventually told BBC News, peeking into the inner workings of government systems felt like "a parent finding their child's diary...you know you shouldn't look at it, but you just can't help yourself."

And that urge to peek into the government's business is where the *real* trouble started.

VIRTUAL SHOOT-OUT AT THE ROME LABS CORRAL

Meanwhile, across the pond in upstate New York, a computer systems manager sat down to start her workday at the computer lab on Griffiss Air Force Base. Located in Rome, New York, the Griffiss lab was one of the air force's premier command and control research facilities in the United States, working on sensitive projects like artificial intelligence (how avant-garde for 1994!) and radar guidance for, you know, blowing stuff up.

It was a Monday—March 28, 1994—and I can imagine the computer systems manager, Mavis perhaps, sighing into her novelty *I Hate Mondays* Garfield mug as she logged in to her computer. Then, suddenly, her eyes narrowed. She noticed something strange. A file in her system that...wasn't supposed to be there. Her nostrils flared, wafting in the scent of stale coffee and jet fuel, apropos because she—along with the swarm of agents from the Air Force Information Warfare Center and the Air Force Office of Special Investigations who would eventually descend on the Rome Labs system to sort out this mess—soon figured out that the unauthorized file was something called a *sniffer*, a tool that hackers use to secretly collect information passing through a network. It's on the lookout for user IDs and passwords—the information a hacker can then use to gain control of a computer system. In this case, the computer system of a highly sensitive military installation that contained many a potential government secret. Bet you can't guess who'd installed that sniffer on the Rome Labs network!

Yup. Looks like our ol' cyber cowpokes Richard and Mathew were at it again. But this time they were *just maybe* a little out of their depth. In fact, when Richard had started this hack from his attic bedroom, he'd basically just gotten lucky, letting his computer run all night so that it could pick up as many passwords as possible on the Rome Labs system. The weak link that cracked the code? A USAF lieutenant was using his pet ferret Carmen's name as a password. It's short and simple. Richard's computer landed on it in no time.

Richard had been emailing Mathew for tips along the way as he breached the system. And eventually, the two were able to take control of the Rome Labs network, launching more than 150 attacks, and gaining access to sensitive research data, military command messages, even peeking into the systems at NASA's Goddard Space Flight Center and defense contractor systems around the country.

Of course, the government officials watching this go down didn't know that all of these data breaches were coming from a sixteen-year-old's attic bedroom. *They* thought that these hackers must be part of some big bad Eastern European spy ring. So, instead of tracking down the hackers right away, they monitored their activity across the system, gathering information about them slowly but surely.

That is, until April 15, 1994, when Datastream Cowboy and Kuji—as the US government now knew them—went just a *little* too far down the ol' dusty cyber trail.

That was the day that Richard kind-of, sort-of accidentally-on-purpose hacked into the network of the Korean Atomic Research Institute (KARI), downloaded the contents of their database, and then deposited them in the Rome Labs system. And it wasn't because Richard was planning some kind of nefarious government takedown. He just wanted to see how far he could flex his keyboard cowboy skills. Well, when Mavis saw *that* little stunt, she must've done a spit take right into her Garfield mug.

Remember that showdown between Richard and the cops in his bedroom? Well, this is the stunt that prompted New Scotland Yard to break down his door. Because at the time, the United States was in the middle of sensitive negotiations with the North Koreans about their nuclear weapons program. So the US officials monitoring the hack freaked out, because if the KARI was located in North Korea, and the North Koreans *saw* that the US Air Force had intruded on their system (even if that intrusion was *actually* carried out by a British teenager), that transfer of data could be perceived as an aggressive act of war. Whoops! Luckily for Richard, the officials tracking the hack quickly realized that the research institute was located in *South* Korea. Crisis averted.

But that potential act of war kicked the search for the hackers into high gear. One US official got so hot and bothered that they referred to Mathew specifically as the "single biggest threat to world security since Adolf Hitler." WHOA, Nelly!

LASSOED BY EMAIL

The threat level may have been high, but the US government's approach to exposing Richard and Mathew was anything *but* high-tech. In fact, it was your run-of-the-mill undercover informant who blew Richard's cover.

The informant posed as just another wannabe-hacker on the forums. From there, Richard and the informant exchanged emails wherein Richard told him, well, basically everything he wanted to know. He said he lived in the UK, and that his handle was Datastream Cowboy. He even gave the informant his *home phone number*, and told him that his favorite hacking targets were "dot mil" sites because their security was so lax.

Ah, to be young and carefree. Seems like *your lips* are a little lax, Richard! Based on the trove of new information, New Scotland Yard started monitoring Richard's home phone, and guess what they found: a *phreak*-a-thon. Richard was still into phone phreaking, and his phreak attacks matched the security breaches at Rome Labs. He was even routing his attacks and phone phreaks through the same systems around the world, in South America, Europe, Mexico, and Hawai'i.

That was enough for New Scotland Yard to bust into Richard's house with a search warrant that day in mid-May 1994. Accounts vary, but the *Times* of London reported that after the cops busted in, Richard curled up in the fetal position and wept.

After New Scotland Yard arrested Richard, they figured that it'd be a breeze to find his accomplice, the notorious Kuji, what with all the hard drives they found in Richard's bedroom, which held enough top secret info to fill *3,000* A4 sheets of paper. SMH.

But even with all that evidence, the cops didn't close in on Mathew for another *two years*. All the while they assumed he was a dangerous foreign agent.

Meanwhile, Mathew carried on with his life. He barely batted an eye when his buddy Richard disappeared from their favorite forum, and when he later saw the newspaper articles stating that Richard had been arrested, Mathew breathed a sigh of relief: He thought he was in the clear. Not so fast, buddy.

Finally, in June 1996, the agents who'd been working on the case, desperate for a break, dove back into the hard drive they'd retrieved from Richard's room two years earlier. Over three weeks they scoured its contents. Then, finally, within the depths of the machine, they found the name Kuji and a telephone number. To their disappointment the number wasn't connected to some far-flung Russian hideout. It was, of course, based in Cardiff, Wales.

The cops drove to the listed address and burst in. Mathew was at his office—where he worked as a computer programmer—but when they threw the door to his room open, the agents found the walls plastered with *X-Files* posters. Not exactly the lair of a high-powered Russian operative. More like a keyboard cowboy's sci-fi den.

They arrested Mathew at the office later that day.

END OF THE LINE, PARDNER

In the end, it was the law that brought our two cyber cowboys face-to-face for the first time. They finally met IRL on July 11, 1996, when they were arraigned at Bow Street Court in London and charged with conspiracy and offenses under the Computer Misuse Act. Their little stunt with Rome Labs had cost the US government about $200,000.

The threat of being thrown in the pokey proved too much for young Richard, and he pleaded guilty to the charges, paying a 1,200-pound fine. After the trial his mother told the *Daily Telegraph*, "This has been a ludicrous and almost surreal situation...Surely the United States government cannot believe that it will get good publicity from insisting on this prosecution. It was not Richard's fault that their security systems were lax." Gnarley burn, Mrs. Pryce!

And in Mathew's case...the courts came to the same conclusion as Richard's mom. They dropped the charges against Mathew, saying that an expensive and lengthy trial was no longer in the public interest. Basically, they didn't have enough hard evidence for the charges to stick. So, Mathew kicked the dust off his boot heels and walked away from the courthouse a free man.

Eventually he parlayed his notoriety into a career as a cyber security adviser and white hat hacker—using his keyboard cowboy powers for good. (And hopefully he held on to all those *X-Files* posters. Now *that's* a serious stash of memorabilia to sell on eBay if you ever fall on hard times...Add a few Beanie Babies to the pile and you're looking at a cushy retirement!)

And Richard? Well, he got a D on his computer science A-levels and ended up picking up that double bass again: After the trial he started school at the Royal College of Music. He's probably plucking a groovy tune somewhere out there as we speak.

But maybe that hacking-shaped void makes Richard a little sad sometimes. Perhaps as he sits down to tune his double bass, he wistfully wonders what might have been if he hadn't pursued the thrill of chasing government secrets all those years ago.

Well, wouldn't you know it, sometimes even cyber cowboys get the blues.

BEANIE BREAKDOWN:

THE TOY THAT TAINTED THE NINETIES

How one man turned normal adults
into crazed stuffed animal collectors
by bluffin' with his fluffin'.

"The Princess Diana Bear is mine!"

The year was 1999. We were on the precipice of a new millennium dubbed Y2K. The film *10 Things I Hate About You* had just hit theaters, "Livin' la Vida Loca" was blaring from car stereos, and your Tamagotchi was either overweight or dead. Inside an air-conditioned courtroom in Las Vegas, Frances Mountain said to the people in the gallery, "I don't agree with the judge's decision to do this. It's ridiculous and embarrassing."

On the floor in front of Frances and her ex-husband, Harold, lay a pile of plush treasure: Beanie Babies. Not just any Beanie Babies—it was a collection worth an estimated $2,500 to $5,000. And like the rest of their possessions, these Beanies were supposed to have been split evenly four months ago, when they divorced. The judge overseeing the proceedings said to the couple, "Because you folks can't solve it, it takes the services of a district court judge, a bailiff, and a court reporter." Frances approached the pile and took the first stuffed animal—Maple the Bear. Next Harold chose one, and they would proceed this way, splitting the Beanies up one by one until Harold ceded his right to half and let his ex-wife take the lot.

This is the story of how one toy became such a hot commodity that it was found in drug busts, inspired parents to invest college funds in stuffed plushies, and ultimately reduced adults...to children.

A GOOD CAT

Ty Warner grew up in La Grange, a sought-after suburb of Chicago. Fun fact: His childhood home was designed by Frank Lloyd Wright. But he likes to leave that part out of his story. In fact, he prefers to share as little information about himself as possible, revealing only that he "emerged from an unhappy family and a youth devoid of educational advantages" (or so he claimed in a court memo when fighting a lawsuit, but we'll get to that later). That youth devoid of educational advantages included boarding school and, from there, Kalamazoo College, from which he dropped out after freshman year, choosing to pursue an acting career in Los Angeles.

In the City of Angels, Ty supported himself by working as a valet, fruit market vendor, and elevator operator. After five years of trying and failing to make it as an actor (don't worry, Ty; we've all had our ups and downs), he returned to Chicago, where his dad landed him a job at the toy company Dakin. Ty would travel door-to-door selling toys, and he did so in style. He recounts that he would pull up to customers' homes in a Rolls-Royce, decked out in a fur coat. His thought process here? If he looked interesting, people would be interested in buying whatever he was selling. And he was right. Ty was pulling in a six-figure salary—and we're talking *in the eighties*!

But his success was short-lived. Ty not only sold toys but he designed and crafted his own. This "hobby" led to him being unceremoniously fired from Dakin because, in addition to selling their toys on house calls, he had started selling *his own toys*.

After being fired, Ty did what any of us might do, and spent some time in Italy. Three years to be exact. And while taking this not-so-brief hiatus, he discovered a line of stuffed animal cats unlike any he'd seen stateside. To this day, Ty Warner has only ever given one in-depth interview about his life. It was with Joni Blackman for *People* magazine in 1999. He told her, "I decided to come back and do something that no one has done. Make a good cat."

When he returned to the United States in 1986, Ty Inc. was born.

BEANIE BOOM

It took a few years for Ty to find his stride. His first line of Italian-inspired cats was life-size and lifelike, but by 1993 he had hit on a design that you'd find familiar: the Beanie Baby.

That year at the World Toy Fair in New York City, Ty (both the company and the man) debuted an understuffed, plastic-pellet-filled plush that soon became the hottest toy of the nineties. And from there, things took off quickly.

So what prompted the Beanie boom? Maybe the true genius stemmed from charging an affordable $5 for the toys, whereas other stuffed animals at the same price point were not nearly as well made, at least in Ty's opinion. Or perhaps it was the sales strategy; Ty Inc. only sold the stuffed fluffs to mom-and-pop gift shops and limited each gift shop's inventory to thirty-six of each style of Beanie. They would also cut off Beanie supplies to retailers who sold Beanies under lump-sale promotions such as the classic "buy five Beanies, get one free," keeping tight reins on the value of their stuffed animals. The other trick Ty had developed was what I like to call the Daniel Day-Lewis Stratagem: to launch new types of Beanie Babies into stardom, only to quickly retire them, ramping up demand as customers realized they wouldn't be available forever. Trust me, I've watched *Phantom Thread* an unhealthy number of times.

Plus, the Beanies were just really freakin' cute. I still think about Patti the Platypus—her beautiful webbed feet (?) and fuzzy purple fur. But I digress.

Just two years after the Beanie Baby debuted, the company was profiting $700 million. Children and adults alike flocked to local toy stores and gift shops to wait in line for the latest Beanie Baby drop. People had begun straight up "investing" in Beanies to turn a profit, selling "mint" ones on the "gray market," aka the new online retailer, eBay, where the dollar value of those little sacks climbed, in some cases, as high as $5,000. Every serious collector knew you had to keep the tags on and intact, or your precious plushie would plummet in value. There were even special protectors made (by other companies) to keep the tags in mint condition. If you don't believe me, you can ask my grandma—she still switches up her Beanie Baby display seasonally, and every single one has a tag protector.

By 1997, America's Big Brands had gotten in on the game. McDonald's came calling, and started including Beanies in their Happy Meals—scaled-down versions aptly dubbed "Teenie Beanie Babies." They, too, became wildly

collectible, with stories of customers ordering hundreds of Happy Meals and asking the staff to "hold the food."

The craze intensified, so much so that police officers began spotting Beanie Babies in surprising places. In one incident in Ohio, a cop recalled finding the Princess Bear—a special edition Princess Diana–themed collectible Beanie—sprawled on the floor during a raid tracking down stolen property. He told the *New York Times*, "I thought, Good Heavens, this bear is worth $400. What's it doing here?" (And because you know I love an inflation calculator, that's $790 in today's dollars.) And in another incident in Columbus, Ohio, $20,000 worth of Beanies was stolen and eventually found its way to a fencing operation, which is just a fancy term for a group of people who buy and sell stolen goods.

Hey, Ohio, are you guys okay?

SPILLING THE BEANS

By 1999, the Beanie wave had hit its peak and was about to crash. In September of that year, Ty Inc. made an announcement: They would be retiring *all* Beanie Babies. The hard-core collectors were crushed, but everyone else was beginning to wake up to the scheme of jacking up the demand for the Beanies by making them scarce. The backlash toward Ty Inc. was intense, with customers reaching out to the company to express their displeasure. Or at least that's what the company claimed when they made another announcement three months later. Like Will Smith, the Blues Brothers, and many other icons of the twentieth century, they would be cashing in on the calendar flip itself: Ty Inc. would be starting a new millennium line.

It was unclear if Ty's decision was in response to collector outrage or just another cheap sales tactic. For many people, this marked the end of the Beanie roller coaster—time to unbuckle their seat belts and get off the ride. Previously obsessed buyers questioned why they had once clamored to get their hands on these small stuffed creatures in the first place. How was it possible that anyone considered them an investment? That's what everyone over the age of seven was thinking anyway.

Harold and Frances Mountain got off easy when they had to split their treasure after ending their marriage. Others had it much worse. Take Chris Robinson, a former soap opera star who bought $100,000 worth of Beanies with his family's savings in an ill-planned attempt to pay for his five kids' college educations. What Chris's son, also named Chris, remembers of that time is eating Happy Meals multiple times a day to get the Teenie Beanies. Today those Beanies retail for less than a dollar apiece online, meaning the collection is worth less than $20,000 (and that's *if* there are any interested buyers). It felt like the only person getting rich off the Beanies was Ty Warner himself.

Throughout all the ups and downs, Ty was able to remain just outside the limelight. He portrayed himself as a reclusive mastermind, a Howard Hughes meets Willy Wonka type character who wanted the public to know just enough about him to be curious for more—but not enough to actually judge him.

But in 1996 he made a move that would come back to haunt him when he started stashing money away in a Swiss bank account to evade paying taxes.

What started out as $3.1 million in foreign sales ballooned into more than $100 million—at which point the IRS caught wind of the situation. In 2013, the pellets came pouring out of the seams. Ty was convicted of tax evasion and forced to pay a $53 million fine. But perhaps the authorities were nostalgic about the little critters, as Ty was able to avoid any jail time. The fine itself was small beans for him because, unlike his former customers, he foresaw that the Beanie boom would eventually come to an end. In 1999, he bought the Four Seasons in New York and has only continued to diversify his assets through the purchase of other hotels and resorts.

Ty Inc. still makes Beanie Babies and other stuffed toys, but consumers treat them just like any other stuffed animal—cute, affordable, and readily available. Ty himself remains just elusive enough to garner interest. I mean, we're talking about him, aren't we? In 2023, Apple TV+ made a movie about Ty and his Beanie empire based on the 2015 book *The Great Beanie Baby Bubble: Mass Delusion and the Dark Side of Cute*. The movie's narrative suggests that three of the women in Ty's life have as much, if not more, claim to the success of Ty Inc. as Ty does. Is there an element of truth to this? It's hard to know, but *The Great Beanie Baby Bubble* would be a good place to start if you're curious. As for my grandma, I've done my best to keep all this information away from her. She doesn't need her pure love of the Beanies tainted.

Last I checked, Ty Warner was the 458th-richest person in the world with a net worth of $6.5 billion.

Not bad for a guy who set out to make "a good cat."

MARS ORBITER:

THE PROBE TO NOWHERE

In 1999, a Mars probe mysteriously
careened off course, and a bewildered
team of rocket scientists realized
their rookie math mistake was to blame.

In the early morning hours of September 23, 1999, on another gorgeous SoCal day, flight operations manager Dr. Sam Thurman and his team sat slumped in their chairs at NASA's Jet Propulsion Laboratory in Pasadena, California. The glumness on their faces clocked somewhere between "Our Caribbean cruise has been canceled" and "All of our kittens just died." The spacecraft on their screens, the $125 million Mars Climate Orbiter, was overdue in sending the signal to confirm it had successfully been caught by Mars's orbit.

In the tense preceding days, two things had become clear: that the Orbiter was way off its target trajectory at the worst possible time, and that nobody had a clue why. But their despair had a basement level. Even if the signal never came and the craft was lost to the void, which does happen from time to time in the business of insanely complex space missions, the team would have no time to work through their stages of grief over a piña colada.

The Mars Climate Orbiter, with its primary mission of studying Mars's atmosphere and climatic history for signs of water, was also designed to play second fiddle to its sister craft, the Mars Polar Lander, due to complete its own 200-million-mile journey to Mars mere weeks later. The Lander was built and launched in tandem with the Orbiter; a problem built into one could also have ended up in the other. As the day wore on, Dr. Sam Thurman and his bewildered gang of rocket scientists waited. And waited. And waited. But no signal came.

FASTER, BETTER, CHEAPER

For most of the nineties, NASA felt like a party that would never end. After the devastating 1986 *Challenger* disaster, the agency's space shuttle program worked its way back into public acceptance, reviving a sense of optimism and giving space exploration a newfound whiff of affordability.

And the American public, whose tax dollars kept the agency's coffee machines bubbling, were being rewarded with tangible nuggets of wonder: Three of the four "Great Observatories" were sent to space in the nineties, including the Hubble Space Telescope, which provided some of the most beautiful images of space we've ever secured.

Despite all this progress, Daniel S. Goldin, NASA administrator from 1992 to 2001, also espoused a "faster, better, cheaper" mentality. He prioritized leaner and more frequent missions. This approach reduced the time it took to develop a spacecraft by 40 percent and slashed costs by two-thirds. With an emphasis on efficiency, manned missions were becoming harder to justify. After all, humans were the neediest of all space cargo!

So, after the successful 1998 launch of the Lunar Prospector, NASA had the moon pretty well covered. It was Mars time, baby. And this mission to the Red Planet? As Goldin said, it had to be fast and cheap. Too bad they forgot about the "better" part.

LOOKING FOR LIFE

Dr. Thurman, flight operations manager for both the Climate Orbiter and the Polar Lander, heeded the call. Tall, lanky, and prone to turtlenecks, with dark, neatly combed hair showing some first gray around his temples, Dr. Thurman looked like a young Reed Richards before he discovered his elastic super-powers and became Mr. Fantastic. The son of an air force interceptor pilot, he had spent his 1960s childhood steeped in military aviation. As he gazed in awe at the mythological Apollo missions, a career was born.

Dr. Thurman was already something of a veteran of the Jet Propulsion Laboratory by 1999, having worked in various roles since 1987 and earning praise as an expert in project management. Now, under the thumb of NASA's increasingly stringent calls for efficiency, his Climate Orbiter ground support team was positively lean at eighty people, down from two hundred people for the Mars Observer mission just seven years earlier.

"We're trying to do a whole lot more with less," Thurman told the *New York Times*. "The public and Congress have told us, 'Space is neat, but it's got to be done at less than a billion dollars a pop.'"

The Mars Climate Orbiter was a real steal at $125 million. Still, white-collar grumbling abounded about the project's cost having ballooned 44 percent throughout its construction by Lockheed Martin, go-to contractor for all things weapons and space. The craft itself was a 6.9-foot-tall, 1,387-pound cube wrapped in wrinkled orange foil. It was strikingly asymmetrical, with a large rectangular array of solar panels jutting out of one side and a dish antenna perched precariously on its top surface. Low gravity would be a relief: The Orbiter looked like it wanted to fall over.

Over the course of a Martian year, or 668 Martian sols (for any Earthling readers out there, that's 687 days), the probe would take daily photos and atmospheric readings, monitor real-time changes on the Martian surface due to wind, and detect clouds of water vapor to help scientists piece together the nature of water on Mars. Liquid water could mean life. Would David Bowie finally get an answer to the question he'd been caterwauling about since 1971? Was there life on Mars?

But before it could start collecting those juicy data sets, the Orbiter would set up shop in a nice, round, sun-synchronous polar orbit and wait for the Mars Polar Lander to arrive. It would serve as a communications satellite, relaying messages from the Lander back to Earth, and as an eye in the sky, taking weather and geographical readings to aid the Lander in a smooth touchdown on the Martian south pole.

Time to countdown: 5, 4, 3, 2, 1...

METRIC MISHAP

The Climate Orbiter launched on December 11, 1998, from Cape Canaveral. Initially, the mission was exceeding expectations, according to Dr. Thurman. The Jet Propulsion Lab tracked the probe's location by detecting changes, or Doppler shifts, in radio signals that were continuously sent back to Earth, correcting discrepancies between the observed flight path and the target flight path through several controlled burns of directional rockets. It was normal and even expected to see discrepancies. All spacecraft needed a bit of a nudge from time to time. Even if we're talking about a 200-million-mile nudge!

But after the first few corrections, a sense of unease began to grow at NASA. The craft itself was just...kind of finicky. According to the engineering magazine *Spectrum*, which later did its own independent review, the Orbiter's gigantic, asymmetrical side-mounted solar array subjected it to constant energy bursts from the sun, slightly spinning it like the blade of a wind turbine in a light breeze. To counteract that rotation, heavy flywheels inside the craft could be spun up at varying speeds. This technique is the same way a Segway holds itself upright. (The next time you're rippin' down the sidewalk behind a Segway tour guide, just remember that spacecraft work the same way.)

Due to the Orbiter's peculiar design, though, its thrusters were placed out of balance with its center of mass, meaning that every time they fired them up to correct a rotation, a "cross coupling of forces" occurred, leading to a drift from original position that engineers refer to as a "translation." Translation: The probe was slipping and sliding all over the place.

Dr. Thurman and his team were navigation experts. Their job was to take the craft they were given and steer it to Mars. The team that had actually designed and built the spacecraft, the engineers at Lockheed Martin, wasn't involved in its navigation until mere hours before the craft was due to arrive at Mars. This left the navigation team guessing about extremely important details like, "Uh, how close to Mars can the Orbiter get without exploding?" Without any input from Lockheed, the navigation team deemed that, while their target flyby altitude was approximately 224 kilometers (which would have been a safe distance), the craft would survive a pass as close as 85 kilometers. This, by the way, wasn't based on actual analysis by Lockheed's engineers. It was also wrong—and they'd learn that the hard way.

To make matters worse, later investigations would reveal that Dr. Thurman and his navigators were stubbornly clinging to a belief that the margin of error in their numbers was approximately 10 kilometers in either direction, whereas in reality the spread was closer to 100 kilometers. According to an expert who spoke to *Spectrum*, this should have had people "screaming down the halls," as it showed that the navigators had no idea where exactly their craft was.

The idiosyncrasies of the Orbiter's design and the poor communication between the engineers and the navigators made troubleshooting the Orbiter's navigation woes extremely difficult. Going through the code alone would take

months, and the fact that there was no project manager with total oversight meant that the teams would be on nearly introductory terms with each other's work. Was the Orbiter's tendency to drift off course the result of poor location readings? Was there a physical problem with the thrusters? Had Dr. Thurman forgotten to upgrade his PC to Windows 98?

There was no time to dig for answers. The craft had arrived at Mars.

In an article published on NASA's website on September 20, Dr. Thurman sounded remarkably cheery, given the circumstances: "The curtain goes up on this year's Mars missions with the orbit insertion of Mars Climate Orbiter. If all goes well, the happily-ever-after part of the play will be the successful mission of the Mars Polar Lander that begins in December followed by the mapping mission of the orbiter that is set to begin next March." You can almost see the beads of sweat on his forehead.

Spoiler alert: The orbit insertion didn't go well. It went very, very badly. And when something crashes and burns, people with clipboards come staggering out of the night and form an investigatory panel.

In the following weeks, an investigation would tear apart every blueprint, every shred of data, every snippet of code. And what they would discover as

the root cause of the Orbiter's failure was so forehead-slappingly basic that a humiliated NASA would be forced to implement sweeping changes at every level of the agency.

Each time the Orbiter had fired up its rockets to correct course, its onboard computer had sent back to Earth a record of exactly what each awkwardly placed thruster did, so that engineers could calculate the unwanted drift and adjust accordingly. The thruster performance data was then processed by Lockheed and emailed to the Jet Propulsion Laboratory in pound-force seconds, which are English units—the kind of units we use for measuring nearly all things here in these great United States. Wait, why do we use English units in the first place? Hold that thought.

Dr. Thurman and his JPL team had been taking *those* numbers and entering them into their navigation software as newton-seconds. And guess what? Those are *metric* units. The kind of units that are used in space navigation.

That's right: The fate of a highly anticipated, years-in-the-making, $125 million mission through 200 million miles of space boiled down to a dumb-as-moonrocks mismatch of measurement units. Sent by *email*.

"To be very blunt, it was overlooked," Neil Hinners, vice president for flight systems at Lockheed Martin, said to the *Washington Post*. Everyone at the Jet Propulsion Lab just *assumed* the numbers they were receiving in Lockheed's emails were in metric units, because that was the widely accepted standard in jet propulsion work. They were unlabeled, by the way. And since the resulting calculations were within the same order of magnitude, the mismatch went undetected for the entirety of the ten-month trip.

On the morning of orbit insertion day, some last-minute estimates came in that placed the craft's approach altitude at around 110 kilometers—more than 100 kilometers closer than planned. Lockheed Martin engineers were finally consulted. According to *Spectrum*, they were "frightened." An altitude like that would subject the Orbiter to debilitating heat and turbulence far outside the bounds of its limited warranty.

As the Pasadena sun rose, a sense of gloom descended over the Jet Propulsion Lab. The number was updated several minutes later: 95 kilometers. At that altitude, air friction would generate heat equivalent to a "bank of propane torches." The minutes ticked by. A final altitude estimate came in: 57 kilometers. The heat generated at 57 kilometers would have been ten times higher than at 95 kilometers. The Orbiter likely plowed straight into Mars's atmosphere, exploding immediately.

CAUTIONARY TALE

The absurdity of the mission's failure was not lost on the scientific commu-nity. John Logsdon, director of George Washington University's Space Policy Institute, said it best to the *Los Angeles Times*: "That is so dumb."

Speaking of dumb, why does America use English units at all? In 1793, the adoption of the metric system in the United States was of such importance to Thomas Jefferson that he requested artifacts from France that the Americans could use to calibrate their tools. A French botanist named Joseph Dombey was sent across the Atlantic with a standard kilogram in his cargo, but his ship was blown off course, and he was kidnapped by pirates. He died in captivity.

If it weren't for those meddling pirates, would the Mars Climate Orbiter be whistling a merry tune around the Red Planet to this very day, beaming back images of Martian vapor clouds while the Denver Broncos play a home game at 1.60934-Kilometer-High Stadium?

It would feel *so* nice and tidy to place the blame for the failure of the Cli-mate Orbiter on that one fateful error. Sure, Lockheed Martin should have supplied the Jet Propulsion Lab with glitch-free software. Yes, JPL should have double-checked their homework. Of *course* those mean pirates shouldn't have stolen that sweet French man.

But to reduce the entirety of the Orbiter's failure to a mismatch of mea-surements would be to ignore Congress's underfunding, NASA's swaggering overconfidence, and bad management that trickled down into a culture of poor communication and fear of questioning authority.

To top it all off, weeks later, the Mars Polar Lander was also lost because of an entirely different mistake. A software error shut off the burners early, causing it to crash into the Martian surface.

After the loss of both spacecraft and months of reviews by several panels, NASA made a slew of changes. They rebuilt project management structures, implemented stricter review processes, and emphasized the importance of training. In a sense, you could say these changes worked, considering nine of the eleven missions to Mars since 1999 were successful, including the twin Mars rovers *Spirit* and *Opportunity* and the atmospheric orbiter *MAVEN*, whose mission was similar to that of the Climate Orbiter.

Whether NASA's changes were enough to ensure its continued success in the future is still an evolving question. Its budget remains a fraction of what it was in the Apollo years—just about .36 percent of the US federal budget. A tiny budget leads to small team sizes. How thorough can you really be if you're overworked and spread thin?

As for the less measurable changes to NASA's culture, is it even *possible* to convince a sprawling tech agency to slow down and embrace a more thoughtful approach in the twenty-first century? An official NASA document from 1970 called "What Made Apollo a Success" included this surprisingly folksy passage from NASA engineer Bob Tindal:

> *Of course, the way we got this job done was with meetings...hundreds of meetings! The thing we always tried to do in these meetings was to encourage everyone, no matter how shy, to speak out, hopefully (but not always) without being subjected to ridicule. We wanted to make sure we had not overlooked any legitimate input.*

By my extremely careful measurements, that's about 200 million miles from Dan Goldin's "faster, better, cheaper." Which, according to one eyewitness, allegedly led Goldin to hurl a projector at the wall when someone suggested a backup plan in case a Russian module didn't arrive on schedule (in the end, it was indeed late).

Sometimes the work needs to be slow. Sometimes it isn't about the money. And despite your best efforts, sometimes you will fail. Because going to space is extremely difficult. But it is most definitely worth it. Just ask Major Tom from David Bowie's "Space Oddity," floating in his capsule high above the world, marveling at a sight few of us will ever see, contemplating the progress of humanity and the strange peace of the great beyond. He sings that:

"I'm feeling very still / And I think my spaceship knows which way to go."

Sure does, Major Tom. Well, assuming they all used the same units.

PART SIX

AUGHTS
AND
ONWARD

SAME OLD SHIT,
NEW CENTURY

The turn of the century offered a fresh start for everyone. New Year's resolutions were now New Millennium resolutions, and perhaps anything felt possible. Secondhand smoke evaporated overnight. Napster led to Spotify, and Oprah became her *own* empire. Heck, even Will Smith transformed from rapper and extraterrestrial enforcer to an Oscars darling. People didn't know what to expect post-Y2K madness, but the coming years would unequivocally reshape human perspective. While the early aughts began innocently enough, soon the 9/11 attacks, the Iraq War, those darn hanging chads, and Hurricane Katrina forced a new era upon us all.

And by the late 2010s, the rapid delivery and consumption of information transformed the way we live. Smartphones could be found in every pocket with an instantaneous connection to GPS, ride-sharing apps, and the whole dang world. As a result, every morsel of news, scandal, and pop culture moment infused our everyday rhetoric. I mean, I don't know how many times I've stood up to leave a peaceful campfire only to hear my wife shout behind me, "The tribe has spoken!"

But alas, despite the new digit at the beginning of our yearly planners, the same ol' issues came bubbling back up: everything from military secrets and war games to missile debacles. After all, trend cyclicity wasn't just for the stock market and mom jeans. While instant gratification and information overload became tantamount with the aughts, so did a variety of SNAFUs that seem hauntingly familiar if you stare at them long enough.

EMERGENCY LANDING:

THE LITTLE HARD DRIVE THAT COULDN'T

When an American spy plane pulled an emergency
landing in Chinese territory, the crew had
to think fast to destroy state secrets.

At around five A.M. on April 1, 2001, Lieutenant Shane Osborn and his crew of two dozen airmen took off from Kadena Air Force Base in Okinawa, Japan. Osborn was a God-fearing Nebraskan who was always obsessed with flying; his dad took him on his first flight when he was just three years old, and ever since then Osborn had known he wanted to be a pilot. He attended college on an ROTC scholarship, and by 2001, when Osborn was twenty-six years old, he had already been in the navy for nearly five years.

On that fateful April Fools' Day, Osborn was piloting an EP-3E surveillance plane, equipped with all sorts of advanced receivers and antennae and souped-up computers, with the purpose of doing recon on Chinese communications. The plane was high-tech, but it looked surprisingly old-school: It was a prop plane powered by four propellers.

The mission was going along as expected. Then, at 9:55 A.M. Okinawa time, as Osborn flew over the South China Sea, he spotted a pair of Chinese Navy F-8 Finback II fighter jets on his tail. And you know as I always say, spot a pair of Finback II fighter jets on your tail, it's time to bail!

What happened next would trigger a diplomatic crisis, leave the American flight crew in limbo, and prompt finger-pointing and recriminations between the two most powerful countries in the world.

MAYDAY

One of the two Chinese fighter jets was helmed by thirty-two-year-old Chinese Navy pilot Wang Wei. Wang grew up in Huzhou, a two-hour drive from Shanghai, and like Osborn, he had been obsessed with flying since he was a kid. He grew up near an air force base, and whenever he heard planes overhead, he'd drop everything and run outside just to watch. He joined military flight school at age eighteen and had spent his entire adult life as a pilot.

It's fairly routine for fighters to patrol their national airspace and politely see off unwanted rubberneckers, but Wang was also known for being a particularly aggressive pilot. He'd flown dangerously close to American spy planes before—there was one incident when he zipped right up to a US plane and held up a piece of paper with his email address on it. Seriously, Wang, there are easier ways to get a pen pal.

So with our two lifelong navy pilots—one from Nebraska, the other from Huzhou—hurtling through the skies dangerously close to each other, perhaps it was inevitable that something bad would happen. Wang flew a little too close to the sun...metaphorically speaking, of course. He pulled up just five feet from the US plane and mouthed something to the crew—I can only imagine it was his AIM username this time.

Wang pulled back, and as he made one more approach, his fighter tragically collided into one of the EP-3E's propellers. Wang's jet split in half, tumbling 22,500 feet and splashing into the ocean.

Osborn's EP-3E depressurized, rolled upside down, and plunged 14,000 feet. Talk about turbulence. As one crew member later said in *The Intercept*, "We're falling like a rock and...everyone thought we were going to die."

MOVE FAST AND BREAK THINGS

Osborn ordered the crew to put on their parachutes and prepare to bail. But incredibly, he was able to stabilize the plane—now he just needed to land it ASAP.

Osborn knew there was no chance of safely landing on the water. He had only one option: to land on the People's Liberation Army's Lingshui Air Base on Hainan Island, with no prior warning or permission from China.

Knowing that they'd soon be surrounded by soldiers who wouldn't exactly be friendly, the crew had only twenty minutes to destroy as much sensitive

material as possible before landing. Now, every airman on that plane was *supposed* to have received training in emergency destruction procedures (i.e., How to Destroy a Laptop). So of course they knew exactly what to do in this worst-case scenario...right?

Wrong. Because it turned out that only *one* crew member ever received that training.

With the rickety, damaged aircraft shuddering its way toward land, the crew set to work. They tried to destroy their chunky, matte-black government-issued laptops by throwing and stomping on them—without even knowing which hard drives were particularly sensitive. They tore up papers by hand since there wasn't a shredder onboard. Someone grabbed a fire ax meant for emergency evacuations and tried using it to destroy equipment, but the blade was too dull to be of any use. Instead, one crew member weaponized a mysteriously heavy briefcase and swung it around wildly, smashing anything in sight—until the briefcase sprang open, spewing its contents across the plane. Big whoops! Because it turns out that case was actually something called a "COMSEC box," and it was filled with classified material. Now it was scattered willy-nilly all over the floor.

"By the time we landed, the plane was in total disrepair," one crew member told *The Intercept*. "We had screwed up the inside of that plane as much as we could." And with smashed laptops, shredded papers, emptied briefcases, and tangled wires scattered—as if a robot had thrown up its guts all over the place—Shane Osborn had miraculously landed the plane with the entire crew uninjured. After taxiing to a stop, he stood up, walked to the door, and opened it. If it were me, I would have then vomited violently. Another famous idiom of mine: Never let your crew see you spew.

HOTEL CALIFORNIA

Dubbed the "Hawai'i of China," Hainan is best known for its tropical climate, five-star beach resorts, and duty-free luxury shopping. But the crew of the EP-3E hadn't booked a travel package and didn't exactly get a warm welcome.

As soon as the EP-3E landed, PLA soldiers surrounded the plane. After Osborn opened the door, a Chinese officer spoke to him through an interpreter, ordering everyone off. Osborn and his crew complied; they were taken onto a bus and driven to...well, not a scary torture chamber, as you might imagine, but the on-base canteen. In his memoir, written with Malcolm McConnell, Osborn described his first meal in China: "several scoops of boiled rice, some stewed green vegetable, and hacked-up chunks of medium-size boiled fish." Which honestly doesn't sound too bad—probably better than your average take-out place.

After a few bites of boiled rice, two officers introduced themselves as official interpreters. "Call me Lieutenant Tony," said one of them. "I am Lieutenant Gump," said the other (wonder what his favorite Tom Hanks movie is). Lieutenants Tony and Gump led the Americans to a mildewy concrete building, where they'd live for the next ten days while US diplomats negotiated with their Chinese counterparts for the crew's release. During their stay in the barracks, Chinese officials interrogated the Americans daily and deprived them of sleep. But it wasn't all bad. Their hosts kept them well fed, gave them English-language newspapers to read, and even playing cards for entertainment. It was like the world's weirdest cross-cultural summer camp—with some light torture thrown in.

At the end of their detention, Lieutenants Tony and Gump even wrote some goodbye messages in English and Chinese for the crew. In return, one crew member taught them the lyrics to "Hotel California": "You can check out anytime you like. But you can never leave." Thankfully, Lingshui Air Base was a bit more accommodating.

THE BLAME GAME

While Osborn's crew was jamming to the Eagles with Tony and Gump, American and Chinese officials were busy pointing fingers. The Americans blamed the Chinese for flying too aggressively. The EP-3E was big, difficult to maneuver, and equipped with giant propellers—what was Wang Wei thinking when he flew so close to the plane?

The Chinese blamed the Americans for encroaching on their sovereign airspace. What was Osborn doing flying so close to Chinese territory—wasn't that a deliberate provocation?

With both sides blaming each other, the US ambassador to China sent a letter to the Chinese foreign minister, which came to be known as the "Letter of two sorries." China claimed that the Americans said in the letter that they were "very sorry" for (1) entering Chinese airspace and landing in Hainan without clearance; as well as (2) the death of Wang Wei, who unfortunately was never found and later presumed dead. But the Americans claimed that they never apologized—they just expressed regret and sorrow for the whole thing.

Either way, the letter was contrite enough that it smoothed things over. Osborn and his crew checked out of the Hotel Hainan and went home, and the Chinese returned the EP-3E to the United States. And what became of our starring pair of American and Chinese navy pilots, Shane Osborn and Wang Wei? Well, Osborn would later pursue a career in politics and be elected state treasurer of Nebraska. Wang Wei was posthumously awarded the title of "revolutionary martyr," and a tombstone was erected for him in Anxian Cemetery near his hometown.

As for all the top secret materials on the plane, a joint US Navy–NSA investigation later found that there was classified data onboard that didn't really *need* to be there and was needlessly put at risk. There was also sensitive information about intelligence personnel on board, including their full names, addresses, and social security numbers. Talk about an identity theft risk. Most importantly, when the Chinese searched the plane, they found information detailing how the United States collected data from China.

And, folks, this one is a cautionary tale on why you never, ever call out sick on employee training day. You never know when you'll miss crucial instructions on how to destroy a laptop, safely land a plane, or smooth over rapidly escalating international tensions. And as we've learned here, a few Don Henley and Glenn Frey lyrics always help.

THE MILLENNIUM CHALLENGE:

OR, HOW TO RIG A GAME... TO LOSE IT

When America's generals were
humiliated in their own war game,
they rigged the game instead.

In the early aughts, lots of millennials spent their evenings the same way—huddled around television sets in their parents' basement, controller in hand, playing video games. *Madden, Super Smash Bros., Mortal Kombat.* Different from my own dalliances with Mrs. Pac-Man in the eighties, but not *so* different. This was how a generation grew up, immersing themselves in fantasy worlds, competing against friends and strangers.

But what would often happen when someone lost? They'd throw a tantrum, eject the disc, and start the game over. Pretty childish, right? Well, in the early 2000s, the US military pulled a similar move, when a simulation *they created* wasn't exactly going its way.

You see, after 9/11, the United States had begun the *quote-unquote* War on Terror, and it seemed inevitable that this would escalate conflict in the Middle East. To help prepare the troops, Pentagon officials oversaw the creation of a war game, a series of live-action sequences and computer simulations that would get American grunts ready for the real deal. The military even gave the game a title fit for the Nintendo console: Millennium Challenge 2002.

But this game didn't fit in an arcade cabinet. This war game would bring together more than 13,000 troops from all four wings of the military under Pentagon command (Army, Navy, Air Force, Marines), cost more than $250 million, and took two years to plan. The goal was to test a new set of combat strategies that emphasized speed, precision, and coordination, rather than blunt force.

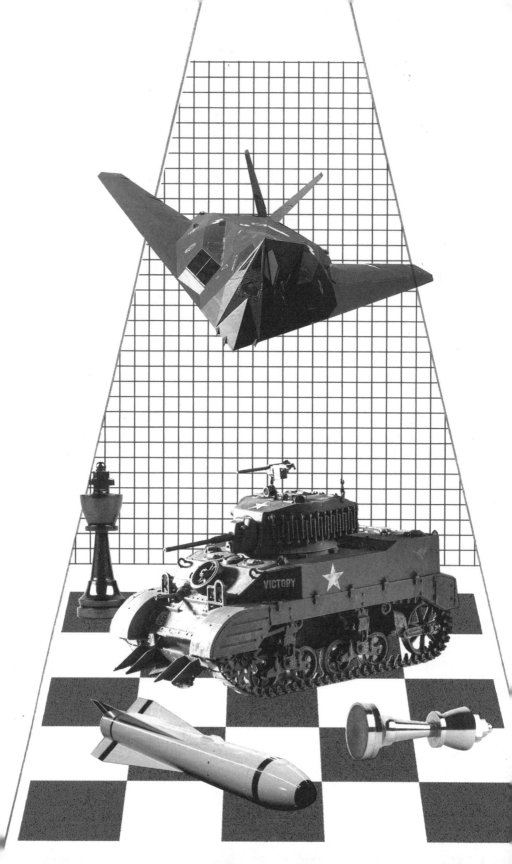

The game would be set five years into the future, in 2007, and pit two teams against each other. The Blue Team, which was a stand-in for the United States. And the Red Team, which was reportedly designed to resemble Iraq or Iran.

Red versus Blue? That makes it sound like the joint chiefs were pulling up for a little Rock 'Em Sock 'Em Robot action. But believe me when I tell you: They took this one *oh so seriously.*

GAME ON?

The games commenced less than a year after 9/11, over the course of three weeks in July and August 2002. At first, to the outside world, all seemed to be going well. Word was that the new strategies had passed the test—until the *Army Times* leaked an email sent by Paul K. Van Riper, a retired lieutenant general of the Marine Corps, who was also the leader of the Red Team.

Van Riper had a long and distinguished military career. He'd won so many personal decorations, including the Silver Star medal and the Purple Heart, he seemed to run out of room on his uniform. He'd also participated in previous war games with the military.

Toward the end of the Millennium Challenge 2002, Van Riper apparently wrote an email raising serious concerns about the integrity of the game and its outcome. "Instead of a free-play, two-sided game...it simply became a scripted exercise," Van Riper wrote. He added: "It was in actuality an exercise that was almost entirely scripted to ensure a Blue 'win.'"

Not exactly a fair fight. But when the details finally came out, they made the US military look even worse.

At the start of the game, Van Riper's Red Team was set up the way that the US military leaders saw America's enemies: He had far fewer troops, and lesser technology. Red Team was like the little brother who comes out to play street hockey with hand-me-down stick and skates. But then imagine that kid is a little Wayne Gretzky. Despite being set up to fail, Van Riper and the Red Team managed to outmaneuver the Blue Team with a series of creative tactics. He always had his troops moving, keeping the Blue Team on its toes. If he needed to send messages to his troops, he sometimes used couriers on motorcycles, to avoid the Blue Team intercepting important digital communications.

One retired army officer told the *Army Times*, "What he's done is, he's made himself an expert in playing Red, and he's real obnoxious about it. He will insist on being able to play Red as freely as possible and as imaginatively and creatively...He can be a real pain in the ass, but that's good" because, the officer noted, "he's doing all those things for the right reasons."

Somehow running the line between goody-two-shoes and rebellious at exactly the same time. Like I said, *just like* a little brother.

SORE LOSERS

As the Blue Team entered the virtual Persian Gulf, General Van Riper sent a fleet of Red Team boats to move in aimless circles around them, as if to lull the Blue Team to sleep—and then began a surprise attack. The Red Team boats were smaller, more agile, and they swarmed the Blue Team ships.

Van Riper also equipped some of the Red Team boats with explosives, essentially turning them into suicide bombs. The attack sank more than a dozen Blue Team vessels. If it were a real event, the *Guardian* pointed out, it would have been "the worst naval disaster since Pearl Harbor." The whole attack lasted less than fifteen minutes. In the game, it was a humiliating defeat.

"A phrase I heard over and over was: 'That would never have happened,'" Van Riper told the *Guardian*. "And I said: nobody would have thought that anyone would fly an airliner into the World Trade Center...but nobody seemed interested."

Surely feeling a bit embarrassed, the officials managing the game hit pause and "refloated" the sunk ships from the Blue Team, wiping out General Van Riper's victory.

The game managers also ordered Van Riper not to use certain military tactics or weapons against the Blue Team, but to move or turn off air defense systems, and to reveal the location of his own troops to the Blue Team. They had, in a way, tied both of his hands behind his back.

In the end, General Van Riper quit in protest and wrote that soon-to-be-leaked email, trying to raise alarms. He was concerned that the military would order troops to follow the game strategy in real-life combat scenarios, when its results had been totally rigged. "You don't come to a conclusion beforehand and then work your way to that conclusion," he wrote. "You see how the thing plays out."

FEARS REALIZED

Less than six years later, in January 2008, three US Navy warships were traveling in the Strait of Hormuz, through a narrow corridor entering the Persian Gulf, when they were confronted by five Iranian speedboats.

The smaller, more nimble Iranian vessels maneuvered aggressively between and around the larger American ships. Around the same time, the Americans reportedly received a radio message saying, "I am coming at you, and you will explode in a few minutes." The Iranian boats also dropped boxes in the pathway of one of the American ships—boxes that could have been interpreted as explosives.

One American ship took aim with a high-powered machine gun. But the Iranian speedboats backed off before any shots were fired. No one ended up getting hurt.

In the aftermath, US military officials criticized the Iranians for their reckless, provocative behavior. That's understandable—but at the same time, maybe they should have seen this coming.

Retired Lieutenant General Paul K. Van Riper had tried to warn them. Back in 2002, during the $250 million war game, he'd deployed tactics similar to those used by real Iranian boats. His Red Team had even attacked the Blue Team in the same stretch of water, where the Strait of Hormuz meets the Persian Gulf.

After the 2008 real-life incident in the Persian Gulf, reporters spoke with Van Riper about that disastrous war game. He said he'd developed that attack strategy drawing on the Marine Corps' research around animals that move in packs, and work together, in order to attack larger prey.

US military leaders perhaps could have been prepared for the Iran confrontation, if only they had listened to Van Riper back in 2002, if only they had played their war game fair and square and learned from it, rather than whining and rigging the game in their favor.

So the next time you hit *GAME OVER*: Instead of chucking the controller across the room...pick up the sticks, learn from the loss, and be better the next time. It's what General Van Riper would have wanted.

AGENT BTZ:

THE EARLY BIRD GETS THE WORM

How a single dongle dinged the
Department of Defense and remade
US military cybersecurity.

November 26, 2008, Washington, DC: George W. Bush was about to get some bad news. I imagine it went something like this:

The president received an emergency call—a security briefing in the Oval Office. Bush called in his boys. Robert Gates, the secretary of defense, filed in with *his* boys. They circled up, unfurling their canary-yellow legal pads just in time for the door to fly open.

Admiral Michael Mullen, chairman of the joint chiefs, marched in with his own set of boys bouncing up behind him. (Man, we really gotta decommission the phrase "boys" when it comes to political gatherings. Anywho...) By now, Mullen was used to delivering bad news. In fact, it was his testimony in a Senate hearing the year before that confirmed, in front of the entire nation, that the situation in Iraq had gone from something like *My neighbor's house is on fire* to *Shit, now I'm caught in my neighbor's house fire*. Still, what he was about to say to the president had him looking grim. A hush fell over the room as the camera zoomed in on his face. (There's a camera, okay?)

He looked at the president. His voice sounded like a hearse with a flat tire: "Mr. President...we have a worm."

PARTY TIME

As the *Los Angeles Times* reported it later that week, the "worm" Admiral Mullen briefed the president on was "a severe and widespread electronic attack on Defense Department computers." In mid-aughts-speak, it meant the US military *just got served.*

The past decade was incredibly tense for the United States. Invasions of Afghanistan and Iraq sent American troops halfway around the world in numbers that hadn't been seen for almost two decades. It was the height of the War on Terror. Republicans had just been ousted from the White House by Barack Obama, and at the end of 2008, with the Bush administration about to hand over the reins, they were doing everything they could to cement their legacy and/or pass the buck on some, you know, pretty big loose ends.

At the same time, the world was becoming increasingly reliant on technology. The iPhone had been unleashed on the public just the year before. Facebook was ballooning with new users, and, heck, we even saw the invention of bullets that shoot bullets. (No, really, google it!)

No one could keep up with how quickly the digital world was changing. (Some of us are still betting on BlackBerry to make a comeback. Don't laugh. It's sad, okay?) The world was more connected than ever, in more *ways* than ever, and that included the far-flung troops of the American military.

Enter the worm.

The virus started at an unnamed American military base in the Middle East. Within days of the discovery that a worm had infiltrated American systems, the news was everywhere. It was "Pentagon Computer Networks Attacked!" in the *Los Angeles Times* and "Cyber Attack Has Pentagon Worried!" in the *Chicago Tribune*. Okay, I added the exclamation points, but you get the picture. The worm had us trembling from coast to heartland.

So what exactly was this worm? It was a nasty little bug nicknamed *agent.btz*. The security firm that identified it just slotted it into its list of names behind the last worm they'd identified—*agent.bty*. It was their standard naming process. But this worm wasn't going to linger in obscurity. It was about to take the name *agent.btz* into the headlines. Sure, it didn't do a lot at first, but what it did do, was travel.

When agent.btz entered a computer system, it started a manic series of copies of itself, sending them everywhere they could go in a computer system. If we're talking about a *network* of computers—like at an internet café (remember those?) or, say, a military base—then the worm would crawl through the entire network, copying itself into every hard drive, disk drive, and flash drive every step along the way.

Once computer worms have a foothold in a system, they start sending out a signal into the internet: an invitation to the worm party. Then, other malicious programs would be able to creep and crawl in through that open door: for instance, programs that might track every key that's typed into a computer, programs that gobble up passwords, or programs that scrape up secret documents—like battle plans or top secret blueprints—and send them out to the hackers who launched the worm. Or the worm could bring in programs that are simply bigger, hungrier worms to do their own gobbling and share their own invitations.

When agent.btz hit the US military systems in 2008, the Department of Defense had—and still has—a worldwide network for communication that they ran in secret. Or, at least, that's the idea. The government *also* has a separate network that's supposed to be used by all the American intelligence agencies. These are two of the crucial networks that our government uses for sensitive communication around the globe.

The worm infected both.

But it didn't stop there. Like our friend the Very Hungry Caterpillar, the worm was still hungry, so it ate its way into the US Central Command network, the system used by the US military to coordinate between headquarters and combat zones. One spooked official warned the public about the dangers of the worm mucking up this system: "This is how we order people to go to war." If the worm was on the inside, it could stop orders from reaching the troops, or even change them.

So, clearly, this worm had infiltrated the most important and most sensitive American computer systems. That might leave you wondering: How the hell did the worm get through the door in the first place?

Surely it was a supersecret heist, right? Or a cyberbattle between two teams of lightning-fast computer ninjas typing so fast that their fingers blurred into ghostly shadows. Something cool like that, right?

Friends, the real world is so much stupider.

Let's go back to the beginning, to the parking lot of an American military base in an unnamed Middle Eastern country.

THIS GUY IS ALL THUMBS

Once again, I imagine it went something like this:

It was around midmorning when a car pulled through the security gate and crunched over the desert gravel into the parking lot. The door opened up, and out stepped our friendly Department of Defense employee, fresh from a leisurely breakfast and ready to clock in for a day manning a glowing terminal for Uncle Sam.

After grabbing up their briefcase and thermos of coffee, they turned to go inside when a small, dark object on the ground caught their eye. It was right next to the car tires. They must have barely missed it when they pulled in.

They walked over and took a look. It was a normal object in their line of work: a small, plastic USB thumb drive.

Well, our partially caffeinated officer mused, *someone must have dropped this on their way into the building. Maybe I can tell whose it is if I take a peek at what's inside.* So they dropped that thumb drive in their pocket, and strolled into the office past the security desk. (*Hey, Jud!*)

When they reached their desk, they dropped into a chair and flipped open their US military laptop. They logged in. Then, the crucial moment—*let's see what's on here*—they plugged in the drive.

And that's all it took.

When the little drive connected, the worm *autoran.* Meaning it started up automatically, as it was programmed to do. And it autoran directly into the system. Agent.btz was off to the races.

No hacker battle. No flashing red lights and bunker alarms as firewalls were breached. Just one casual mistake, probably with the best intentions.

Now, if you've ever had to sit through one of those corporate network security videos, then you've heard the lecture: Do *not* plug anything mysterious into your computer.

This would be why.

The biggest vulnerability in any computer system, no matter how many safeguards and firewalls and strict orders you slap on, is always the person at the keyboard. At best, the culprit forgot their security training and let their curiosity take over. Maybe they were just trying to be helpful. But finding a thumb drive in the parking lot would be like finding a hot dog in a Chicago gutter. I *guess* you could pick it up if you wanted to, but only to throw it away.

You should never carry it inside and stick it into your computer.

THE VERY HUNGRY AGENT.BTZ

For what it's worth, the US military has never confirmed (nor denied) the *details* of how it actually happened, or how far, exactly, the worm tunneled. But the story of a hapless DoD employee infecting a connected laptop is the best guess of the security experts who talked to the press.

We *do* know that it infiltrated American networks that held the kinds of secrets that generals never want their enemies to see: the battle plans for the campaigns they were fighting in Iraq and Afghanistan.

And once all the worms were partying together, they were programmed to do another thing the United States most feared: search through American computer hard drives for documents, then send those files out onto an internet server in a tidy package, for America's enemies to scoop up.

Right away, the United States tried to blame Russia. After all, the United States *was* in a kind of testy stare-down with Russia around the world, and particularly in the Middle East. But the truth is, it wasn't clear who had created the virus. Hackers—and really, the tech world in general—were miles ahead of the Department of Defense. So much so that there wasn't a group in the DoD ranks ready to address cyberattacks. But with a worm loose in military servers, they scrambled to catch up.

It was an NSA analyst who first spotted the worm party invitation coming from deep within secret American systems. Oddly enough, it was a worm that had been spotted in the wild by cybersecurity pros earlier that summer—back when they had given it that *agent.btz* handle. It had infected a handful of banks, so in a way it was a known entity. It was something they *could* have prepared for.

But they simply...did not. After all, the worm was still out in the yard. No one was going to carry it inside and add it to the secret sauce.

Until they did.

NO WIGGLE ROOM FOR FAILURE

Once all the alarms were blaring, leaders stuffed an elite team of military and intelligence hackers into a windowless room at the headquarters of the National Security Agency.

They called the project "Operation Buckshot Yankee." I'm not exactly sure why. In context, it conjures up an image of someone trying to kill worms

with a shotgun. You see it now, don't you? Wouldn't be my first choice, but I guess that's just where we found ourselves as the calendar flipped over into 2009, and George W. passed the buck(shot) to Obama.

The first thing the Department of Defense did was issue an order: Thumb drives were completely banned. In fact, no form of outside data storage was allowed to be connected to a DoD computer. The ban also forbade CDs, flash media cards, disks, DVDs, and "all other removable data storage devices." No more reruns of *The Office* season 3, I guess, but at least new copies of the worm were kept outside.

Once this digital quarantine was in place, a small team of military and intelligence hackers loaded an infected computer on a truck and drove it to a hidden warehouse. They booted it up, then tried firing all kinds of digital weapons at it. Or, you know, maybe they just ran a line of code they wrote overnight. But picture it with me! The point is: They were looking for a counterattacking code that would delete the worm without melting down the system it inhabited. It took some time, but they crafted something that would work.

Once our high-tech Avengers had crafted a bespoke worm crusher, then came the bigger challenge: the long, grinding process of running their worm

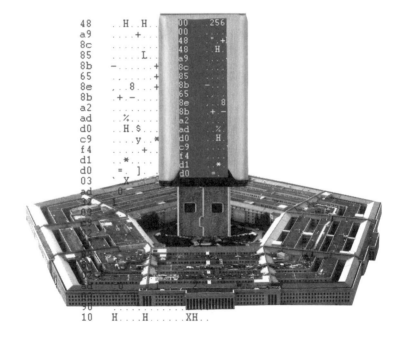

whomper through every secret government computer. They couldn't do it all at once. They had to go server by server, laptop by laptop.

Knowing that, it might be a surprise that it took the DoD *only* fourteen months to finally beat the worm. But eventually, as they reformatted their final hard drive, they did it.

By the end of 2009, US leaders had even launched a new way to coordinate between the different branches of the military and the various American intelligence agencies. Now, they would be *together* to deal with digital threats. It's the kind of thing that maybe should have already been in place, but I guess this is a better-late-than-never sort of situation. It was a new unit they assembled, the US Cyber Command. I imagine it like the nerdy Avengers: Each branch of the military sends their *most* bespectacled computer nerd into America's server hub, where they compare pocket protectors like the business card scene from *American Psycho*. Army! NSA! Department of Defense! Very nice. All joined together thanks to their first big effort: exterminating that worm.

The party was finally over...or was it?

After fourteen months, they did declare victory—*mission accomplished*—but that turned out to be a little premature.

In fact, *three years later* they were *still* fighting to fully wipe it out in government networks. And despite the painstaking worm-slaying of Buckshot Yankee, "new, more potent variations of agent.btz" were still popping up in America's sensitive military computer systems. The Gobbly Worms had indeed let in, for lack of a better phrase, Even More Gobbly Worms.

At first, news reporting had called the agent.btz attack "severe and widespread." But after some time had passed, American officials realized it was *even worse* than that. It had evolved into the worst breach of US military computers in history.

In the years since, the cyberattacks have kept coming. Well-meaning people keep making dumb mistakes. Messes get made and need to be cleaned up. And as long as there are humans at the keyboard, someone (only trying to be helpful) may possibly, accidentally, open the door...and get the worm party started.

EMERGENCY ALERTS ✕

Emergency Alert
BALLISTIC MISSILE THREAT INBOUND TO HAWAII. SEEK IMMEDIATE SHELTER. THIS IS NOT A DRILL.

THE HAWAI'IAN MISSILE ALERT:

A DRILL, NOT A DRILL, NOT *NOT* A DRILL

What happened when a public alert system told the Hawai'ian Islands they were doomed?

BALLISTIC MISSILE THREAT INBOUND...

It was eight A.M. on January 13, 2018. Across the Pacific Ocean from the United States, North Korea had been testing their newly developed nuclear warheads, detonating them deep underground. The leaders of the two nations—Donald Trump and Kim Jong Un—had been spitting in each other's metaphorical faces for over two years. Global tensions were rising.

And smack-dab in the middle, looking back and forth between the White House and Pyongyang like stable hands at the OK Corral, were Hawai'i, Maui, O'ahu, Kaua'i, and the rest of the Hawai'ian Islands.

And they had reason to be terrified.

Less than two weeks earlier, on January 2, 2018, Trump taunted Kim Jong Un that the American nuclear button was *much bigger* than whatever kind of button *he had* in North Korea. In other words, the metaphorical guns they were pointing at each other had been loudly cocked.

Eleven days later...a government alert lit up every phone in Hawai'i:

BALLISTIC MISSILE THREAT INBOUND TO HAWAII. SEEK IMMEDIATE SHELTER. THIS IS NOT A DRILL.

World War III was about to begin.

Or so we thought.

NUKES ON THE BRAIN

If you're like me, you've been waiting for thermonuclear Armageddon since at *least* the eighties. And it's not (just) paranoia!

We built up a stockpile of like 30,000 nukes during the Cold War. Over time, sure, we've decommissioned missile by missile, payload by payload, but recent reports say we still have almost 4,000 warheads in bunkers, on bombers, and under the oceans on submarines. It's an arsenal more than big enough to turn the world into a smoking ball of glass at a moment's notice.

Now, based on the conversations I have with the mailman and the cashier at the grocery store, most people *don't* think about this as much as I do. But you know who does? The good people at the Hawai'i Emergency Management Agency (we'll call 'em HIEMA).

Now, usually, it's their job to keep an eye on the warning signs of a natural disaster, like, say, a tsunami. That's their mission: Detect and prevent catastrophic events that would threaten life in the Hawai'ian Islands.

So after the Pyongyang pissing contest—and especially after North Korea's underground nuke test—keeping a weather eye on the sky for incoming *nukes* had been added to the list of priorities. For the last couple of months of 2017, HIEMA dusted off a Cold War–era system…just in case—like knocking the cobwebs off a pair of ski goggles that had been hanging in the corner of the garage for a few decades. The forecast was showing a new cold front moving in. And when it comes to weathering cold wars, I join HIEMA in saying: Better safe than sorry.

Of course, the old system was just…sirens. So the team thought, *How about updating that just a scooch,* and they started testing the siren of the twenty-first century: cell phone emergency alerts.

For the first few months, the system tests went well. Alert messages were written and dispatched to a select number of phones: the staff directory of HIEMA. Press the alert button, and *bleep bloop*: Missile test warnings were blinking in front of the agency staff. Just the way they wanted them to.

Then came January 13.

EASY BAKE PAYLOAD

You thought you hated your Instagram notifications. But what if the latest social app was telling you that you're about to be incinerated in a huge ball of fire?

At 8:07, Hawai'i local time, the notification of an incoming ballistic missile reached thousands of phones on the island, plus blasting TVs with a scrolling banner. The accompanying audio message played a recording: "The US Pacific Command has detected a missile threat to Hawai'i. A missile may impact on land or sea within minutes. This is not a drill. If you are indoors, stay indoors. If you are outdoors, seek immediate shelter."

Worst voice note ever.

I mean, hell, those words send me diving under a desk, and I'm not even in Hawai'i right now! But remember, it had been *decades* since the last missile alert. This one came out of the blue.

Wherever they were, whatever they were doing, Hawai'ians and visitors alike were told that the big day was finally here: a boom so big it would wipe the slate clean. Okay, to be clear, the warning didn't say that sentence *exactly*, but everyone knew what it meant. Obviously, it sent people into a panic. Parents sent their kids down manholes to escape the blast. A state rep gathered his family in the bathtub, hoping it would hold up in a nuclear detonation. When one woman's boss told her she wasn't allowed to leave her job to *survive a nuclear blast*, she shot back: DON'T TELL ME THIS MISSILE THING IS REAL, I AM NOT DYING AT COOKIE CORNER. Yeah, I wouldn't want to be incinerated bagging fast-food cookies, either.

Well, lucky for our disgruntled cookie bagger, it turned out: This missile thing was *not* real.

Phew. Everyone, breathe a sigh of relief. After the alert went out, the good folks at HIEMA scrambled to set the story straight. Between 8:07 and 8:12, HIEMA staff started calling Hawai'ian leaders to inform them that something had gone wrong. No missile. No boom. Just a mysterious problem to solve.

Then they turned to social media: A HIEMA employee posted on his personal Facebook page at 8:13 that it was a false alarm, and other accounts followed. Hawai'ian reps in Congress and the governor of Hawai'i also started tweeting that it had been a mistake. Don't worry! Nothing to see here.

But I ask you: If, on one hand, you've got an official emergency message on your phone, saying a missile's about to put the kibosh on your pickleball game, and on the other hand you've got someone on Twitter (maybe a bot?)

saying THERE IS NO INCOMING MISSILE TO HAWAI'I...who are you going to believe?

Finally, at 8:45, a second notification went out to all phones in Hawai'i: The first alert *was* a false alarm. I can only imagine how folks in Hawai'i felt during those thirty-eight minutes between *You're gonna die* and *Oh, okay, never mind.*

I guess that's a win for the ALL CAPS Twitter brigade, but if you ask me, that's thirty-eight minutes too many. At least the only burns people got that day were from the sun...oh, and those hot, gooey chocolate chips in their cookies from Cookie Corner.

NO, NO, THE OTHER BUTTON

So what really happened?

Well, it's as stupid as it gets. It turns out, there *was* a drill scheduled for eight A.M. that morning, and it was supposed to happen just before a shift change. You remember the *bleep bloop* tests that would only ping HIEMA staff? Yeah, this was *supposed* to be that.

It turns out the computer menu screen that was used to send *both* the test alert to staff and the *real* alert to everyone...was the *same* screen. You could select one option that said "TEST MISSILE ALERT" or another one that said "MISSILE ALERT."

Guess which one got pushed.

In the weeks that followed, the HIEMA leadership decided to throw "the button pusher" under the bus—without ever sharing their name. They even told the public that it was a disgruntled employee who had done it on purpose. But don't worry, folks, the worker was fired, and it was all put to bed. Neat and tidy. That's how they wanted it.

Later, the worker gave an anonymous statement to the press saying it was an accident, and one they felt terrible about. Apparently, they were just stepping into the office for the day when the graveyard shift was closing up shop. The team that had been there all night said, *Hey, run this drill...See ya!* Our button pusher, freshly clocked in for the new shift, just kind of *went a little too fast* through the menus. Maybe the coffee was still too hot to drink and they were still a little sleepy. It's like I always say: Don't make me simulate nuclear evaporation until I've had my mocha.

Whichever story is true, the aftermath involved a *lot* of finger-pointing and blame-shifting.

What we do know is that after you press the first button, there's also a second popup window that appears, saying: *Do you confirm your choice?* And, somehow, they clicked that, too. Hard to blame them for that one, though. When was the last time you *actually* read one of those little agreements you have to accept when you install something on your computer?

Now, if you go looking, you can find a literal *minute-by-minute* rundown of who said what to whom and when exactly the governor was called on the phone, et cetera. It's not exactly a thrilling read. But it does reveal that the governor took five hours to essentially go out there and say, *Oops, sorry, folks!*

Other people were trying to keep their hands clean of the whole thing. Like the feds. They ordered a retired National Guard officer to investigate, but he said to the Hawai'ian press: "Guys, this is a *Hawai'i* problem. Keep us out of it!"

The way I see it, if it comes time to parcel out blame like a fresh, hot Cookie Corner cookie, there are crumbs to sprinkle around everywhere.

I'd like to throw some blame-crumbs at the White House and Pyongyang for telling everyone it was nuke o'clock again.

And the system designers who thought it would be a great idea to put the two buttons *right* next to each other.

And I'd like to throw a few crumbs, the smallest morsels, to the most relatable guy in the story. Just click that button, bro. What could go wrong?

THE SUEZ CANAL:

LARGEST ENEMA *EVER GIVEN*

A massive cargo ship froze the global economy when it became wedged in the Suez Canal—until the moon came to its rescue.

In the spring of 2021, an unlikely series of memes broke the internet. All of them featured the same cargo ship jamming up a waterway, photoshopped into absurd situations. In one viral image, a Spirit Halloween banner was superimposed onto the side of the barge. In another, millions of helium balloons were tied to the ship, ostensibly to carry all 200,000 tons of her into the sky. Clever as the memes were, the ship in the picture embodied a dire situation and one of the greatest blows to commercial trading in human history.

On March 23, that meme-able cargo ship became mistakenly lodged in the Suez Canal, bringing the global economy to a standstill. The culprit? Some say it was an errant gust of wind. Others claim it was a massive sandstorm—a haboob, as they're called in Arabic—which regularly drift across the desert plains of North Africa and the Arabian Peninsula where this disaster began. Or it may have been a good old-fashioned man-made fuckup, as was speculated by the head of the Suez Canal Authority, Admiral Osama Rabie, when he spoke to the world press. Of course, he kept his response tight and artificial... kind of like the Suez itself...

STUCK ON SUEZ

The sun was about to set over the Nile when the *Ever Given* entered the Gulf of Suez from the Red Sea, some 264 miles south of the entrance to the canal. The *Ever Given* meandered north to Port Tawfik, the southern entrance of the Suez Canal, where Captain Reda Ahmed was tending to the traffic through the

120-mile waterway. Reda, a serious-looking professional sailor with aviator-style glasses and a classic cadet's cap, was in charge of safely guiding ships through this narrow point of entry.

You see, when the canal was built in 1869 by the British to effectively connect the Mediterranean Sea and the Indian Ocean, it was only 25 feet deep and about 300 feet wide—but this was a *helluva* lot better than having to sail all the way around the port of Africa, as had been the custom for centuries. After several enlargements, the canal today is roughly double that size: 79 feet deep and 673 feet wide. But since the 1950s, cargo ships have *tripled* in length—today's ultra-large container vessel can be the length of four NFL football fields. So Reda's main job was to manage a team of sailors that coordinate these mammoth vessels through the canal—*single file*. Since 1973 it had been relatively smooth sailing...until that fateful day in March.

The *Ever Given* is 1,312 feet long, nearly twice as long as the canal is wide. So she could easily clog the pipes from end to end if steered even slightly off course. Thus, it was essential that her captain traverse the path in the middle of the canal with hairline precision, not too far to the left and not too far to the right. Even more daunting was the fact that there were ships in front of and behind her, sailing the same tightrope with millions of dollars of cargo at stake. Luckily, this wasn't *Ever Given*'s first rodeo. She had traversed the Suez twenty-two times before. But unfortunately for her, and for the entire maritime world, there's a first time for everything.

It was early morning by the time she reached Port Tawfik as part of a twenty-ship convoy. The turquoise water was calm, the weather serene. But suddenly, at around seven A.M., a breeze swept across the Suez. In a trice, that breeze transformed into a gale-force wind, the term sailors use to describe a gust moving faster than forty miles per hour. Satellite imagery analyzed by the BBC captured the moment when *Ever Given* steered through the port of entry as she was being blasted from the weather. She wasn't anywhere near the center line of the canal, veering dangerously close to the west bank. Moments later she drifted over to the east bank, unable to steer herself steady. Finally, in a vain attempt to glide back toward the middle, she overshot and forged ahead along the west bank for a few minutes before losing control completely. She spun out, plowed nose-first into the east bank of the canal, and buttressed her tail into the opposite bank. At a thirty-five-degree angle, *Ever Given* was hopelessly wedged from front to back, blocking all maritime traffic from passing. Around the aft, a minute amount of water passed through in a tight flow. (Not quite as tight as "Essence" by Wizkid and Tems. Now, they had flow, but I digress.) The point is: Anything bigger than a paper sailboat would never get through.

The ships trailing behind had to act fast. The *Maersk Denver*, an American cargo ship that weighed 110,000 tons (about half of *Ever Given*'s size), was plowing full steam ahead when *Ever Given* lodged herself across the canal. The *Maersk Denver* immediately threw her engines in reverse. With only minutes to spare, she was able to cast a line to land and anchor herself along the sand bank. Another ship, the *Asia Ruby III*, was mere meters away from colliding with the *Denver*—which would have hurled them both toward the stagnant *Ever Given* in a devastating crash.

But the *Maersk Denver* was not crushed in a two-ship citrus juicer that day. With the hair-raising pace of an action movie, she re-angled herself with just enough room for the *Asia Ruby III* to come to a halt. It was the most high-stakes game of bumper boats imaginable, but most importantly to the state governments involved, billions more dollars in damage were narrowly averted. They came so close that the crew of one ship could have tossed a baseball onto the deck of the other.

When the metaphoric smoke cleared, the crews on all three ships—and the fifty-eight vessels that were stalled behind them—assessed the scope of the crash. Headlines around the world were already reporting the plight of the *Ever Given*, one of the worst accidents of its kind. Though shipping-related incidents aren't uncommon around the world, a SNAFU of this literal scale and strategic location is unprecedented. The only alternative route was *all the way around Africa*, adding two weeks to their journeys. Hopefully those crews are unionized. But more daunting was the task that befell Captain Ahmed, who was now responsible for dislodging the biggest bowel obstruction of his career. And as he learned over the next week, no amount of prune juice could achieve the impossible.

OVERNIGHT FAME

"A giant container ship ran aground in the Suez Canal after losing power, at around 200,000 tonnes and over 400 meters long. 50 ships a day normally pass through the canal, carrying 12 percent of the world's trade," the BBC announced on its broadcast the morning of March 24, a day after *Ever Given* made her world debut. In the world of maritime shipping, she already had a reputation—*Ever Given* is one of the world's largest shipping containers, Japanese-owned and operated by Taiwanese transport company Evergreen Marine. She belongs in the heavyweight class of cargo ships, officially designated an "ultra-large container vessel" that regularly traverses oceans and continents. On this trip, she set sail from China bound for Rotterdam, made her way through the Singapore Strait and across the Indian Ocean, and continued east through the Arabian and Red Seas. It was through this sliver of a waterway at the port of Suez that the unwieldy giant was forced to a grinding halt. This, my friends, is why roller coasters have size requirements. Would you let Dwayne "the Rock" Johnson onto the teacup ride at Disneyland?

Aside from the goods that were on the ship itself (much of which were perishable), the monetary damage wrought by the stagnant ship was immediate. With the Suez out of commission, hundreds of boats trailing behind *Ever Given*, carrying thousands of tons of cargo to various destinations, had to be suddenly rerouted.

Every major network was fixated on the spectacle. Did this story gain traction because the situation was actually as grave as the news cycle described it, or were we all just stir-crazy and desperate for any kind of comic relief? Whatever the reason, *Ever Given* was *the it girl*, literally the moment's biggest star and protagonist of a drama of global proportions.

COSMIC SAVIOR

Meanwhile, Admiral Osama Rabie and Captain Reda Ahmed were assembling a rescue team. And like the construction of the canal itself, the dislodging was a multinational effort. The Dutch maritime company Boskalis lent their high-powered tugboats to assist the Egyptians, and helped calculate the angles and pressure needed for *Ever Given's* big push. Their first course of action was deceptively simple, but ultimately naive. Thirteen tugboats—as small as mice at the feet of an elephant—attempted to push into the bow and stern of the *Ever Given* to wedge her out of the sand. She wouldn't budge. Their next course of action was to remove the sand along the banks of the canal. An arsenal of bulldozers was deployed, slowly hacking away at the embankment until the container ship could break free.

Over the next two days, it was all hands on deck. The team worked tirelessly at this process of "digging and sucking" the sand away. Workers armed with bulldozers started to work the canal on land while a team of seafarers operated a special Dutch-made "cutter suction dredger" in the water. Named the *Masshour*, this special dredging ship had an extended propeller of blades attached to its bow that ground the sediment at the bottom of a riverbed. As the mud was released into the water, a tube next to the blades sucked sediment through a long pipe that expelled the sand, gravel, and rocks onto land. Think of it like an electric whisk breaking up the dry ingredients as they settled at the bottom of the world's nastiest brownie batter.

Not only was the work dangerous, but the ol' dig and suck was painfully slow. Every hour, millions of dollars were lost. The companies whose cargo was on the *Ever Given* were not the only parties affected. The hundreds of ships stuck in congestion, or forced to completely reroute, were expected in ports all around the world. And while the final destination of the *Ever Given* may have been the port of Rotterdam, hundreds of smaller ships were expected to receive the many tons of cargo to be taken elsewhere throughout Europe. In a hyper-globalized world, no matter where you are, it seems that everything comes from somewhere else. Think of it like a string of cheap Christmas lights. If one bulb burns out, the whole tree goes dark. The desert heat paled in comparison to the pressure of the job: The weight of the world economy was literally on their shoulders.

In an interview for the BBC's documentary *Why Ships Crash*, a digger described his fear as he excavated the sandy embankment where *Ever Given*'s bow was lodged several meters deep. "When we arrived, the ship was gigantic and we had to work under it," said Abdullah Abdul-Gawal, a member of the first team of diggers. "Anyone would be afraid." He was afraid that if they were indeed successful in dredging *Ever Given* out of the sand, she would immediately capsize and crush them. Lucky for Abdullah—but to the misfortune of the world economy—they failed. But tragedy did ensue later that night, when a rescue ship capsized alongside the *Ever Given*. One crewmember lost their life, and the circumstances of the death remain murky.

As the work dragged on, Rabie and Ahmed hatched a plan to leverage a cosmic alignment. Like the ancient Egyptians, whose architecture and infrastructure were designed in response to astronomical patterns, the SCA team clocked that at the end of the month the power of a supermoon would be at their disposal—high tide was going to hit at noon and raise the level of the canal. The moon's gravitational pull would outperform any man-made device, no matter how advanced. Until then, they carried on dredging and pushing with tugboats—sort of like loosening the lid on the pickle jar until someone stronger can open it.

Six days into the disaster on March 29, freedom finally seemed possible. With the full moon high in the sky, Dutch, Egyptian, and Japanese tugboats sailed in formation. After hours of tugboats pushing *Ever Given* from one end, and pulling her from the other, she budged an inch. An inch became a meter. Then as night faded to day, her stern finally broke free of her sandy shackles.

The workers hugged, cheered, and proclaimed *Allahu Akbar* from the east and west banks. Crew members aboard other vessels in the canal sang and danced for their phone cameras, blaring their fog h;orns in jubilation. By four P.M. that afternoon, the full ship was floating free in the canal.

The Egyptian president Abdel Fattah el-Sisi hailed the success of the SCA as a nationalist achievement. The waters of the Red and the Mediterranean Seas flowed into each other once more.

EVER AFTER

The accident had a massive ripple effect. On the day *Ever Given* was dislodged, there were already 367 ships in waiting, and the European ports soon flooded with congestion as all of these vessels arrived at their destinations simultaneously. News media covered the imbroglio religiously, and millions of people first learned the baffling mechanics of standard supply chains. Like many of my fellow Americans, I finally learned the true significance of that one skinny link in the chain that ran through Egypt.

Ever Given's legal battle was about to be a veritable multinational shit show. Yes, the initial release was immediately followed by a literal flood of relief, but she was hardly out of hot water. Once she was refloated, she was taken to an Egyptian court (not physically, of course), where a judge ruled in favor of the SCA to impound her and set the bail at a whopping *$916 million*. In response, UK Club—one of the ship's insurers—called bullshit. "The SCA has not provided a detailed justification for this extraordinarily large claim, which includes a $300 million claim for a 'salvage bonus' and a $300 million claim for 'loss of reputation,'" they said in response. Thus began a drawn-out negotiation, where the warring parties haggled with each other to the tune of hundreds of millions.

What made the case even *more* convoluted was that the defendants comprised the Japanese proprietors, the Taiwanese tenants of the defendants ship with German managers, and the English insurers employing an Indian crew of seafarers (who were legally bound to the ship while she was impounded, essentially rendering them temporarily stateless). And, all the while, the company was registered in Panama, in Egyptian jurisdiction. On top of that, businesses in Europe who were expecting the deliveries of expensive inventory simply had to foot the bill while the case dragged on.

To make matters more complicated, the crew onboard was as global a hodgepodge as the ship's stakeholders: The captain was from India, and his crew were Indians, but when a ship passes through the Suez Canal, a different team of Egyptian "pilots" climbs onboard to momentarily guide the ship through the waterway. For this brief period of time, the captain is no longer in complete control.

On the day of *Ever Given's* crash, the Arabic-speaking pilots had a brief conversation with the Tamil-speaking captain in *English* (thanks but no thanks, Brits!) about whether they should enter the canal at all given the weather. But ultimately the economic cost of waiting would be too great...or so they thought.

It took more than 100 days after the crash for the negotiating parties to reach an agreement about who was to blame. Was it the captain, the Canal Authority, or the weather? As of June 2021, the Suez Canal Authority reduced their demand to $550 million, to which the boat's insurers agreed. (At the time, none of the subject parties disclosed the details of this agreement.) When the *Ever Given* was finally released from her imprisonment, she set sail through the Suez once again. Everyone held their breath. This time she made it through as she had countless times before. Then she sailed across the warm waters of the Mediterranean toward the North Atlantic and, on July 29, arrived safe and sound in Rotterdam. Only a few months late! By the time *Ever Given* finally completed her journey, the world had largely forgotten the fate of the colossus they meme-ified. All in all, she'd broken the Suez Canal, the world's flow of goods, and, surprisingly, the internet.

TOP FIVE...

NEAR EXTINCTIONS IN THE NEW MILLENNIUM

Endangered species have become more prevalent for peculiar reasons, thanks to some hapless human hubris in the twenty-first century.

You may have noticed that we're not alone on this planet. No, I'm not talking about conspiracies over lizard-skinned extraterrestrials. I'm talking about all of our planetary buddies in the animal kingdom: vertebrates (the phylum Chordata) and invertebrates (phyla Porifera, Cnidaria, Platyhelmintes, Nematoda, Annelida, Mollusca, Arthropoda, and Echinodermata). WHEW! Say those five times fast). Unfortunately, our widespread industrialization and domination over land and sea have wreaked havoc on the homes of plenty of our furry, feathered, and yes, lizard-skinned friends (again, talking *reptiles* here).

When you look at the numbers, the degree of biodiversity loss is mind-boggling. Experts at the International Union for Conservation of Nature indicate that the accelerating loss we're witnessing today is 1,000 to 10,000 times higher than the normal background extinction rate, which is the rate that extinctions would occur if we humanoids weren't around. So if we're coexisting with roughly 2 million species (and I'm lowballing it here), that means we're losing an estimated 200 to 2,000 different species *per year*. Even the lowball numbers are depressingly wild!

Some of the most bizarre twists in our entanglement with critters around the world lie in our own self-centered practices and antics. Deforestation plays a large part, though it's not the only culprit. I've tallied our top five wackiest pomposities below.

5. THAT AXOLOTL GLOW

This little guy is like a cross between a salamander and a luck dragon (Falkor, my man!). They exist in the wild in only one area of Mexico, Lake Xochimilco. They once roamed much farther in the Mexico Valley, but dwindled thanks to poor wastewater management and the pet market. They've been bred to highlight a distinct protein that makes them "glow" under fluorescent lights, turning them into domestic designer pets. It would seem, though, that life finds a way. While a minuscule *fifty or fewer* are estimated to remain in the wild, they are at least thriving in their newfound homes, with more than 1 million in captivity. To quote Michael Ende, the author of *The Neverending Story*, "Nothing is lost, everything is transformed."

4. CLAWS OF THE COCONUT CRAB

These hefty fellas are kind of like hermit crabs, only they can grow up to nine pounds and nearly three feet around. (That's one clunker of a crustacean!) And they are notorious for stealing locals' silverware and other trinkets, only to run off with them into their sandy hideaways. Despite their mischievous ways, that's not why they're a threatened species. Near their native home of the Philippines and around the Indo-Pacific Ocean, they're considered a delicacy and, thus, overharvested both as a local food source and for the tourist trade. Luckily, plans are in place to protect those precious pincers.

3. DON'T LOOK HIM IN THE AYE-AYE

Endemic to Madagascar, the aye-aye is a nocturnal mammal who thrives under the cover of darkness. With bulging eyes, razor-sharp teeth, bat-like ears and a middle finger that would make Johnny Cash jealous, the aye-aye is one badass primate. And one can only imagine how startling it might be to come across those protuberant peepers in the middle of the night. Their endangerment stems from the superstitious fright we humans bestowed upon the creature. They were once feared as harbingers of evil, sickness, or even death if you stumbled across them. It was even colloquially referred to as "heh heh" so as not to speak a proper name unto the beast. Sadly, as tradition would have it, the creature was killed on the spot. But conservation efforts are remedying those misconceptions, and our lemur-like pal is making its way back, with numbers ranging from 1,000 to 10,000 today.

2. LITTLE SOLDIER OF ARARIPE

The araripe manakin bird, nicknamed in Portuguese as "soldadinho-do-araripe" is the shortest-lived specimen on our list. Like Tiger Woods, it only burst onto the scene in 1996. First discovered in a very limited habitat in Brazil, it was named for the bright red helmet-like crown on its noggin. Local legend told of a story about a redheaded bird that was the "o dono do agua," or "owner of the waters," and if this waterbird were ever injured, the waters would cease to flow. As we can't have nice things and rarely heed the warnings of our ancestors, we humans have since destroyed the araripe's home by developing roads, piping its springs, and building a theme park with waterslides, pushing it toward critical extinction. But fairy tales should end happily. So in 2014 (and again in 2018), an alliance of conservation groups purchased hundreds of acres to add to the local reserve and establish safe breeding grounds.

*Honorable Mention:

Before our number one creature is revealed, there is one bonus beastie that I want to share. He unfortunately is one that involves standard human habitat infiltration, but he also speeds up his own demise in a precarious fashion.

• **Bonus: Sex Drive of the Silver-headed Antechinus**—This Australian bloke has the looks of a tiny desert mouse, but in fact is an insect-eating marsupial. He's cute, but when mating season strikes in the looming spring of August, he becomes a sex-starved monster. For two to three weeks, the antechinus fornicates with as many females as *marsupially* possible. He sexes so hard; his body is literally disintegrating when he's done. (Now that's what I call a hero's death.) He metabolizes his own muscles, his fur falls out, his immune system shuts down, and gangrene sets in. The official term for this is semelparity, meaning a single reproductive episode before death. It stems from the Latin phrase "to beget once." Why does the little antechinus partake in such suicidal sex matters? Like I said, he's a hero—evolutionarily speaking, of course. Because they are marsupial, the young born from this August mayhem must rely on the mother for months on end, as opposed to other species that practice semelparity, whose young require sustenance for only a few days or weeks. Thus, the male, selfless in his lovemaking, is also selfless in death, sacrificing himself to ensure adequate food supplies during the peak season harvest for the next generation.

And now, for our top folly of humankind versus mother nature...

1. THE UNFORTUNATE NAZI NOMENCLATURE OF THE HITLERI BEETLE

In an attempt to collect as much classic Nazi memorabilia as possible, neo-Nazis have been hoarding the *Anophthalmus Hitleri* beetle to the point of near extinction. The reason? Simply because it was named for Adolf Hitler in 1933. The beetle itself is small, its exoskeleton is reddish orange in color, and it lacks any form of toothbrush mustache (which is perhaps for the best). It is blind as well. *Anophthalmus* means "without eyes," and *Hitleri*, well, that was pinned to the insect by an amateur entomologist, who was totally obsessed with both beetles *and* Nazism. In recent years, the Bavarian State Collection

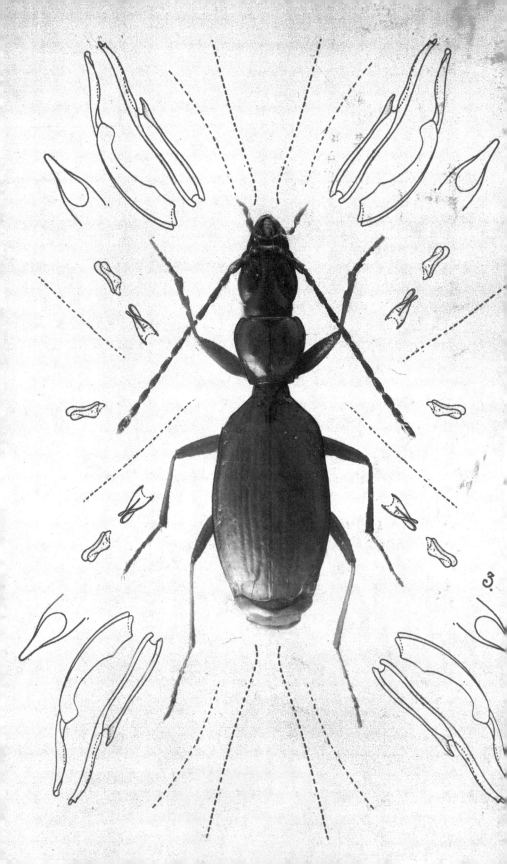

of Zoology located in Munich has stated that numerous specimens have even been stolen from their collection. Each beetle's worth is estimated around $1,200 on the black market. It is found only in roughly fifteen different caves in Slovenia, and scientists nowadays are thankfully pushing for the poor innocent insect to be renamed.

So what's the answer here? It's obvious we're in a bit of a pickle. All species play an important role in the web of life and if certain strands start fading away, all we'll be left with is a dangling thread of despair. We count on these creatures for a lot more than ostentatious mating rituals in a David Attenborough doc. (Imagine his color commentary for the antechinus.) Food security, traditional and modern medicines, even clearing carbon from our atmosphere: all modern human necessities these animals help support via our collective ecosystem.

And if these SNAFUs showcase anything, it's the sliver of a silver lining. I could go all Jeff Goldblum in *Jurassic Park* here, but what I'm trying to say is that life can certainly thrive as long as we humans are attentive and collectively champion a reasonable path forward. Let's chart a path filled with hope for our future, and theirs (so the aye-aye will finally stop giving us the finger).

Cutting back on illegal logging would be a great start. And next time you need to name a newly discovered wasp, maybe aim for cherished actors and musicians over vile dictators. The *Aleiodes Helmsi* has a nice ring to it.

ACKNOWLEDGMENTS

This book would have been an actual SNAFU of epic proportions without an incredible team effort from many creative, dedicated, funny, and smart people.

To Colin Dickerman at Grand Central Publishing—thanks for "getting it" from our first meeting. I hope to do many more of these together. (Please keep an eye out for our next submission, *SNAFU: Medieval Times*.) Ian Dorset, thank you for your close reads of each and every chapter, as well as fielding many frantic emails from our team at all hours. Thanks to our all-star design team: Albert Tang, Paul Kepple, and Mark Harris. You somehow found the perfect balance of tone. Bravo! Infinite gratitude to marketing and publicity wizards Tiffany Porcelli and Jimmy Franco. Our copy was accurate and clean and punctual, thanks to Carolyn Kurek and Rebecca Holland. I appreciate your patience and diligence so very much. To anyone else who touched the book at Grand Central/Hachette, especially the sales team: our infinite gratitude for believing in it with blind optimism.

Gigantic thank-you to my UK publisher, Headline, particularly editor Phillip Connor and publicist Joe Thomas, for helping *SNAFU* take the UK by storm.

Thanks to our literary agent, Eric Lupfer at UTA, for advising and hand-holding a bunch of film/TV/podcast people throughout the publishing process. It's been truly invaluable to have you on our side. Much gratitude to our UK agents Alexander Cochran and Richard Pike at C&W. And a big thanks to my entire fantastic team at UTA: Jason Heyman, Martin Lesak, Greg Cavic, Gregory McKnight, Nick Nuciforo, Sam Stone, Logan Eisenberg, Luke Murphy, Lauren Hochhauser, and Geoff Suddleson. And of course all of their assistants who, let's be honest, do A LOT of heavy lifting.

Thank you to Gilded Audio, the amazing production studio behind *SNAFU*. Huge thanks to Carl Nellis, who oversaw this book from end to end with sharp editorial insight and thousands of obscure, historical references. Much gratitude to Mark Van Hare for keeping us on a very long, winding track. And, of course, to Whitney Donaldson for her kind and thoughtful partnership in all things *SNAFU*.

This book wouldn't exist without the extraordinary dedication of an incredible group of researchers and writers who poured their time, talent, and energy into making it come alive. From hunting down the funniest factoids, the most colorful characters, and the craziest screwups of the past seventy years, you've all worked relentlessly to make this book a reality. Your hard work and passion are woven into every page, and you should feel a deep sense of ownership and pride in what we've created together. A heartfelt thank-you to Kelsey Albright, James Boo, Olivia Canny, Kyra Castelli-Foley, Ekemini Ekpo, Cecile Garcia, Nevin Kallepalli, Michelle Muto, Carl Nellis, Tim Rohan, Sam Skarstad, Tory Smith, Nicki Stein, Boen Wang, Stephen

Wood, and Sarah Wyman. This book is as much yours as it is mine!

Thank you Charles Richter, our astute fact-checker. You allow me to sleep peacefully at night. Special thanks to Matt Gossen, whose stellar designs for the original *SNAFU* podcast and book pitches, as well as the book cover, were integral. Thank you to the fine folks at The Collected Works, for their design partnership and making SNAFU Media look so freakin' cool!

A shout-out to the core team of producers, writers, and editors who were crucial to the *SNAFU* podcast over three seasons. Without our dear show, and you all, there would, in fact, be no book (a travesty!). Epic thanks to Sara Joyner, Stephen Wood, Carl Nellis, Albert Chen, Ben Chugg, Nicki Stein, Nick Dooley, and Andrew Chugg. I love working with you all!

To my phenomenal colleagues at the Pacific Electric Picture Co.—you guys are amazing. First, to my partner in crime, Mike Falbo—the human equivalent of a triple-shot espresso—your boundless energy, legendary work ethic, and ability to challenge us to aim higher (without making us feel like slackers) keep this ship sailing at full tilt. You are the heart, soul, and snappiest dresser of Pacific Electric, and we all know it. To Brett Harris, Ami Saad, and Liam Oznowich, the unsung heroes of our operation: Brett, your sharp insights and tireless hustle make every project better. Ami, you're the wizard behind the curtain, ensuring the gears of this company hum efficiently. And Liam—my assistant, my brain, and, let's face it, my emotional support human—you take my chaos and turn it into something almost coherent. Without

you, I'd accomplish 10 percent of what I do, and the world would be a much messier place. Thanks, gang, for being not just brilliant and dedicated creative partners, but also dear friends.

A massive thank-you to the dream team at FilmNation Entertainment—Milan Popelka, Alyssa Martino, and Tory Smith—my amazing collaborators who have been truly instrumental in the entire journey of *SNAFU*, from the seed of an idea, to a hit podcast and now a book, and whatever else we cook up. Milan, your high-altitude insights are like our North Star, keeping us on course with vision, clarity, and a fabulous dry wit. Alyssa, you are a cat-herder extraordinaire, wrangling schedules, details, and occasionally my wandering focus with an impossible mix of grace and grit—honestly, I sometimes think you are part Jedi. Tory, you're the sly quip machine, mixing sharp insight with much-needed humor on those long, brutal recording sessions and Zoom calls. You're all relentlessly hardworking, wildly creative, and just ridiculously delightful to work with. None of this would be happening without you. THANK YOU!

Additional thanks to the rest of the FilmNation team for working on our first-ever book together. I'm so grateful for the foundational support from Glen Basner, Alison Cohen, Andy Kim, Bob Peck, Ben Ryzak, Daniel Welsh, Caroline Johnson, and Megan Hallson. And a huge TYSM (as the Gen Z say...) to the many iterations of FilmNation podcast interns who helped us on a yearlong treasure hunt for SNAFUs.

SNAFU also would not have been possible without our wonderful partners at iHeartPodcasts, who heard a Zoom pitch for a comedic history series and immediately said, "Oh, hell yes!" Huge thanks to Will Pearson, Carrie Lieberman, Conal Byrne, Nikki Ettore, Nathan Otoski, Dylan Fagan, Alex Koral, Jenn Powers, and everyone else over there for helping make each season a hit. I'm so grateful for your continued partnership and belief in our team's storytelling.

To my incredible legal team—Ira Schreck, Isaac Dunham, Adam Horne, Lorien Kirkup, and Liza Montesano—thank you for your unmatched acumen in entertainment and publishing law, your professionalism, and your collaborative spirit. You are true masters of the minutiae, always a step ahead, and forever ensuring I'm protected from the circling vultures of showbiz. Knowing you have my back gives me the freedom to focus on the fun stuff, and for that, I am endlessly grateful!

To Matt Haberman and Liz Mahoney, my brilliant publicists at Narrative PR: You are true wizards of media and messaging, guiding me through the insane, and occasionally terrifying maze of pop culture with grace and confidence. And you do it all with style and good humor. I am so grateful to have you in my corner!

A quick shout-out to all the history teachers out there who sparked my love for the subject and continue to inspire younger generations with the wild wonders and powerful lessons of our shared human story. You dedicate your lives to unpacking the beautiful, tragic, hilarious, and heartbreaking tapestry of history, and the world is so much better for it. Teaching is hard work, and you are appreciated!

To my amazing wife, Sarah, and our two exquisite daughters: Sarah, you are a saint of patience and grace, tolerating my creative chaos and somehow finding the heroic strength to laugh at my relentless jokes and ideas. Your unconditional love and support are the fuel for everything I do, and somehow you also hold me to the highest standards with grace and compassion. You, and our two amazing girls, inspire me every day to be a better dad, a better husband, a better artist, a better collaborator, and just a better human all around. You three are my heart, my joy, and my absolute everything, and I'm forever grateful to you!

And finally—because we love to save the best for last—I want to sincerely thank our *SNAFU* fans. To everyone who preordered or gifted this book, downloaded the podcast, left a rating or review (we're looking at you, Pounding Beers McSlammington!), or told their weird history-loving uncle to check it out, I'm honored you've given me your ears, and, now, your eyes, in a world that demands so much attention on every front. I hope to continue to live up to the great challenge of teaching and entertaining you with these massively f*cked-up moments from history. But I also hope that maybe one day, the world will have a lot fewer SNAFUs to put in my podcasts and books. Sadly, we have not yet reached that day...but fortunately for me and you, that means there's much more to come for *SNAFU*, so stay tuned.

SOURCE NOTES

ATOMIC ENERGY LAB

"Gilbert U-238 Atomic Energy Lab," Museum of Radiation and Radioactivity, ORAU, https://orau.org/health-physics-museum/collection/toys/gilbert-u-238-atomic-energy-lab.html.

"Atomic Advertising in the 20th and 21st centuries," National Museum of Nuclear Science and History, https://www.nuclearmuseum.org/virtual/vex1/D161482C-D525-4CE7-814E-955192691390.htm.

"The Spinthariscope and the Smithsonian," Smithsonian Institution Archives, accessed April 4, 2024, https://siarchives.si.edu/blog/spinthariscope-and-smithsonian.

"Gilbert Mysto Magic Sets," A. C. Gilbert Heritage Society, https://www.acghs.org/?page_id=4488.

"About A.C. Gilbert," Gilbert House and Children's Museum, accessed April 4, 2024, https://acgilbert.org/about-a-c-gilbert/.

Bruce Watson, *The Man Who Changed How Boys and Toys Were Made* (Viking, 2002), 21–22.

Ellen Tyrell, Library of Congress Blogs, "A.C. Gilbert's Successful Quest to Save Christmas," accessed April 4, 2024, https://blogs.loc.gov/inside_adams/2016/12/a-c-gilberts-successful-quest-to-save-christmas/.

"'I Am Become Death' Comes to Tularosa Basin: The Trinity Test 74 Years Later," International Campaign to Abolish Nuclear Weapons (ICAN), July 16, 2019, https://www.icanw.org/_i_am_become_death_comes_to_tularosa_basin_the_trinity_test_74_years_later.

Alison Marsh, "Fun—And Uranium—for the Whole Family in This 1950s Science Kit," IEEE Spectrum, accessed April 4, 2024, https://spectrum.ieee.org/fun-and-uranium-for-the-whole-family-in-this-1950s-science-kit.

"The Gilbert Patents," Eli Whitney Museum and Workshop, accessed April 4, 2024, https://eliwhitney.org/museum/-gilbert-project/-collections/patents.

Jan Howard, "A.C. Gilbert—An Inventive Connecticut Yankee Made Learning Child's Play," *Newtown Bee*, March 14, 2001, https://www.newtownbee.com/03142001/a-c-gilbert-an-inventive-connecticut-yankee-made-learning-childs-play/.

THE CHOSIN FEW

"CEO RECEIVES AWARD FOR TO...," Marine Corps Recruiting Command, photo by Sgt. Alfredo Ferrer, September 9, 2016, https://www.mcrc.marines.mil/In-the-News/Photos/igphoto/2001628722/.

Associated Press, "MacArthur Fired by Truman in Sensational Late Hours Statement; Ridgeway Named as Successor," *Daily World*, April 11, 1951, https://www.newspapers.com/image/950291812/.

"'Chosin Few Memorial' Honors Korean War Survivors," NBC 5 Dallas-Fort Worth, July 27, 2022, https://www.nbcdfw.com/news/local/something-good/chosin-few-memorial-stands-tall-at-dfw-national-cemetery-honoring-korean-war-veterans/3032861/#:~:text=The%20Dallas%2DFort%20Worth%20National%20Cemetery%20is%20now%20home%20to,fought%20in%20the%20Korean%20War.

"Code Name 'Tootsie Rolls': Soldier Candy Rations: Iowans in Korea," PBS LearningMedia, August 25, 2023, https://illinois.pbslearningmedia.org/resource/code-name-tootsie-rolls-soldier-candy-rations-vide/the-forgotten-war-iowans-in-korea/.

Don Dare, "'Tootsie Roll Drop: How a Codeword Mix-up Led to Marines Getting a Sweet Treat," WATE 6 On Your Side, December 29, 2023, https://www.wate.com/news/veterans-voices/tootsie-rolls-honors-korean-war-marines-after-ammunition-mix-up/.

Jim Wilson, *Retreat, Hell! We're Just Attacking in Another Direction* (William Morrow, 1988).

Gail B. Shisler, *For Country and Corps: The Life of General Oliver P. Smith* (Naval Institute Press, 2009).

The Battle of Chosin, directed by Randall MacLowry. (Boston, MA: WGBH Educational Foundation, 2016), Amazon Video, https://www.pbs.org/wgbh/americanexperience/films/chosin/.

JIMMY CARTER'S NUCLEAR NUTS

Jonathan Alter, *His Very Best: Jimmy Carter, a Life*, first Simon & Schuster hardcover edition (Simon & Schuster, 2020).

Peter G. Bourne, *Jimmy Carter: A Comprehensive Biography from Plains to Post-Presidency* (Scribner, 1997).

Brief History of: The NRX Reactor Accident, YouTube, accessed March 28, 2024, https://www.youtube.com/watch?v=ntbYi9n2-O0.

Jimmy Carter, *A Full Life: Reflections at Ninety*, first Simon & Schuster hardcover edition (Simon & Schuster, 2015).

Jimmy Carter, *Why Not The Best?: Why One Man Is Optimistic About America's Third Century*, first edition (Broadman Press, 1975).

Chris Cox, "U.S. National Security and Military/Commercial Concerns with the People's Republic of China," Congressional Report, 105th Congress, 2nd Session. Vol. 1, U.S Government Printing Office, Washington DC, 1999, https://www.congress.gov/105/crpt/hrpt851/CRPT-105hrpt851.pdf.

William G. Cross, "The Chalk River Accident in 1952," in *Symposium on "Historical Perspective on Reactor Accidents,"* Seattle, Washington, 1980.

"Before He Was President, Jimmy Carter Saved Nuclear Reactor After Meltdown," FOX 5 Atlanta, February 23, 2023, https://www.fox5atlanta.com/news/jimmy-carter-nuclear-meltdown-clean-up-canada-navy-history.

"Inaugural Addresses of the Presidents of the United States: From George Washington 1789 to George Bush 1989," Avalon Project, Lillian Goldman Law Library, Yale University, accessed March 15, 2024, https://avalon.law.yale.edu/20th_century/carter.asp.

Jimmy Carter: Rock and Roll President, documentary, music, Greenwich Entertainment, 2020.

W. B. Lewis, "The Accident to the NRX Reactor on December 12, 1952," Atomic Energy of Canada Ltd. Chalk River Project, Chalk River, Ontario (Canada), July 13, 1953, https://www.osti.gov/biblio/4379334.

James A. Mahaffey, *Atomic Accidents: A History of Nuclear Meltdowns and Disasters: From the Ozark Mountains to Fukushima*, first Pegasus Books edition (Pegasus Books, 2014).

Arthur Milnes, "When Jimmy Carter Faced Radioactivity Head-on," *Ottawa Citizen*, January 28, 2009, https://web.archive.org/web/20110217161647/http://ottawariverkeeper.ca/news/when_jimmy_carter_faced_radioactivity_head_on.

"Reactor Accidents: The Human Fallout," Canadian Coalition for Nuclear Responsibility, accessed March 15, 2024, https://www.ccnr.org/paulson_legacy.html.

MKULTRA

John Jacobs and Bill Richards, "The Bizarre Tale of a CIA Operation," *Washington Post*, August 26, 1977, via CIA, https://www.cia.gov/readingroom/docs/CIA-RDP90-01208R000100210006-4.pdf.

John Marks, *Manchurian Candidate"* (Allen Lane, 1979), first published in the USA by Times Books and in Canada by Fitzhenry & Whiteside Ltd., https://www.cia.gov/library/abbottabad-compound/12/129E144131F2E093FB1E441C737ACF92_SearchForTheManchurianCandidate.rtf.pdf.

"Operation Midnight Climax: How the CIA Dosed S.F. Citizens with LSD," *SF Weekly*, March 4, 2012, https://www.sfweekly.com/archives/operation-midnight-climax-how-the-cia-dosed-s-f-citizens-with-lsd/article_6f361f04-2146-5321-9a82-69c7091c5d30.html.

John Crewdson, "Abuses in Testing of Drugs by C.I.A. to Be Panel Focus," *New York Times*, September 20, 1977, https://www.nytimes.com/1977/09/20/archives/abuses-in-testing-of-drugs-by-cia-to-be-panel-focus-senate-panel-to.html.

US Congress, Senate Select Committee on Intelligence, *Project MKULTRA, the CIA's Program of Research in Behavioural Modification*, 95th Congress, 1st session, 1977, https://www.intelligence.senate.gov/sites/default/files/hearings/95mkultra.pdf.

Stephen Kinzer, *Poisoner in Chief: Sidney Gottlieb and the CIA Search for Mind Control* (Henry Holt, 2019).

"A precursor of the MK-ULTRA program began in 1945 when the Joint Intelligence Objectives Agency was established and given direct responsibility for Operation Paperclip...purpose was to study mind-control, interrogation, behavior modification and related," https://www.cia.gov/readingroom/document/06760269.

"Project MKULTRA," CIA FOIA (foia.cia.gov), https://www.cia.gov/readingroom/document/06760269.

Allen W. Dulles, "Brain Warfare—Russia's Secret Weapon," *US News & World Report*, May 1953, https://www.cia.gov/readingroom/docs/CIA-RDP70-00058R000100010023-4.pdf.

Allen W. Dulles, "Brain Warfare," Summary of Remarks at the National Alumni Conference, Princeton University, 10 April 1953," https://www.cia.gov/readingroom/docs/CIA-RDP80R01731R001700030015-9.pdf.

Joshua Fried, "What a Trip," *Stanford Magazine*, January/February 2022, https://stanfordmag.org/contents/what-a-trip.

Kali Holloway, "The Secret Black History of LSD," *Nation*, March 22, 2022, https://www.thenation.com/article/society/lsd-acid-black-history/.

Paul Magnusson, "Patients Stood in for Spies in Tests," *Detroit Free Press*, August 28, 1977, https://www.cia.gov/readingroom/docs/CIA-RDP88-01315R00040046 0007-4.pdf.

Michael Rezendes, "After Learning of Whitey Bulger LSD Tests, Juror Has Regrets," AP News, February 22, 2020, https://apnews.com/article/us-news-ap-top-news-whitey-bulger-crime-weekend-reads-8dff185e1324cb7079b8a86c48c2ec56.

Howie Carr, "Bulger's LSD Diaries Reveal Ravings of a… Psychedelic Head Case," Opinion, *Boston Herald*, July 10, 2011, https://www.bostonherald.com/2011/07/10/bulgers-lsd-diaries-reveal-ravings-of-a-psychedelic-head-case/.

James Bulger, "Whitey Bulger: I Was a Guinea Pig for CIA Drug Experiments," *OZY*, May 9, 2017, https://web.archive.org/web/20181030231252/https://www.ozy.com/true-story/whitey-bulger-i-was-a-guinea-pig-for-cia-drug-experiments/76409.

MARS BLUFF BOMB

Department of Defense, *Narrative Summaries of Accidents Involving U.S. Nuclear Weapons 1950–1980*, accessed March 12, 2024, https://nsarchive.files.wordpress.com/2010/04/635.pdf.

Luke Dittrich, "A Perfectly Understandable Mistake," *Esquire*, May 1, 2005, https://web.archive.org/web/20120414031117/http://www.esquire.com/features/ESQ0505BOMB_122.

David Klepper, "Man Recalls Day a Nuclear Bomb Fell on His Yard," *Sun News*, November 24, 2003, https://rense.com/general45/Manrec.htm.

Cyriaque Lamar, "An Interview with a Woman Who Survived the 1958 Atomic Bombing of South Carolina," Gizmodo, May 8, 2012, https://gizmodo.com/an-interview-with-a-woman-who-survived-the-1958-atomic-5908493.

Bo Petersen, "The Atomic Bomb That Faded into South Carolina History," *Army Times*, August 19, 2022, https://www.armytimes.com/news/2018/03/31/the-atomic-bomb-that-faded-into-south-carolina-history/.

Clark Rumrill, "'Aircraft 53-1876A Has Lost a Device,'" *American Heritage*, September 2000, https://www.americanheritage.com/aircraft-53-1876a-has-lost-device.

"Armed Forces: Mars Bluff," *Time*, March 24, 1958, https://content.time.com/time/subscriber/article/0,33009,868306-1,00.html.

Carlton Truax, "Review of the Day an A-Bomb Fell near a S.C. City," *State Sun*, January 29, 1961.

UPI, "London Is Angry, Jittery After U.S. A-Bomb Mishap," *Cincinnati Enquirer*, March 13, 1958.

UPI, "Reds Propagandize A-Mishap," *Cincinnati Enquirer*, March 13, 1958.

UPI, "Review of A-Bomb Is Blown to Bits in Drop, Searchers Learn," *Cincinnati Enquirer*, March 13, 1958.

UPI, "Shut Area Clawed by Tame A-Bomb," *Daily News*, March 12, 1958.

A119

Mark Piesing, "The Crazy Plan to Explode a Nuclear Bomb on the Moon," *BBC*, May 2023, https://www.bbc.com/future/article/20230505-the-crazy-plan-to-explode-a-nuclear-bomb-on-the-moon.

Riddle, Lincoln, "Nukes on the Moon: The A119 Cold War Project," *War History Online*, December 7, 2017, https://www.warhistoryonline.com/instant-articles/nukes-moon-a119-cold-war.html.

Vince Houghton, "Why the Air Force Almost Blasted the Moon with an H-Bomb," *History*, July 19, 2019, https://www.history.com/news/nuclear-bomb-moon-cold-war-plan.

Christopher Klein, "How Lewis Strauss Shaped the Atomic Age—and Orchestrated Robert Oppenheimer's Downfall," *History*, July 26, 2023 https://www.history.com/news/lewis-strauss-nuclear-program-oppenheimer#.

PROJECT ICEWORM

International Union of Geodesy and Geophysics. *IUGG Electronic Journal*, vol. 24, no. 1, December 2023, https://iugg.org/wp-content/uploads/2023/12/IUGGej2401.pdf.

Henry Nielsen and Kristian Hvidtfeldt Nielsen, *Camp Century* (Columbia University Press, 2021).

"Nuclear City Buried Under Ice Featured," *Bradenton Herald*, January 13, 1961, p. 5, https://www.newspapers.com/image/717041905/?clipping_id=147296409.

The U.S. Army's Top Secret Arctic City under the Ice! "Camp Century" Restored Classified Film. n.d., www.youtube.com, accessed March 22, 2024.

Walter Wager, *Camp Century: City Under the Ice* (Chilton Books, 1962).

Kent Goering, "Eagle Under the Ice," *Boys' Life*, March 1961.

Christian Wenande, "In the Name of the King or Traitor to the Crown?" *Copenhagen Post*, March 5, 2018, https://cphpost.dk/2018-03-05/business-education/in-the-name-of-the-king-or-traitor-to-the-crown/.

Philip Ewing, "FACT CHECK: Did Harry Truman Really Try to Buy Greenland Back in the Day?" NPR, August 22, 2019, https://www.npr.org/2019/08/22/753192368/fact-check-did-harry-truman-really-try-to-buy-greenland-back-in-the-day.

Nikolaj Petersen, "Negotiations on Greenland: Denmark and the United States in 1946–47," *Scandinavian Political Studies*, 1975, https://tidsskrift.dk/scandinavian_political_studies/article/view/32916/31281#:~:text=The%20negotiations%20started%20in%20Copenhagen,concerning%20the%20Defense%20of%20Greenland.

North Atlantic Treaty Organization, "Letter from Marshal Bulganin to the Danish Prime Minister," NATO Archives, March 28, 1957, https://archives.nato.int/uploads/r/null/3/8/38124/RDC_57_156_ENG.pdf.

North Atlantic Treaty Organization, "The Danish Prime Minister's Reply to Marshal Bulgarin's Letter of 28th March, 1957," NATO Archives, 1957, https://archives.nato.int/uploads/r/null/3/8/38154/RDC_57_177_ENG.pdf.

North Atlantic Treaty Organization, *Report on Danish-Greenland Defense Negotiations*, NATO Archives, 1957, https://archives.nato.int/uploads/r/null/3/8/38124/RDC_57_156_ENG.pdf.

Søren Gregersen, "Jeg har været 60 meter nede i indlands-isen" [I've been 60 meters down into the ice sheet], *Politiken*, February 19, 1961, p. 13.

Eric Niler, "When the Pentagon Dug Secret Cold War Ice Tunnels to Hide Nukes," *History*. March 27, 2019, https://www.history.com/news/project-iceworm-cold-war-nuclear-weapons-greenland.

Hans M. Kristensen, "U.S. Nuclear Weapons Deployments Disclosed," *Nuclear Policy*, Nautilus Institute, October 20, 1999, https://nautilus.org/projects/nuclear-policy/u-s-nuclear-weapons-deployments-disclosed/.

Geological Survey of Denmark and Greenland, "Camp Century Is Staying Under the Ice," *GEUS*, March 18, 2021, https://eng.geus.dk/about/news/news-archive/2021/march/camp-century.

UNRIC, "The Politics of Language in Greenland," *UNRIC*, March 24, 2021, https://unric.org/en/the-politics-of-language-in-greenland/.

Greenland and Iceland in the New Arctic: Recommendations of the Greenland Committee Appointed by the Minister for Foreign Affairs and International Development Co-Operation, Government of Iceland, Ministry for Foreign Affairs, 2020, https://www.government.is/library/01-Ministries/Ministry-for-Foreign-Affairs/PDF-skjol/Greenland-Iceland-rafraen20-01-21.pdf.

Vittus Qujaukitsoq, "The Danish Government Is Violating Agreements on Indigenous Peoples' Rights by Not Dealing with American Pollution in Greenland," *ArcticToday*, . October 19, 2016, https://www.arctictoday.com/the-danish-government-is-violating-agreements-on-indigenous-peoples-rights-by-not-dealing-with-american-pollution-in-greenland/.

W. Colgan, H. Machguth, M. MacFerrin, J. D. Colgan, D. van As, and J. A. MacGregor, "The Abandoned Ice Sheet Base at Camp Century, Greenland, in a Warming Climate," *Geophys. Res. Lett.* 43 (2016): 8091–8096, doi:10.1002/2016GL069688.

ACOUSTIC KITTY

Victor Marchetti and John D. Marks, *The CIA and the Cult of Intelligence* (Laurel, 1983).

John Ranelagh, *The Agency* (Touchstone, 1987).

Robert Wallace, H. Keith Melton, and Henry R. Schlesinger, *Spycraft: The Secret History of the CIA's Spytechs, from Communism to Al-Qaeda* (Bantam, 2008).

"[Deleted] Views on Trained Cats for [deleted] Use," National Security Archive—George Washington University, https://nsarchive2.gwu.edu/NSAEBB/NSAEBB54/st27.pdf. Accessed March 27, 2024.

"CIA Documents on Animal Testing / Acoustic Kitty," The Black Vault, https://documents.theblackvault.com/documents/cia/acoustickitty-cia.pdf, accessed March 27, 2024.

"THE MARCHETTI CASE, NEW CASE LAW | CIA FOIA (Foia.cia.gov)," www.cia.gov, April 12, 2006, https://www.cia.gov/readingroom/document/cia-rdp80s01268a000200020024-4. Accessed March 27, 2024.

"Robert Wallace—Advisor at International Spy Museum." THE ORG, https://theorg.com/org/international-spy-museum/org-chart/robert-wallace, accessed March 27. 2024.

"Bob Wallace." International Spy Museum, https://www.spymuseum.org/host-an-event/spy-speaker-series/bob-wallace, accessed March 27, 2024.

OPERATION POPEYE

U.S National Archives, "Vietnam War U.S. Military Fatal Casualty Statistics: Electronic Records Reference Report," last reviewed on August 23, 2022, https://www.archives.gov/research/military/vietnam-war/casualty-statistics.

Jeffrey J. Clarke, *United States Army in Vietnam: Advice and Support: The Final Years, 1965–1973*, (Center of Military History, United States Army, 1988), 275.

"Protests and Backlash, from the Collection: Vietnam War," PBS, accessed April 18, 2024, https://www.pbs.org /wgbh/americanexperience/features/two-days-in -october-student-antiwar-protests-and-backlash/.

Eleanor Cummings, "With Operation Popeye, the U.S. Government Made Weather an Instrument of War," *Popular Science*, March 20, 2018, https://www.popsci.com /operation-popeye-government-weather-vietnam-war/.

Amélie Robert, "At the Heart of the Vietnam War: Herbicides, Napalm and Bulldozers Against the A Luoi Mountains," *Open Edition*, journals, 2016, https://journals .openedition.org/rga/3266.

Pamela McElwee, "The Origins of Ecocide: Revisiting the Ho Chi Minh Trail in the Vietnam War." Environment & Society Portal, *Arcadia* (Spring 2020), no. 20, Rachel Carson Center for Environment and Society, https:// www.environmentandsociety.org/arcadia/origins -ecocide-revisiting-ho-chi-minh-trail-vietnam-war.

James Fleming, *Fixing the Sky: The Checkered History of Weather and Climate Control* (Columbia University Press, 2010).

US Congress, Senate Committee on Foreign Relations, Subcommittee on Oceans and International Environment, *Weather Modification*, 93rd Congress, 2nd session, March 20, 1974, https://www.govinfo.gov/app/details /CHRG-93shrg29544O/context.

Brett Forest, "It Won't Refill Lake Mead, but State Lawmakers Are Betting on Nevada Cloud Seeding Program," News 3, June 29, 2023, https://news3lv.com/news/local /it-wont-refill-lake-mead-but-state-lawmakers-are -betting-on-nevada-cloud-seeding-program.

Mark Feldstein, *Poisoning the Press: Richard Nixon, Jack Anderson, and the Rise of Washington's Scandal Culture* (Farrar, Straus and Giroux, 2010).

CATCHING FIRE ON THE CUYAHOGA

Jonathan Adler, "Fables of the Cuyahoga: Reconstructing a History of Environmental Protection," *Fordham Environmental Law Journal*, Special Edition: Case Western Reserve University School of Law: Paper-Only Symposium, 14, no. 1 (Fall 2002): 89–146, https://www .jstor.org/stable/44174399.

"Carl B. Stokes and the 1969 River Fire" (U.S. National Park Service), accessed June 3, 2024, https://www.nps.gov /articles/carl-stokes-and-the-river-fire.htm.

"The Shocking River Fire That Fueled the Creation of the EPA," History, October 4, 2023, https://www.history .com/news/epa-earth-day-cleveland-cuyahoga-river -fire-clean-water-act.

Lorraine Boissoneault, "The Cuyahoga River Caught Fire at Least a Dozen Times, but No One Cared Until 1969," *Smithsonian Magazine*, June 19, 2019, accessed June 3, 2024, https://www.smithsonianmag.com/history /cuyahoga-river-caught-fire-least-dozen-times-no-one -cared-until-1969-180972444/.

Robin Goist, "One Dead in Fiery Tanker Crash on Ohio 8 in Akron," Cleveland com, August 25, 2020, https://www .cleveland.com/news/2020/08/one-dead-in-fiery -tanker-crash-on-ohio-8-in-akron.html.

David Stradling and Richard Stradling, *Where the River Burned: Carl Stokes and the Struggle to Save Cleveland* (Cornell University Press, 2015).

"The TIME Vault: August 1, 1969," TIME.com, accessed June 3, 2024, http://time.com/vault/issue/1969-08-01 /page/51/.

Megan Trimble, "Fish from Infamous Cuyahoga River Are Now Safe to Eat," *US News & World Report*, March 19, 2019, sec. National News, https://www.usnews.com/news /national-news/articles/2019-03-19/fish-from-ohios -cuyahoga-river-are-now-safe-to-eat-ohio-epa-says.

Barry Wittenstein and Jessie Hartland, *The Day the River Caught Fire: How the Cuyahoga River Exploded and Ignited the Earth Day Movement*. (Simon & Schuster Books for Young Readers, 2022).

TOP FIVE...FAILED PLOTS TO ASSASSINATE EL COMANDANTE

Duncan Campbell, "Close but no Cigar: How America Failed to Kill Fidel Castro," *Guardian*, November 26, 2016, https://www.theguardian.com/world/2016/nov/26 /fidel-castro-cia-cigar-assasination-attempts.

"Castro and the Cold War," PBS, https://www.pbs.org/wgbh /americanexperience/features/castro-and-cold-war/.

Arnaldo M. Fernandez, "Antonio Veciana, with Carlos Harrison, Trained to Kill (2)," Kennedys and King, April 18, 2017, https://www.kennedysandking.com/john-f -kennedy-reviews/antonio-veciana-with-carlos -harrison-trained-to-kill-2.

"Manuel Antonio de Varona; Cuban Leader Forced into Exile," LA Times Archives, November 2, 1992, https:// www.latimes.com/archives/la-xpm-1992-11-02-mn -1064-story.html.

Dylan Matthews, "7 bizarre Ways the US Tried to Kill or Topple Fidel Castro," Vox, November 26, 2016, https:// www.vox.com/2016/11/26/13752514/us-fidel-castro -assassination.

Office of the Historian, "278. Despatch from the Embassy in Cuba to the Department of State," US Department of State, https://history.state.gov/historicaldocuments /frus1958-60v06/d278#:~:text=The%20Partido%20 Socialista%20Popular%20.

Office of the Historian, "The Bay of Pigs Invasion and its Aftermath, April 1961–October 1962," US Department of State, https://history.state.gov/milestones/1961-1968 /bay-of-pigs.

"634 Ways to Kill Fidel," Seven Stories Press, https://www .sevenstories.com/blogs/258-634-ways-to-kill-fidel.

Alexander Smith, "Fidel Castro: The CIA's 7 Most Bizarre Assassination Attempts," NBC News, November 28, 2016, https://www.nbcnews.com/storyline/fidel -castros-death/fidel-castro-cia-s-7-most-bizarre -assassination-attempts-n688951.

SILENCIO

Conelisa N. Hubilla, "Zone of Silence: Exploring the Strange Phenomenon in the Mexican Desert," *Science Times*, June 29, 2023, https://www.sciencetimes.com/articles /44610/20230629/zone-silence-exploring-strange -phenomenon-mexican-desert.html.

"Experimental Launch & Test Division/Rocket System Launch Program," Los Angeles Air Force Base, https:// www.losangeles.spaceforce.mil/About-Us/Fact-Sheets /Display/Article/1217574/experimental-launch-test -divisionrocket-system-launch-program/.

Jim Eckles, "The Athena That Got Away," White Sands Missile Ranch, https://history.utah.gov/wp-content /uploads/2019/04/UHQ-The-Athena-That-Got-Away.pdf.

T. E. Wilson, "Exploring Mexico's Zone of Silence, Where Radio Signals Fail and Meteorites Crash: The Mexican Version of the Bermuda Triangle Has Its Fair Share of Alien Rumors," Atlas Obscura, November 3, 2016, https://www.atlasobscura.com/articles/exploring-mexicos-zone-of-silence-where-radio-signals-fail-and-meteorites-crash.

PROJECT AZORIAN

"7000 Romaine St.," Google Maps, accessed March 19, 2024, https://www.google.com/maps/@34.0889185,-118.3422462,3a,75y,183.28h,91.01t/data=!3m6!1e1!3m4!1sdn9Th6zKrxsJOVWiWLnrg!2e0!7i16384!8i8192?entry=ttu.

@CIA, "We Can Neither Confirm nor Deny That This Is Our First Tweet," Twitter, June 6, 2014, https://twitter.com/CIA/status/474971393852182528.

"Abyssal Zone," Woods Hole Oceanographic Institution, accessed March 19, 2024, https://www.whoi.edu/know-your-ocean/ocean-topics/how-the-ocean-works/ocean-zones/abyssal-zone/.

Neal Agarwal, "The Deep Sea," Neal.fun, accessed March 19, 2024, https://neal.fun/deep-sea/.

Matthew Aid, "Project Azorian: The CIA's Declassified History of the Glomar Explorer," edited by William Burr and Thomas Blanton, National Security Archive, February 12, 2010, https://nsarchive2.gwu.edu/nukevault/ebb305/.

Jack Anderson and Joseph Spear, "Witness Tells of CIA Plot to Kill Castro," Washington Post, October 31, 1988, https://www.washingtonpost.com/archive/business/1988/11/01/witness-tells-of-cia-plot-to-kill-castro/0708d92a-204c-49d1-b64c-557012350762/.

Burial at Sea of Soviet Submariners from Hughes Glomar Explorer, YouTube, August 25, 2014, https://www.youtube.com/watch?v=aJAJUJ41PBI.

"Chile Dictatorship Victim Toll Bumped to 40,018," CBC News, August 18, 2011, https://www.cbc.ca/news/world/chile-dictatorship-victim-toll-bumped-to-40-018-1.998542.

Josh Dean, The Taking of K-129: How the CIA Used Howard Hughes to Steal a Russian Sub in the Most Daring Covert Operation in History (Dutton Caliber, 2018).

Seymour Hersh, "C.I.A. Salvage Ship Brought Up Part of Soviet Sub Lost in 1968, Failed to Raise Atom Missiles," New York Times, March 19, 1975, https://www.nytimes.com/1975/03/19/archives/cia-salvage-ship-brought-up-part-of-soviet-sub-lost-1968-failed-tohtml?module=ArrowsNav&contentCollection=Archives&action=keypress&region=FixedLeft&pgtype=article.

"Howard Hughes Headquarters," Art Deco Society of Los Angeles. Accessed March 19, 2024. https://artdecola.org/howardhughesheadquarters.

James Phelan, "An Easy Burglary Led to the Disclosure of Hughes-C.I.A. Plan to Salvage Soviet Sub," New York Times, March 27, 1975, https://www.nytimes.com/1975/03/27/archives/an-easy-burglary-led-to-the-disclosure-of-hughescia-plan-to-salvage.html.

Phillippi v. Central Intelligence Agency, Casetext (United States Court of Appeals, District of Columbia Circuit 1976).

"Project Azorian: The Story of the Hughes Glomar Explorer," Studies in Intelligence, 1985, https://nsarchive2.gwu.edu/nukevault/ebb305/doc01.pdf.

Sherry Sontag, Christopher Drew, and Annette Lawrence Drew, Blind Man's Bluff: The Untold Story Of American Submarine Espionage (Public Affairs, 1998).

Lila Thulin, "During the Cold War, the CIA Secretly Plucked a Soviet Submarine from the Ocean Floor Using a Giant Claw," Smithsonian Magazine, May 10, 2019.,https://www.smithsonianmag.com/history/during-cold-war-ci-secretly-plucked-soviet-submarine-ocean-floor-using-giant-claw-180972154/.

PIGEON PALS

"Avians Project Evaluation," Central Intelligence Agency, 1975, https://www.cia.gov/readingroom/docs/AVIANS%20PROJECT%20EVALUATION%5B15687503%5D.pdf.

"A Program for Providing High-Resolution Oblique Photography over Denied Area," Central Intelligence Agency, 1976, https://www.cia.gov/readingroom/docs/A%20PROGRAM%20FOR%20PROVIDING%20H%5B15687573%5D.pdf.

"Feasibility Research on a System to Provide High Resolution Photography Over Denied Areas,' Central Intelligence Agency, 1978, https://www.cia.gov/readingroom/docs/FEASIBILITY%20RESEARCH%20ON%20A%5B15688715%5D.pdf.

"Leningrad Target for Project TACANA," Central Intelligence Agency, 1976, https://www.cia.gov/readingroom/docs/LENINGRAD%20TARGET%20FOR%20PROJ%5B15687498%5D.pdf.

"ORD Report Card—Status of the LSR/ORD Avian Program," Central Intelligence Agency, 1976, https://www.cia.gov/readingroom/docs/ORD%20REPORT%20CARD%20-%20STATUS%20%5B15687593%5D.pdf.

"Proposal for Avian Operational Support," Central Intelligence Agency, 1978, https://www.cia.gov/readingroom/docs/PROPOSAL%20FOR%20AVIAN%20OPERAT%5B15687539%5D.pdf.

Gordon Corera, "CIA Unveils Cold War Spy-Pigeon Missions," BBC, https://www.bbc.com/news/world-us-canada-49692534. Accessed June 10, 2024.

Steven Ewin, "When the CIA Spied on American Citizens—Using Pigeons," Atlas Obscura, https://www.atlasobscura.com/articles/cia-cold-war-pigeon-spies, accessed June 10, 2024.

Courtney Humphries, Superdove: How the Pigeon Took Manhattan...and the World (HarperCollins, 2009).

Rosemary Mosco, A Pocket Guide to Pigeon Watching: Getting to Know the World's Most Misunderstood Bird (Workman, 2021).

OPERATION SNOW WHITE

Richard Behar, "The Thriving Cult of Greed and Power," Time, June 24, 2001, https://web.archive.org/web/20140525200902/https://content.time.com/time/magazine/article/0,9171,156952,00.html.

Charles Stafford, "Scientologists' Downfall Began with Phony IDs," Tampa Bay Times, December 28, 1979, 1, 8.

Douglas Frantz, "Scientology's Puzzling Journey from Tax Rebel to Tax Exempt," New York Times, March 9, 1997, https://www.nytimes.com/1997/03/09/us/scientology-s-puzzling-journey-from-tax-rebel-to-tax-exempt.html.

Elaine Povich, "Christine Hansen Was One of the First 12 Women...," UPI, July 31, 1981, https://www.upi.com/Archives/1981/07/31/Christine-Hansen-was-one-of-the-first-12-women/9647365400000/.

Glenn Currie, "FBI Discrimination," UPI, July 31, 1981, https://www.upi.com/archives/1981/07/31/FBI -discrimination/8828365400000/.

Hugh Urban, *The Church of Scientology: A History of a New Religion* (Princeton University Press, 2011).

John McCormick, "More Firsts for Betty," *Quad-City Times*, October 2, 1977, 74.

Jon Atack, *A Piece of Blue Sky: Hubbard, Dianetics, and Scientology*, 4th ed. (Richard Woods, 2013).

Robert Gillette and Robert Rawitch, "Scientology: A Long Trail of Controversy," *Los Angeles Times*, August 27, 1978, https://time.com/archive/6697626/religion -mystery-of-the-vanished-ruler/.

Robert Rawitch, "Church Sues FBI Agents," *Los Angeles Times*, July 19, 1977, https://www.cia.gov/readingroom /docs/CIA-RDP88-01315R000400410042-0.pdf.

Robert Wood, "HBO's Going Clear Exposes Scientology Tactics, Wealth, and IRS Church Status." *Forbes*, April 13, 2015, https://www.forbes.com/sites/robertwood /2015/03/31/hbos-going-clear-exposes-scientology -tactics-wealth-and-irs-church-status/.

Russell Miller, *Bare-Faced Messiah: The True Story of L. Ron Hubbard* (Silvertail Books, 1987).

Scientology, "Why Auditing Works," https://www.scientology -losangeles.org/what-is-scientology/the-practice -of-scientology/why-auditing-works.html.

Sentencing memorandum, *United States of America v. Jane Kember*, 487 F. Supp. 1340 (D.D.C. 1980), no. 78-401 (2) & (3), 20–21.

Tony Ortega, "Double Crossed," *Phoenix New Times*, December 23, 1999, https://web.archive.org/web/200703 12025501/http://www.phoenixnewtimes.com/1999-12 -23/news/double-crossed/full.

Tony Ortega, *The Unbreakable Miss Lovely: How the Church of Scientology Tried to Destroy Paulette Cooper* (Silvertail Books, 2018).

"Woman Charges FBI with Sex Discrimination," *Missoulian*, September 6, 1978, 34.

UPI, "Class-Action FBI Suit Filed," *Tyler Morning Telegraph*, September 6, 1978, 9.

SKYLAB

Christopher Borrelli, "Who Created the McDonald's Happy Meal? 40 Years Later, the Answer Is Complicated," *Chicago Tribune*, July 5, 2019, https://www.chicagotribune .com/2019/07/05/who-created-the-mcdonalds-happy -meal-40-years-later-the-answer-is-complicated/.

Garry Carman, "From the Archives, 1979: They're Off and Racing in the Skylab Stakes," *WAtoday*, July 12, 2021, https://www.watoday.com.au/national/western-austra- lia/from-the-archives-1979-they-re-off-and-racing -in-the-skylab-stakes-20210709-p588el.html.

Jim Carrier, "Skylaugh...Humor Built Around Skylab," *Williamson Daily News*/Associated Press, July 9, 1979, https://books.google.com/books?id=H6hDAAAA IBAJ&pg=PA1&dq=skylab&article_id=4047 ,5799537&hl=en&sa=X&ved=2ahUKEwiy7bC4kry GAxUbGFkFHW_-AF0Q6AF6BAgLEAI#v= onepage&q=skylab&f=false.

Andrew Chamings, "A Space Station Fell to Earth. An Australian Boy Brought It to San Francisco," SFGATE, May 4, 2023, https://www.sfgate.com/sfhistory/article /the-skylab-race-to-san-francisco-18074888.php.

James Coates, "Skylab Danger Isn't as Small as NASA Hints," *Chicago Tribune*, July 1, 1979, accessed June 10, 2024, https://news.google.com/newspapers?nid=1291 &dat=19790701&id=h9gPAAAAIBAJ&pg=6094 ,67904&hl=en.

William David Compton, Charles D. Benson, and Paul Dickson, "What Goes Up...," in *Living and Working in Space: A NASA History of Skylab*, 361, 368, Courier Corporation, 2011, https://sma.nasa.gov/SignificantIncidents/assets /living-and-working-in-space.pdf.

Tony Dunnell, "Skylab's Remains—Esperance, Australia," Atlas Obscura, February 19, 2018, https://www.atlas obscura.com/places/skylabs-remains.

Jane Green, "The Story of the Skylab Space Station," *BBC Sky at Night* magazine, January 10, 2024, https://www .skyatnightmagazine.com/space-missions/skylab.

Elizabeth Howell, "International Space Station: Everything You Need to Know About the Orbital Laboratory," Space.com, February 23, 2024, https://www.space .com/16748-international-space-station.html.

Judd Bridget, "A Space Station Falling at 550kph, Where It Would Land, a Mystery. Enter Balladonia, WA," ABC News, May 30, 2020, https://www.abc.net.au/news /2020-05-31/nasa-skylab-fell-to-earth-esperance -retrofocus/12282468.

Eunice Lee, "Radio DJ Heads to Australia to Pay NASA Litter Fine," *Victorville Daily Press*, June 7, 2009, https:// www.vvdailypress.com/story/news/2009/07/07/radio -dj-heads-to-australia/37071108007/.

Kelli Mars, "50 Years Ago: Second Skylab Crew Begins Record-Breaking Mission," July 31, 2023, https://www .nasa.gov/history/50-years-ago-second-skylab-crew -begins-record-breaking-mission/.

Allison Marsh, "Skylab: The Space Station That Fell on Australia," IEEE Spectrum, April 30, 2023, https://spectrum .ieee.org/skylab.

"Space Food, Turkey and Gravy, Skylab," National Air and Space Museum, accessed June 26, 2024, https://air andspace.si.edu/collection-objects/space-food-turkey -and-gravy-skylab/nasm_A19850816000.

Valerie Neal, "Skylab Is Falling!," National Air and Space Museum, July 11, 2014, https://airandspace.si.edu /stories/editorial/skylab-falling.

Kiona N. Smith, "The Summer the Skylab Space Station Crashed, 41 Years Later," *Forbes*, June 12, 2020, https:// www.forbes.com/sites/kionasmith/2020/07/12/the -summer-the-skylab-space-station-crashed-41-years -later/.

"Stanley Thornton & Jeff Jarvis," *Sunday Record*, July 15, 1979, https://www.newspapers.com/article/the -record-stanley-thornton-jeff-jarvi/128072316/.

John Uri, "40 Years Ago: Skylab Reenters Earth's Atmosphere," NASA History (blog), July 11, 2019.

John Uri, "50 Years Ago: Skylab 3 Astronauts Splash Down After Record 59 Days in Space," September 25, 2023, https://www.nasa.gov/history/50-years-ago-skylab -3-astronauts-splash-down-after-record-59-days -in-space/.

John Noble Wilford, "Astronauts 'Fixits' on Earth, Too," *New York Times*, June 24, 1973, https://www.nytimes.com /1973/06/24/archives/astronauts-fixits-on-earth-too -the-hammer-tradition.html?_r=0.

"The Real Story of the Skylab 4 'Strike' in Space," NASA, November 16, 2020, https://www.nasa.gov/history/the -real-story-of-the-skylab-4-strike-in-space/.

SWINGING SPIES

"Meet the Koechers: How a KGB Super-Spy Infiltrated CIA 'Swinger' Clubs," *Spyscape*, https://spyscape.com /article/the-czech-super-spy-who-infiltrated-the-cia -and-a-spy-swingers-club.

Christopher Burgess, "The Salacious Swingers Arrested for Espionage This Day in 1984," *Clearance Jobs*, November 27, 2021, https://news.clearancejobs.com/2021/11/27 /the-salacious-soviet-swingers-arrested-for-espionage -this-day-in-1984/.

Benjamin Cunningham, *The Liar: How a Double Agent in the CIA Became the Cold War's Last Honest Man* (Hachette, 2022).

Benjamin Cunningham, "How a Czech 'Super-Spy' Infiltrated the CIA," *Guardian*, June 30, 2016, https://www .theguardian.com/world/2016/jun/30/how-a-czech -super-spy-infiltrated-cia-karel-koecher.

Todd Farley, "This Double Agent Spied for the CIA and KGB—and Was a Famous Swinger," *New York Post*, August 13, 2022, https://nypost.com/2022/08/13/this -double-agent-cia-and-kgb-spy-was-also-a-famous -swinger/.

Natasha Frost, "The Sex-Loving Soviet Spy Who Infiltrated the CIA," *History.com* May 5, 2023, https://www.history .com/news/soviet-spy-sex-parties-cia-agent.

"This Day in History: Soviets Announce Boycott of 1984 Olympics," *History.com*, May 8, https://www.history .com/this-day-in-history/soviets-announce-boycott-of -1984-olympics.

Ron Kessler, *Inside the CIA* (Simon & Schuster, 1994.)

Ron Kessler, *The Secrets of the FBI* (Broadway Paperbacks, 2011, 2012).

Ronald Kessler, "Opinion, Moscow's Mole in the CIA," *Washington Post*, April 16, 1988, https://www .washingtonpost.com/archive/opinions/1988/04/17/ moscows-mole-in-the-cia/a976fac3-622a-475d-8c87 -46b6170b1f4e/.

Rudy Maxa and Phil Stanford, "The Swinging Spies," *Washingtonian*, February 1987, CIA sanitized copy December 2, 2011, https://www.cia.gov/readingroom/docs /CIA-RDP90-00965R000706430001-4.pdf.

Selwyn Raab, "Friend Says Spy Suspect 'Hated Communists,'" *New York Times*, November 29, 1984.

Julia Shapero, "Number of Russian Spies in U.S. Remains 'Way Too Big,' Says FBI Director," *The Hill*, September 8, 2023, https://thehill.com/policy/national-security /4194044-fbi-wray-russian-spies-us/.

Francine Uenuma, "The 1983 Military Drill That Nearly Sparked Nuclear War with the Soviets," *Smithsonian*, April 27, 2022, https://www.smithsonianmag.com /history/the-1983-military-drill-that-nearly-sparked -nuclear-war-with-the-soviets-180979980/.

Kristen Walker and Patrick Smith, "U.S.-Russian tensions Escalate with nuclear Rhetoric from Moscow," *NBC News*, February 22, 2023, https://www.nbcnews.com /news/world/us-russian-tensions-nuclear-moscow -medvedev-putin-biden-rcna71726.

OPERATION MONOPOLY

"The Painfully Obvious FBI Spy House," *Atlas Obscura*, May 3, 2017, http://www.atlasobscura.com/places/fbi-spy -house.

Dara Bitler, "5 of the Most High-Profile Criminals in Colorado Supermax Prison," *FOX31 Denver*, accessed March 21, 2024, https://kdvr.com/news/local/5-of-the-most -high-profile-criminals-in-colorado-supermax-prison/.

Michael Crowley, "Russia's Embassy in Washington Becomes a Different Kind of Battle Zone," *New York Times*, July 3, 2023, sec. U.S., https://www.nytimes.com /2023/07/03/us/politics/russia-embassy-ukraine-war .html.

"Ex-Stripper Describes Her Time with Accused Spy—May 22, 2001," *CNN.com*, November 14, 2004, https://web .archive.org/web/20041114093843/http://archives.cnn .com/2001/US/05/22/hanssen.stripper/.

Benjamin B. Fischer, "Leon Theremin—CIA Nemesis." *Studies in Intelligence*, January 1, 1970, 29–39, https://www .cia.gov/readingroom/docs/DOC_0006122432.pdf.

Megan Friedman, "A Brief History of Charles Schulz's 'Peanuts' Comic Strip," *TIME*, October 1, 2010, accessed March 19, 2024, https://content.time.com/time/arts /article/0,8599,2022745,00.html.

Vince Houghton, "Operation Monopoly," in *Nuking the Moon: And Other Intelligence Schemes and Military Plots Left on the Drawing Board* (Penguin, 2019).

United States of America vs. Robert Phillip Hanssen— Affidavit, in the United States District Court for the Eastern District of Virginia., n.d., https://www.fbi.gov /file-repository/hanssen-affidavit.pdf/view.

Morton Kondracke, and Fred Barnes, *Jack Kemp: The Bleeding-Heart Conservative Who Changed America* (Sentinel, 2015).

Vernon Loeb, "FBI Offered Officials Tours of Secret Tunnel Under Soviet Embassy." *Washington Post*, January 17, 2024, https://www.washingtonpost.com/archive /politics/2001/03/11/fbi-offered-officials-tours-of -secret-tunnel-under-soviet-embassy/c2e7e4fe-67d2 -4c92-b980-da9f7d96dc05/.

Dorian Lynskey, "The Riot That 'Killed' Disco," BBC, September 22, 2023, https://www.bbc.com/culture/article /20230922-the-night-angry-rock-fans-destroyed -disco-music.

"May 16, 1972 Vol. 118, Part 14—Bound Edition." Congressional Record, accessed March 19, 2024, https://www .congress.gov/bound-congressional-record/1972/05/16 /house-section.

Louis Menand, "Getting Real," *New Yorker*, November 6, 2011, https://www.newyorker.com/magazine/2011 /11/14/getting-real.

"New Evidence on Soviet Intelligence: The KGB's 1967 Annual Report." *COLD WAR INTERNATIONAL HISTORY PROJECT BULLETIN*, accessed March 19, 2024, https://www.wilsoncenter.org/sites/default/files/media /documents/publication/CWIHPBulletin10_p6.pdf.

"A Review of the FBI's Performance in Deterring, Detecting, and Investigating the Espionage Activities of Robert Philip Hanssen," Office of the Inspector General, August 14, 2003, https://oig.justice.gov/sites/default/files /archive/special/0308/index.htm.

James Risen, "A Search for Answers: The Spymaster; Spy Handler Bedeviled U.S. in Earlier Case," *New York Times*, February 22, 2001, sec. U.S., https://www.nytimes.com /2001/02/22/us/a-search-for-answers-the-spymaster -spy-handler-bedeviled-us-in-earlier-case.html.

James Risen and Lowell Bergman, "U.S. Thinks Agent Revealed Tunnel at Soviet Embassy," *New York Times*, March 4, 2001, sec. U.S., https://www.nytimes.com /2001/03/04/us/us-thinks-tunnel-at -soviet-embassy.html.

Chris Vognar, "The Day Disco Was Demolished," *New York Times*, October 29, 2023, sec. Arts, https://www.nytimes.com/2023/10/29/arts/television/the-war-on-disco-pbs.html.

Robert Wallace and Harold Keith Melton, *Spycraft: The Secret History of the CIA's Spytechs from Communism to Al-Qaeda* (Penguin, 2008).

Calder Walton, "That Time the Soviets Bugged Congress, and Other Spy Tales," *POLITICO*, May 22, 2017, https://www.politico.com/magazine/story/2017/05/22/donald-trump-russia-soviet-union-spying-congress-bug-215174.

Lindsay Whitehurst, "Former FBI Agent Robert Hanssen, Who Was Convicted of Spying for Russia, Dies in Prison," AP News, June 5, 2023, https://apnews.com/article/fbi-spy-russia-prison-died-hanssen-f16ff609b91ba5f84946a2ccf6363df2.

David Wise, *Spy: The Inside Story of How the FBI's Robert Hanssen Betrayed America* (Random House, 2003).

Caitlin Yilek, Pat Milton, and Arden Farhi, "Robert Hanssen, Former FBI Agent Convicted of Spying for Russia, Dead at 79," CBS News June 5, 2023, https://www.cbsnews.com/news/robert-hanssen-dies-convicted-spying-for-russia-dead-age-79/.

OZONE

Rudy Baum, "Chlorofluorocarbons and Ozone Depletion," *American Chemical Society* (blog), 2017, https://www.acs.org/content/dam/acsorg/education/whatis chemistry/landmarks/cfcsozone/cfcs-ozone.pdf.

Jeff Blyskal and Marie Hodge Blyskal, "The Battle for Corporate Survival: Crisis PR," in *PR : How the Public Relations Industry Writes the News* (William Morrow, 1985), 171, http://archive.org/details/prhowpublicrelat00blys.

Hilary Costa, Erin Sprout, Santani Teng, Melissa McDaniel, Jeff Hunt, Diane Boudreau, Tara Ramroop, Kim Rutledge, and Hilary Hall, "Ozone Layer," *National Geographic*, accessed June 14, 2024, https://education.nationalgeographic.org/resource/ozone-layer.

Ruth Schwartz Cowan, "The Postwar Years," in *More Work for Mother : The Ironies of Household Technology from the Open Hearth to the Microwave*, (Basic Books, 1983), 196, http://archive.org/details/moreworkformothe0000unse.

Barbara J. Finlayson-Pitts, "F. Sherwood Rowland: A Man of Science, Vision, Integrity, and Kindness," *Proceedings of the National Academy of Sciences of the United States of America* 109, no. 35 (August 28, 2012): 13881–82, https://doi.org/10.1073/pnas.1212354109.

Candice Gilet, "Ozone Depletion: Uncovering the Hidden Hazard of Hairspray," *Understanding Science—UC Museum of Paleontology* (blog), 2007, https://undsci.berkeley.edu/wp-content/uploads/2022/08/ozone_depletion_complex.pdf.

Lanie Jones, "Ozone Warning: He Sounded Alarm, Paid Heavy Price," *Los Angeles Times*, July 14, 1988, https://www.latimes.com/archives/la-xpm-1988-07-14-mn-8873-story.html.

"The Effects of Climate Change," National Aeronautics and Space Administration (NASA), accessed June 14, 2024, https://science.nasa.gov/climate-change/effects/.

Naomi Oreskes and Erik M. Conway, "Constructing a Counternarrative: The Fight over the Ozone Hole," in *Merchants of Doubt: How a Handful of Scientists Obscured the Truth on Issues from Tobacco Smoke to Global Warming* (Bloomsbury, 2010).

Benjamin Phelps, "Tragedy at the Pole: Interview with Dr. Susan Solomon," PBS, April 21, 2023, https://www.pbs.org/wnet/secrets/tragedy-at-the-pole-interview-with-dr-susan-solomon/7114/.

Kelsey Piper, "Why the Ozone Hole Is on Track to Be Healed by Mid-Century," Vox, January 10, 2023, https://www.vox.com/future-perfect/22686105/future-of-life-ozone-hole-environmental-crisis-united-nations-cfcs.

Giovanni Prete, "Tuvalu: Why Is the Small Island Nation Sinking?," Earth.org, January 29, 2024, https://earth.org/tuvalus-sinking-reality-how-climate-change-is-threatening-a-small-island-nation/.

Hannah Ritchie and Max Roser, "Global Inequalities in CO2 Emissions," *Our World in Data*, December 28, 2023, https://ourworldindata.org/inequality-co2.

Ann Schaffer, "The Climate Optimist," *MIT Technology Review*, February 27, 2019, https://www.technologyreview.com/2019/02/27/137093/the-climate-optimist/.

"American Meteorological Society University Corporation for Atmospheric Research—Interview with Susan Solomon," September 5, 1997, https://opensky.ucar.edu/islandora/object/archives%3A7645/datastream/OBJ/view.

"Health and Environmental Effects of Ozone Layer Depletion," Reports and Assessments, US EPA, OAR, July 17, 2015, https://www.epa.gov/ozone-layer-protection/health-and-environmental-effects-ozone-layer-depletion.

"Executive Summary. Scientific Assessment of Ozone Depletion: 2022." GAW, World Meteorological Organization (WMO), Geneva, 2022, https://ozone.unep.org/system/files/documents/Scientific-Assessment-of-Ozone-Depletion-2022-Executive-Summary.pdf.

THE COLA COLD WAR

"PEPSI—GLASNOST," AdAge, January 22, 1989, https://adage.com/videos/pepsi-glasnost/1198.

Nena Baker, "Coke, Pepsi Announce Super Bowl Ad Plans" UPI, December 19, 1988, https://www.upi.com/Archives/1988/12/19/Coke-Pepsi-announce-Super-Bowl-ad-plans/8024598510800/.

Anne Ewbank, "When the Soviet Union Paid Pepsi in Warships," Atlas Obscura, January 12, 2018, https://www.atlasobscura.com/articles/soviet-union-pepsi-ships.

Tom Friend and Leonard Shapiro, "Super Bowl XXIII: Really Super This Time, 49ers, 20–16," *Washington Post*, January 23, 1989, https://www.washingtonpost.com/wp-srv/sports/nfl/longterm/superbowl/stories/sb23.htm?itid=lk_inline_manual_44.

"This Day in History: Richard Nixon and Nikita Khrushchev Have a 'Kitchen Debate,'" History.com, https://www.history.com/this-day-in-history/nixon-and-khrushchev-have-a-kitchen-debate.

Flora Lewis, "Foreign Affairs; Soviets Buy American," *New York Times*, May 10, 1989, https://www.nytimes.com/1989/05/10/opinion/foreign-affairs-soviets-buy-american.html.

Becky Little, "How the 'Blood Feud' Between Coke and Pepsi Escalated During the 1980s Cola Wars," History.com, September 19, 2023, https://www.history.com/news/cola-wars-pepsi-new-coke-failure.

Paul Musgrave, "The Doomed Voyage of Pepsi's Soviet Navy," *Foreign Policy*, November 27, 2021, https://foreignpolicy.com/2021/11/27/pepsi-navy-soviet-ussr/.

"USSR Exhibition in New York Booklet," National Museum of American Diplomacy, https://diplomacy.state.gov /items/ussr-exhibition-in-new-york-booklet/#:~:text =The%20Soviet%20exhibition%20came%20first , agriculture%2C%20and%20music%20and%20theater.

Michael Parks, "Doing Business : Bloc-Buster Deal: Pepsico's $3-billion-plus Soviet Expansion Was the 'Deal of the Century,'" Los Angeles Times, July 21, 1992, https://www .latimes.com/archives/la-xpm-1992-07-21-wr-4376 -story.html.

Anthony Ramirez, "Coca-Cola Net Up 20.9% in Quarter," New York Times, October 13, 1989, https://www.nytimes .com/1989/10/13/business/coca-cola-net-up-20.9-in -quarter.html.

Jake Rossen, "Oral History: The Strangest Super Bowl Half-time Show Ever," Mental Floss, February 4, 2018, https:// www.mentalfloss.com/article/74902/oral-history -strangest-super-bowl-halftime-show-ever.

TOP FIVE...BODACIOUS VIRUSES THAT BUGGED US IN THE EIGHTIES

Gary Cohen, "Throwback Attack: Pakistani Brothers Create the Brain Virus to Outthink Software Pirates," Industrial Cybersecurity Pulse, https://www.industrialcybersecurity pulse.com/threats-vulnerabilities/throwback-attack -pakistani-brothers-create-the-brain-virus-to-outthink -software-pirates/.

Michael Cooney, "Security History: Nothing like an Old-Fashioned Boot Sector Virus," Network World, January 19, 2012, https://www.networkworld.com /article/704358/security-security-history-nothing -like-an-old-fashioned-boot-sector-virus.html.

Diego Galan, "Invasion of the data snatchers—Untangling the knotty history of the computer virus," Sleek, October 13, 2020, https://www.sleek-mag.com/article/invasion -of-the-data-snatchers-untangling-the-knotty-history -of-the-computer-virus/.

Kate Johanns, "Tech Time Warp: A Look Back at the Ping-Pong Virus," Smarter MSP, https://smartermsp.com /tech-time-warp-look-back-ping-pong-virus/.

Lindsay Lennon, "The 'Morris Worm': A Notorious Chapter of the Internet's Infancy," Cornell University, https:// alumni.cornell.edu/cornellians/morris-worm/#:~:text= Morris%20became%20the%20first%20person,more %20than%20%2410%2C000%20in%20fines.

Danny Lewis, "Check Out These Vintage Computer Viruses at the Malware Museum," Smithsonian Magazine, February 2016, https://www.smithsonianmag.com /smart-news/check-out-these-vintage-computer -viruses-malware-museum-180958090/.

John Leyden, "The 30-year-Old Prank That Became the First Computer Virus," Register, December 14, 2012, https://www.theregister.com/2012/12/14/first_virus _elk_cloner_creator_interviewed/.

John Markoff, "A 'Virus' Gives Business a Chill," New York Times, March 17, 1988, https://www.nytimes.com/1988 /03/17/business/a-virus-gives-business-a-chill.html.

NORIEGA'S NIFTY PACKAGE

"Panamanian Dictator Manuel Noriega's Complex US Ties Suggest Lessons for Trump Era, Historians Say," ABC News, June 1, 2017, https://abcnews.go.com /International/panamanian-dictator-manuel -noriegas-complex-us-ties-lessons/story?id=47722429.

Jon Lee Anderson, "Manuel Noriega, A Thug of a Different Era," New Yorker, June 2, 2017, https://www.newyorker .com/news/daily-comment/manuel-noriega-a-thug-of -a-different-era.

Stephen Engelberg, with Jeff Gerth, "Bush and Noriega: Examination of Their Ties," New York Times, September 28, 1988, https://www.nytimes.com/1988/09/28/us /bush-and-noriega-examination-of-their-ties.html.

Seymour Hersh, "Panama Strongman Said to Trade in Drugs, Arms and Illicit Money," New York Times, June 12, 1986, https://www.nytimes.com/1986/06/12/world /panama-strongman-said-to-trade-in-drugs-arms-and -illicit-money.html?pagewanted=all&mcubz=0.

David Johnston, "U.S. Admits Payments to Noriega," New York Times, January 19, 1991, https://www.nytimes .com/1991/01/19/us/us-admits-payments-to-noriega .html.

Ed Magnuson, "A Guest Who Wore Out His Welcome," TIME, January 15, 1990, https://time.com/archive /6713904/a-guest-who-wore-out-his-welcome/.

"Operation Just Cause," U.S. SOUTHCOM Public Affairs After Action Report Supplement, https://nsarchive2 .gwu.edu/nsa/DOCUMENT/DOC-PIC/950206_4.gif, accessed July 12, 2024.

George C. Wilson, "Invasion of Panama Reflected Gen. Thurman's Gung-Ho Style," Washington Post, January 6, 1990, https://www.washingtonpost.com/archive /politics/1990/01/07/invasion-of-panama-reflected -gen-thurmans-gung-ho-style/a27ac0e6-8981-4faf -8500-4cea17b40fa9/.

DARK DANTE

Amy Davidson Sorkin, "Introducing Strongbox," New Yorker, May 14, 2013, https://www.newyorker.com/news /amy-davidson/introducing-strongbox.

Julia Layton, "How Did a Programmer Find Sex Offenders on MySpace?" How Stuff Works, October 21, 2006, https://computer.howstuffworks.com/internet/social -networking/information/myspace-predator-code.htm.

Jonathan Littman, "The Last Hacker: He Called Himself Dark Dante. His Compulsion Led Him to Secret Files and, Eventually, the Bar of Justice," Los Angeles Times, September 12, 1993, https://www.latimes.com/archives /la-xpm-1993-09-12-tm-34163-story.html.

Kevin Poulsen, "Exile.com," Wired, January 1, 1999, https:// www.wired.com/1999/01/poulsen/.

Kevin Poulsen, "About the Author," Kingpin (Crown, 2011), https://www.kingpin.com/about/.

"Computer Whiz Is Charged with Fixing Radio Contests in Los Angeles," Baltimore Sun, April 22, 1993, https:// www.baltimoresun.com/1993/04/22/computer-whiz-is -charged-with-fixing-radio-contests-in-los-angeles/.

J. J. Sutherland, "Busted on MySpace," NPR, October 16, 2006, https://www.npr.org/2006/10/16/6277120 /busted-on-myspace.

"The Internet's First Message Sent from UCLA," UCLA, 2019, https://100.ucla.edu/timeline/the-internets-first -message-sent-from-ucla.

"Kevin Poulsen," Unsolved Mysteries, https://unsolved.com /gallery/kevin-poulsen/.

UPI, "War Games Film Cited in Computer Bank Intrusion," New York Times, November 6, 1983, https://www .nytimes.com/1983/11/06/us/war-games-film-cited -in-computer-bank-intrusion.html.

Tyler Wall, "Throwback Attack: Kevin Poulsen Wins a Porsche (and hacks the U.S. government)," Industrial Cybersecurity Pulse, March 31, 2022, https://www.industrialcybersecuritypulse.com/threats-vulnerabilities/throwback-attack-kevin-poulsen-wins-a-porsche-and-hacks-the-u-s-government/#:~:text=A%2025%2Dyear%2Dold%20hacker,Peters.

Elka Worner, 1994, "Hacker Pleads Guilty to Fraud," UPI, June 14, 1994, https://www.upi.com/Archives/1994/06/14/Hacker-pleads-guilty-to-fraud/7490771566400/

SNOW WAY!

"Panamanian Dictator Manuel Noriega's Complex US Ties Suggest Lessons for Trump Era, Historians Say," ABC News, June 1, 2017, https://abcnews.go.com/International/panamanian-dictator-manuel-noriegas-complex-us-ties-lessons/story?id=47722429.

Howard Chua-Eoan, "Confidence Games," TIME, November 29, 1993, https://time.com/archive/6724295/confidence-games/.

Michael Isikoff, "U.S. Probes Narcotics Unit Funded by CIA," Washington Post, November 20, 1993, https://www.washingtonpost.com/archive/politics/1993/11/20/us-probes-narcotics-unit-funded-by-cia/08e49ab4-b23a-4143-ace9-baebab212284/.

Tim Weiner, "Anti-Drug Unit of C.I.A. Sent Ton of Cocaine to U.S. in 1990," New York Times, November 20, 1993, https://www.nytimes.com/1993/11/20/world/anti-drug-unit-of-cia-sent-ton-of-cocaine-to-us-in-1990.html.

Tim Weiner, "Venezuelan General Indicted in C.I.A. Scheme," New York Times, November 23, 1996, https://www.nytimes.com/1996/11/23/us/venezuelan-general-indicted-in-cia-scheme.html.

"The CIA's Cocaine," 60 Minutes, 1993, https://www.youtube.com/watch?v=IF-IYdsFGrw.

BIOSPHERE 2

Joel Achenbach, "BIosphere 2: Bogus New World?" Washington Post, January 8, 1992, https://www.washingtonpost.com/archive/lifestyle/1992/01/08/biosphere-2-bogus-new-world/f2de366a-ed63-42a0-ae39-0393db18ea46/.

John Allen, Me and the Biospheres: A Memoir by the Inventor of Biosphere 2 (Synergetic Press, 2018).

John C. Avise, "The Real Message from Biosphere 2," Conservation Biology 8, no. 2 (June 1994): 327–29, https://doi.org/10.1046/j.1523-1739.1994.08020327.x.

B. Drummond Ayres Jr., "Ecological Experiment Becomes Battleground," New York Times, April 11, 1994, sec. U.S., https://www.nytimes.com/1994/04/11/us/ecological-experiment-becomes-battleground.html.

Melinda Beck, "Biosphere II: Science Or Showmanship?" Newsweek, October 6, 1991, https://www.newsweek.com/biosphere-ii-science-or-showmanship-204676.

Connie Bruck, "How Hollywood Remembers Steve Bannon," New Yorker, April 24, 2017, https://www.newyorker.com/magazine/2017/05/01/how-hollywood-remembers-steve-bannon.

Joe Nick Patoski and Bill Crawford, "The Long, Strange Trip of Ed Bass," Texas Monthly, June 1, 1989, https://www.texasmonthly.com/news-politics/long-strange-trip-ed-bass/.

Jordan Fisher Smith, "Life Under the Bubble," Discover, December 19, 2010, https://www.discovermagazine.com/environment/life-under-the-bubble.

Erica Gies, "Life Inside the Biosphere Bubble," Wired, October 18, 2006, accessed July 4, 2024, https://www.wired.com/2006/10/life-inside-the-biosphere-bubble/.

Chelsea Gohd, "Biosphere 2: Explore the Habitat's History and Mystery in These Amazing Photos," Space.com, May 8, 2020, https://www.space.com/biosphere-2-spaceship-earth-habitat-photos.html.

Robert Lee Hotz and Adam S. Bauman, "Column One : Biosphere 2: Trouble in Paradise : What Began as a Theater Troupe's Fantasy Is Now a Nightmare of Legal Wrangles and Bitter Feuds," Los Angeles Times, April 24, 1994, https://www.latimes.com/archives/la-xpm-1994-04-24-mn-49890-story.html.

Jane Poynter: Life in Biosphere 2, TED Talk, 2009, https://www.ted.com/talks/jane_poynter_life_in_biosphere_2/transcript.

Aaron Katersky, Peter Charalambous, and Kevin Shalvey, "Steve Bannon Reports to Prison for Contempt of Congress Sentence," ABC News, July 1, 2024, https://abcnews.go.com/US/steve-bannon-surrenders-reports-prison/story?id=111569255.

Thomas H. Maugh II, "Woman in Biosphere Cuts Off Fingertip: Science: Two-Year Experiment's Resident Doctor Reattaches Segment, but Victim May Need Outside Surgery If Hand Doesn't Heal Properly," Los Angeles Times, October 11, 1991, https://www.latimes.com/archives/la-xpm-1991-10-11-mn-239-story.html.

Mike Menichini, "Biosphere 2 Struggles to Put Science First," Lewiston Morning Tribune, March 6, 1994.

"Music of the Biospheres with John Allen," in Voices from the Edge: Conversations with Jerry Garcia, Ram Dass, Annie Sprinkle, Matthew Fox, Jaron Lanier, & Others (Crossing Press, 1995), 179.

Jane Poynter, "It Takes Four Months to Make a Pizza," in The Human Experiment: Two Years and Twenty Minutes Inside Biosphere 2 (Thunder's Mouth Press, 2006), 187.

Jane Poynter, "What Honeymoon?," in The Human Experiment: Two Years and Twenty Minutes Inside Biosphere 2 (Thunder's Mouth Press, 2006), 145.

"Two Former Biosphere Workers Are Accused of Sabotaging Dome," New York Times, April 5, 1994, sec. U.S., https://www.nytimes.com/1994/04/05/us/two-former-biosphere-workers-are-accused-of-sabotaging-dome.html.

Rebecca Reider, "The Power of Life," in Dreaming the Biosphere: The Theater of All Possibilities (University of New Mexico Press, 2010), 138.

Arthur H. Rotstein, "Biosphere's Mastermind Quits in Wake of Shakeup," Daily Courier, April 11, 1994.

Clarissa Sebag-Montefiore, "20 Minutes with: Space Perspective Co-Founder Jane Poynter," Barron's, June 6, 2022, https://www.barrons.com/articles/20-minutes-with-space-perspective-co-founder-jane-poynter-01654533003.

Annys Shin, "The Year There Was No World Series," Washington Post, July 6, 2023, https://www.washingtonpost.com/lifestyle/magazine/the-year-there-was-no-world-series/2017/09/05/f1ed4a60-7d0f-11e7-9d08-b79f191668ed_story.html.

Howard Witt, "Talk About a Housing Bubble—This House Is Just That," Free Lance-Star, June 21, 2005.

Carl Zimmer, "The Lost History of One of the World's Strangest Science Experiments," *New York Times*, March 29, 2019, sec. Sunday Review, https://www.nytimes.com/2019/03/29/sunday-review/biosphere-2-climate-change.html.

KEYBOARD COWBOYS

Jack L. Brock Jr., "Computer Attacks at Department of Defense Pose Increasing Risks," United States General Accounting Office, May 22, 1996, https://nsarchive2.gwu.edu/NSAEBB/NSAEBB424/docs/Cyber-010b.pdf.

Duncan Campbell, "More Naked Gun Than Top Gun," *Guardian*, November 26, 1997, https://www.duncancampbell.org/menu/journalism/guardian/nakedgun.pdf.

John T. Correll, "War in Cyberspace," *AIR FORCE Magazine*, January 1998, https://www.airandspaceforces.com/PDF/MagazineArchive/Documents/1998/January%201998/0198cyber.pdf.

"Hacker Mathew Bevan Vents His Spleen on the Inq," *Inquirer*, August 21, 2009, https://web.archive.org/web/20090821213059/https://www.theinquirer.net/inquirer/news/1023776/hacker-mathew-bevan-vents-his-spleen-on-the-inq.

"Joy Riders: Mischief That Leads to Mayhem | The Rome Labs Case: Datastream Cowboy and Kuji Mix It Up with the U.S. Air Force," InformIT, accessed July 10, 2024, https://www.informit.com/articles/article.aspx?p=19603&seqNum=2.

Margaret Ryan, "The 'Spider's Web' of Hacking," BBC News, June 8, 2005, https://web.archive.org/web/20190319185926/http://news.bbc.co.uk/2/hi/uk/4072938.stm.

"Security in Cyberspace APPENDIX B—Case Study Rome Laboratory, Griffiss Air Force Base, NY Intrusion," accessed July 10, 2024, https://irp.fas.org/congress/1996_hr/s960605b.htm.

"Fine for Boy Who Hacked into Pentagon," *Independent*, March 22, 1997, https://www.independent.co.uk/news/fine-for-boy-who-hacked-into-pentagon-1274204.html.

"When Two Young Hackers Played War Games with Pentagon," Black Hat Ethical Hacking, March 29, 2021, https://www.blackhatethicalhacking.com/articles/hacking-stories/when-two-young-hackers-played-war-games-with-pentagon/.

BEANIE BREAKDOWN

Bryan Smith, "Behind the Beanie Babies: The Secret Life of Ty Warner," *Chicago Magazine*, May 2014, https://www.chicagomag.com/chicago-magazine/may-2014/ty-warner.

"Ex-Spouses Go to Court to Split Beanie Babies," Associated Press, *Los Angeles Times* Archive, November 6, 1999, https://www.latimes.com/archives/la-xpm-1999-nov-06-mn-30725-story.html.

"Family Ruined by $100K Beanie Babies 'Investment,'" ABC News, July 6, 2013, https://abcnews.go.com/Business/beanie-babies-mania-ends-bankruptcy/story?id=19785126.

Kevin Lang, "The Beanie Bubble: History vs. Hollywood," historyvshollywood.com, July 26, 2023, https://www.historyvshollywood.com/reelfaces/beanie-bubble/.

Liz Calvario, "Where is Ty Warner, the billionaire subject of 'The Beanie Bubble,' now?" *USA Today*, August 10, 2023, https://www.today.com/popculture/news/ty-warner-now-beanie-baby-founder-rcna98266.

Mariah Espada, "Apple TV+'s The Beanie Bubble Explores the True Story of the Women Behind the Beanie Baby Fad," *TIME*, July 28, 2023, https://time.com/6299371/the-beanie-bubble-true-story-apple-tv/.

Mark Joseph Stern, "Plush Life: Why did people lose their minds over Beanie Babies?," *Slate*, https://slate.com/technology/2015/02/beanie-babies-bubble-economics-and-psychology-of-a-plush-toy-investment-craze.html.

"Metro Business; Four Seasons Hotel Sold for $275 Million," Bloomberg News via *New York Times*, February 5, 1999, https://www.nytimes.com/1999/02/05/nyregion/metro-business-four-seasons-hotel-sold-for-275-million.html.

Natasha Frost, "How the Beanie Baby Craze Came to a Crashing End," History.com, July 28, 2023, https://www.history.com/news/how-the-beanie-baby-craze-came-to-a-crashing-end.

"CRIME; A World Gone Beanie Mad!", *New York Times*, July 5, 1998, https://www.nytimes.com/1998/07/05/magazine/sunday-july-5-1998-crime-a-world-gone-beanie-mad.html.

Tyler Piccotti, "Beanie Babies Made Ty Warner a Billionaire, But His Life Has Been Complicated Ever Since," Biography.com, July 27, 2023, https://www.biography.com/business-leaders/a44661324/beanie-babies-movie-true-story.

"'Ty Warner, creator of Beanie Babies, charged with tax evasion," NBC News, September 18, 2013, https://www.nbcnews.com/businessmain/ty-warner-creator-beanie-babies-charged-tax-evasion-4b11187603.

MARS ORBITER

Blaine Friedlander, "Two NASA Spacecraft Launches, One to Mars and the Other to Research the Birth of Stars, Involve Cornell Astronomers' Projects." *Cornell Chronicle*, December 11, 1998, news.cornell.edu/stories/1998/12/two-nasa-spacecraft-launches-one-mars-and-other-research-birth-stars-involve.

Brian Kennedy and Alex Tyson, "Americans' Views of Space: U.S. Role, NASA Priorities and Impact of Private Companies." Pew Research Center, July 20, 2023, https://www.pewresearch.org/science/2023/07/20/americans-views-of-space-u-s-role-nasa-priorities-and-impact-of-private-companies/.

"Colloquium Detail." Johns Hopkins Applied Physics Laboratory, 2019, www.jhuapl.edu/colloquium/Archive/Detail?colloqid=228.

Diane Ainsworth, "Mars Climate Orbiter on Its Way," Jet Propulsion Laboratory, December 18, 1998, https://www.jpl.nasa.gov/universe/archive/un9812.pdf.

James Oberg, "Why the Mars Probe Went Off Course," IEEE Spectrum, December 1, 1999, spectrum.ieee.org/why-the-mars-probe-went-off-course.

John Noble-Wilford, "Beginning a Bargain-Basement Invasion of Mars," *New York Times*, September 21, 1999, archive.nytimes.com/www.nytimes.com/library/national/science/092199sci-nasa-mars.html.

Kathy Sawyer, "Mystery of Orbiter Crash Solved," *Washington Post*, October 1, 1999, https://www.washingtonpost.com/wp-srv/national/longterm/space/stories/orbiter100199.htm.

Mars Climate Orbiter Mishap Investigation Board. "Report on Project Management in NASA," NASA, March 13, 2000, https://www.dcs.gla.ac.uk/~johnson/Mars/MCO_MIB_Report.pdf.

"Mars Polar Lander / Deep Space 2," NASA Jet Propulsion Laboratory (JPL), 2023, www.jpl.nasa.gov/missions/mars-polar-lander-deep-space-2/.

"NASA's Mars Climate Orbiter: First Martian Weather Satellite," NASA Jet Propulsion Laboratory (JPL), September 20, 1999, www.jpl.nasa.gov/news/nasas-mars-climate-orbiter-first-martian-weather-satellite/.

"Mars Climate Orbiter Mishap Investigation Board Phase I Report," NASA, November 10, 1999, https://llis.nasa.gov/llis_lib/pdf/1009464main1_0641-mr.pdf.

"NATIONAL AERONAUTICS and SPACE ADMINISTRATION Mars Climate Orbiter Arrival," NASA, September, 1999, https://mars.nasa.gov/internal_resources/812/.

Robert Lee Hotz, "Mars Probe Lost Due to Simple Math Error," Los Angeles Times, October 1, 1999, https://www.latimes.com/archives/la-xpm-1999-oct-01-mn-17288-story.html.

Robert Lee Hotz, "String of Missteps Doomed Orbiter; JPL Found at Fault," Los Angeles Times, November 11, 1999, www.latimes.com/archives/la-xpm-1999-nov-11-mn-32228-story.html.

"The 1990s: International Flair and Understanding the Solar System—NASA," NASA, March 29, 2023, www.nasa.gov/history/the-1990s-international-flair-and-understanding-the-solar-system/.

Sam Wesley, "Sam Wesley Thurman, PhD, Presented with the Albert Nelson Marquis Lifetime Achievement Award by Marquis Who's Who," 24-7 Press Release Newswire, October 19, 2020, www.24-7pressrelease.com/press-release/476552/sam-wesley-thurman-phd-presented-with-the-albert-nelson-marquis-lifetime-achievement-award-by-marquis-whos-who.

"What Made Apollo a Success," NASA, March 1970, https://ntrs.nasa.gov/api/citations/19720005243/downloads/19720005243.pdf.

EMERGENCY LANDING

"EP-3 Collision, Crew Detainment and Homecoming," Naval History and Heritage Command, Aug. 18, 2021, www.history.navy.mil/research/archives/Collections/ncdu-det-206/2001/ep-3-collision--crew-detainment-and-homecoming.html.

Nectar Gan and Brad Lendon, "Hainan Island: It's Known as 'China's Hawaii,' but the Vacation Hotspot Is Also a Strategic Military Base," CNN, Feb. 15, 2023, www.cnn.com/2023/02/15/china/china-hainan-island-explainer-intl-hnk/index.html.

"Hero Pilot Wang Wei," Hangzhou China, Apr. 2, 2021, www.ehangzhou.cn/2021-04/02/c_277246.htm, accessed 10 July 2024.

"Hotel California," Genius, Dec. 8, 1976, genius.com/Eagles-hotel-california-lyrics.

Robbie Mitchell, "A Game of Chicken in the South China Sea: The Hainan Island Incident," Historic Mysteries, Mar. 6, 2023, www.historicmysteries.com/history/hainan-island-incident/31078/, accessed July 10, 2024.

Jim Turnbull, "Lt. Shane Osborn: Looking at a Miracle," Naval Aviation News, Sept. 2023, web.archive.org/web/20130513020628/www.history.navy.mil/nan/backissues/2000s/2003/so03/osborn.pdf, accessed July 10, 2024.

Kim Zetter, "Burn After Reading: Snowden Documents Reveal Actual Scope of Secrets Exposed to China in 2001 Spy Plane Incident," Intercept, Apr. 10, 2017, the intercept.com/2017/04/10/snowden-documents-reveal-scope-of-secrets-exposed-to-china-in-2001-spy-plane-incident/, accessed July 9, 2024.

THE MILLENIUM CHALLENGE

Fred Kaplan, "War-Gamed," Slate News, March 28, 2003, https://slate.com/news-and-politics/2003/03/the-officer-who-predicted-saddam-s-moves.html.

IGN Staff, "Smashing Success," IGN, October 28, 1999, https://web.archive.org/web/20180501122854/http://www.ign.com/articles/1999/10/29/smashing-success-2.

IGN Staff, "Xbox Live Subscriptions Double Expectations," IGN, January 7, 2003, https://web.archive.org/web/20120121234008/http://games.ign.com/articles/381/381618p1.html.

Julian Borger, "Wake-up Call," Guardian, September 5, 2002, https://www.theguardian.com/world/2002/sep/06/usa.iraq.

Julian Borger, "War game was fixed to ensure American victory, claims general," Guardian, August 20, 2002, https://www.theguardian.com/world/2002/aug/21/usa.julianborger.

Thom Shanker, "Iran Encounter Grimly Echoes '02 War Game," New York Times, January 12, 2008, https://www.nytimes.com/2008/01/12/washington/12navy.html.

Thom Shanker, "U.S. Explores a New World of Warfare," New York Times, August 20, 2002, https://www.nytimes.com/2002/08/20/world/us-explores-a-new-world-of-warfare.html.

Thom Shanker and Brian Knowlton, "U.S. Describes Confrontation with Iranian Boats," New York Times, January 8, 2008, https://www.nytimes.com/2008/01/08/washington/08military.html.

AGENT BTZ

Julian E. Barnes, "Pentagon Computer Networks Attacked," Los Angeles Times, November 28, 2008, https://www.latimes.com/archives/la-xpm-2008-nov-28-na-cyberattack28-story.html.

Kristen Bialik, "U.S. Active-Duty Military Presence Overseas Is at Its Smallest in Decades." Pew Research Center (blog), August 22, 2017, accessed March 29, 2024, https://www.pewresearch.org/short-reads/2017/08/22/u-s-active-duty-military-presence-overseas-is-at-its-smallest-in-decades/.

"Connect the Dots on State-Sponsored Cyber Incidents—Agent.Btz," n.d., Council on Foreign Relations, accessed March 12, 2024, https://www.cfr.org/cyber-operations/agentbtz.

Dominic L. Epps, "Offensive Cyber Operations Reshaping the Modern Battlespace," Master's Thesis, Utica College, August 2021, https://media.proquest.com/media/hms/PFT/2/7j1SK.

James P. Farwell, "Industry's Vital Role in National Cyber Security," Strategic Studies Quarterly, 6.4 (Winter 2012), 10–41.

"Government Can't Kill Old Worm After Attack on Military," HuffPost, June 17, 2011, https://www.huffpost.com/entry/agentbtz-worm-attack-military_n_878880.

William J. Lynn, "Defending a New Domain: The Pentagon's Cyberstrategy," Foreign Affairs 89 (5): 97–108, https://www.jstor.org/stable/20788647.

Ellen Nakashima, "Cyber-Intruder Sparks Response, Debate," Washington Post, December 9, 2011, https://www.washingtonpost.com/national/national-security/cyber-intruder-sparks-response-debate/2011/12/06/gIQAxLuFgO_story.html.

Ellen Nakashima, "Defense Official Discloses Cyberattack," *Washington Post*, August 25, 2010, http://www.washingtonpost.com/wp-dyn/content/article/2010/08/24/AR2010082406495.html.

NPR Reports and the Associated Press, "Joint Chiefs Nominee Expects More Results in Iraq," NPR, July 31, 2007, sec. National, https://www.npr.org/2007/07/31/12372993/joint-chiefs-nominee-expects-more-results-in-iraq.

Isaac R. Porche III, Jerry M. Sollinger, and Shawn McKay, *Cyberworm That Knows No Boundaries* (RAND, 2011).

Christine Romero-Chan, "Every iPhone Release in Chronological Order: 2007–2024," *Digital Trends*, January 29, 2024, https://www.digitaltrends.com/mobile/every-iphone-release-in-chronological-order/.

Mark R. Schonberg, *Defining the DOD Role in National Cybersecurity*, Thesis, US Army War College, 2013, https://apps.dtic.mil/sti/tr/pdf/ADA590756.pdf.

Noah Shachtman, "Insiders Doubt 2008 Pentagon Hack Was Foreign Spy Attack (Updated)," *Wired*, August 25, 2010, accessed March 12, 2024, https://www.wired.com/2010/08/insiders-doubt-2008-pentagon-hack-was-foreign-spy-attack/.

Noah Shachtman, "Under Worm Assault, Military Bans Disks, USB Drives," *Wired*, November 19, 2008, accessed March 12, 2024, https://www.wired.com/2008/11/army-bans-usb-d/.

Sergei Shevchenko, "Agent.Btz—A Threat That Hit Pentagon," *Threat Expert*, November 30, 2008, accessed March 28, 2024, http://blog.threatexpert.com/2008/11/agentbtz-threat-that-hit-pentagon.html.

"The Worm Turns," *Economist*, December 4, 2008, accessed March 12, 2024, https://www.economist.com/united-states/2008/12/04/the-worm-turns.

"Key Players in Operation Buckshot Yankee," *Washington Post*, December 8, 2012, https://www.washingtonpost.com/world/national-security/key-players-in-operation-buckshot-yankee/2011/12/08/gIQASJaSgO_story.html.

Kim Zetter, "The Return of the Worm That Ate the Pentagon," *Wired*, December 9, 2011, accessed March 12, 2024, https://www.wired.com/2011/12/worm-pentagon/.

THE HAWAI'IAN MISSILE ALERT

Corey Pein, "Blame the Computer," *Baffler*, March 5, 2018, https://thebaffler.com/salvos/blame-the-computer-pein.

"Children Rushed into Manhole for Safety During Hawaii Missile Threat," n.d., ABC7 Los Angeles, accessed July 15, 2024, https://abc7.com/hawaii-missile-threat-safety-war/2940300/.

Cecilia Kang, "Hawaii Missile Alert Wasn't Accidental, Officials Say, Blaming Worker," *New York Times*, January 30, 2018, sec. Technology, https://www.nytimes.com/2018/01/30/technology/fcc-hawaii-missile-alert.html.

Ted Kemp, "North Korea Hydrogen Bomb: Read the Full Announcement from Pyongyang," CNBC, September 3, 2017, https://www.cnbc.com/2017/09/03/north-korea-hydrogen-bomb-read-the-full-announcement-from-pyongyang.html.

Michelle Mark, "38 Minutes of Panic: Here's How People in Hawaii Reacted to a False Ballistic Missile Alert," Business Insider, accessed July 15, 2024, https://www.businessinsider.com/how-people-in-hawaii-reacted-to-a-false-ballistic-missile-alert-2018-1.

Bhavini Patel Murthy, Nevin Krishna, Terrance Jones, Amy Wolkin, Rachel Nonkin Avchen, and Sara J. Vagi, "Public Health Emergency Risk Communication and Social Media Reactions to an Errant Warning of a Ballistic Missile Threat—Hawaii, January 2018," *Morbidity and Mortality Weekly Report* 68 (7): 174–76, https://www.jstor.org/stable/26608600.

Vipin Narang and Heather Williams, "Thermonuclear Twitter?," in *The Fragile Balance of Terror: Deterrence in the New Nuclear Age*, edited by Vipin Narang and Scott D. Sagan, 63–89 (Cornell University Press), https://www.jstor.org/stable/10.7591/j.ctv310vm0j.6.

Nicole Darrah and Kathleen Joyce, "Hawaii's False Missile Threat: Worker 'Feels Terrible' After Pushing the Wrong Button," Fox News, January 13, 2018, https://www.foxnews.com/us/hawaiis-false-missile-threat-worker-feels-terrible-after-pushing-the-wrong-button.

"Oliveira: Feds Don't Need to Be Involved in Missile Alerts," n.d., *Mauinews.Com* (blog), accessed July 15, 2024, https://www.mauinews.com/news/local-news/2018/03/oliveira-feds-dont-need-to-be-involved-in-missile-alerts/.

"Timeline of the Hawaii False Missile Alert Shows How Drill Went Wrong," CNN, January 31, 2018, https://www.cnn.com/2018/01/30/us/hawaii-false-missile-alert-timeline/index.html.

Amy B. Wang, "Hawaii Missile Alert: How One Employee 'Pushed the Wrong Button' and Caused a Wave of Panic," *Washington Post*, October 26, 2021, https://www.washingtonpost.com/news/post-nation/wp/2018/01/14/hawaii-missile-alert-how-one-employee-pushed-the-wrong-button-and-caused-a-wave-of-panic/.

Joby Warrick, Ellen Nakashima, and Anna Fifield, "North Korea Now Making Missile-Ready Nuclear Weapons, U.S. Analysts Say," *Washington Post*, July 6, 2023, https://www.washingtonpost.com/world/national-security/north-korea-now-making-missile-ready-nuclear-weapons-us-analysts-say/2017/08/08/e14b882a-7b6b-11e7-9d08-b79f191668ed_story.html.

THE SUEZ CANAL

Mary-Ann Russon, "The Cost of the Suez Canal Blockage," BBC, March 29, 2021, https://www.bbc.com/news/business-56559073.

Akhilesh Pillalamarri, "India and the Gulf States Share a Long History," *Diplomat*, June 10, 2016, https://thediplomat.com/2016/06/india-and-the-gulf-states-share-a-long-history/.

AFP, "Suez Canal Chief Cites Possible 'Human Error' in Ship Grounding," *Economic Times*, March 28, 2021, https://economictimes.indiatimes.com/international/business/suez-canal-chief-cites-possible-human-error-in-ship-grounding/articleshow/81731210.cms?from=mdr.

Alessandra Bonomolo, director, *Why Ships Crash*, BBC Two, 2022, 59 min.

Elisabeth Braw, "What the *Ever Given* Taught the World About Supply Chains," *Foreign Policy*, November 10, 2021, https://foreignpolicy.com/2021/11/10/what-the-ever-given-taught-the-world/.

Max E. Fletcher, "The Suez Canal and World Shipping, 1869–1914," *Journal of Economic History* 18, no. 4 (1958): 556–73, http://www.jstor.org/stable/2114548.

Joel Benin, "How Egypt's Gamal Abdel Nasser Changed World Politics," Jacobin, November 2, 2021, https://jacobin.com/2021/11/egypt-gamal-abdel-nasser-world-politics-arab-socialism-anti-imperialism-history.

"Milestones: 1953–1960," Office of the Historian, Department of State, n.d., https://history.state.gov/milestones/1953-1960/suez.

Matt Mullen, "Suez Canal Opens," History, November 16, 2021, https://www.history.com/this-day-in-history/suez-canal-opens.

Chris Michael, "Container Ship Ever Given Returns to Suez Canal for Another Attempt," *Guardian*, August 20, 2021, https://www.theguardian.com/world/2021/aug/20/ever-given-round-two-container-ship-returns-to-suez-canal.

"Ship MAERSK DENVER (Container Ship) Registered in USA—Vessel Details, Current Position and Voyage Information—IMO 9332999, MMSI 338418000, Call Sign WMDQ," MarineTraffic.com, n.d., https://www.marinetraffic.com/en/ais/details/ships/shipid:400623/mmsi:338418000/imo:9332999/vessel:MAERSK_DENVER.

"Suez Incident Causes Shipping Backlog," *Seafarers International Union*, May 1, 2021, https://www.seafarers.org/seafarerslogs/2021/05/suez-incident-causes-shipping-backlog/.

Peter S. Goodman and Stanley Reed, "With Suez Canal Blocked, Shippers Begin End Run Around a Trade Artery," *New York Times*, March 29, 2021, https://www.nytimes.com/2021/03/26/business/suez-canal-blocked-ship.html.

Atthar Mirza, Júlia Ledur, and Ruby Mellen, "How the Ever Given Was Freed from the Suez Canal: A Visual Analysis," *Washington Post*, April 2, 2021, https://www.washingtonpost.com/world/interactive/2021/suez-canal-ever-given-freed-visual-analysis/.

Joseph Hincks, "How the Giant Boat Blocking the Suez Canal Was Freed: Dredgers, Tugboats, and a Full Moon," *TIME*, March 29, 2021, https://time.com/5950888/suez-canal-boat-freed-explained/.

Jon Henley and Michael Safi, "How a Full Moon and a 'Huge Lever' Helped Free *Ever Given* from Suez Canal," *Guardian*, March 31, 2021, https://www.theguardian.com/world/2021/mar/30/powerful-tugs-and-an-ebbing-tide-how-the-ever-given-was-freed.

Sophia Ankel, "One Person Reportedly Died While Helping Free the *Ever Given* Ship, the Suez Canal Authority Says," *Business Insider*, June 12, 2021, https://www.businessinsider.com/suez-canal-authority-person-died-during-ever-given-rescue-mission-2021-6.

CNN World, "See tugboat crew celebrate freeing the Ever Given in Suez Canal," CNN video, 1:51, March 3, 2021, https://www.cnn.com/videos/world/2021/03/30/suez-canal-ever-given-freed-wedeman-pkg-intl-hnk-vpx.cnn.

Alex Christian, "The Untold Story of the Big Boat That Broke the World," *WIRED*, June 22, 2021, https://www.wired.com/story/ever-given-global-supply-chain/.

Matt Leonard and Shefali Kapadia, "Timeline: How the Suez Canal Blockage Unfolded Across Supply Chains," *Supply Chain Dive*, July 29, 2021, https://www.supplychaindive.com/news/timeline-ever-given-evergreen-blocked-suez-canal-supply-chain/597660/.

Kit Chellel, Matthew Campbell, and K. Oanh Ha, "Six Days in Suez: The Inside Story of the Ship That Broke Global Trade," *Bloomberg*, June 24, 2021, https://www.bloomberg.com/news/features/2021-06-24/how-the-billion-dollar-ever-given-cargo-ship-got-stuck-in-the-suez-canal?embedded-checkout=true.

"'Ever Given' Re-floated in Suez Canal," UK P&I Club, n.d., https://www.ukpandi.com/news-and-resources/press-release-articles/2021/ever-given-media-statement/.

Ruth Michaelson, "Ever Given Released from Suez Canal After Compensation Agreed," *Guardian*, July 8, 2021, https://www.theguardian.com/world/2021/jul/07/ever-given-released-from-suez-canal-after-compensation-agreed.

"President Sisi Reappoints Osama Rabie as Chairman of Suez Canal Authority," Ahram Online, August 13, 2023, https://english.ahram.org.eg/News/506532.aspx.

Aya Salah, "Egypt's Suez Canal records highest ever daily transit rate," Ahram Online, March 13, 2023, https://english.ahram.org.eg/News/491607.aspx.

TOP FIVE…NEAR EXTINCTIONS IN THE NEW MILLENNIUM

"Aye Aye," Britannica, https://www.britannica.com/animal/aye-aye.

Amber Dowling, "10-of-the-weirdest-endangered-animals-on-the-planet," https://blog.animalogic.ca/blog/10-of-the-weirdest-endangered-animals-on-the-planet.

Dave Kindy, "Scientists want to rename the Hitler beetle—but not for the reason you think," *Washington Post*, September 24, 2023, https://www.washingtonpost.com/history/2023/09/24/hitler-beetle-offensive-species-names/.

Franz Lidz, "What to Do with a Bug Named Hitler?" *New York Times*, December 26, 2023, https://www.nytimes.com/2023/12/26/science/taxonomy-beetle-insects-hitler.html.

Jim Lyons, "Under Threat: The Endangered Species Act and the Plants and Wildlife It Protects," Center for American Progress, https://www.americanprogress.org/article/under-threat/.

Emily Osterloff, "Coconut Crabs: The bird-eating behemoths thriving on isolated tropical islands," Natural History Museum, https://www.nhm.ac.uk/discover/coconut-crabs-bird-eating-giants-on-tropical-islands.html.

Lindsey Jean Schueman, "Aye-aye: The enigmatic life of the world's largest nocturnal primate," One Earth, https://www.oneearth.org/species-of-the-week-aye-aye/.

Lesley Ciarula Taylor, "10 species endangered for stupid reasons," *Toronto Star*, May 20, 2011, https://www.thestar.com/news/world/10-species-endangered-for-stupid-reasons/article_0a717f45-ff4c-5c75-b8c0-312b01a6be7c.html.

World Wildlife Foundation. "5 Fun Facts About the Silver-Headed Antechinus," https://wwf.org.au/blogs/5-fun-facts-about-the-silver-headed-antechinus/.

Ed Yong, "Why a Little Mammal Has So Much Sex That It Disintegrates," *National Geographic*, https://www.nationalgeographic.com/science/article/why-a-little-mammal-has-so-much-sex-that-it-disintegrates?rnd=1730149938165&loggedin=true.